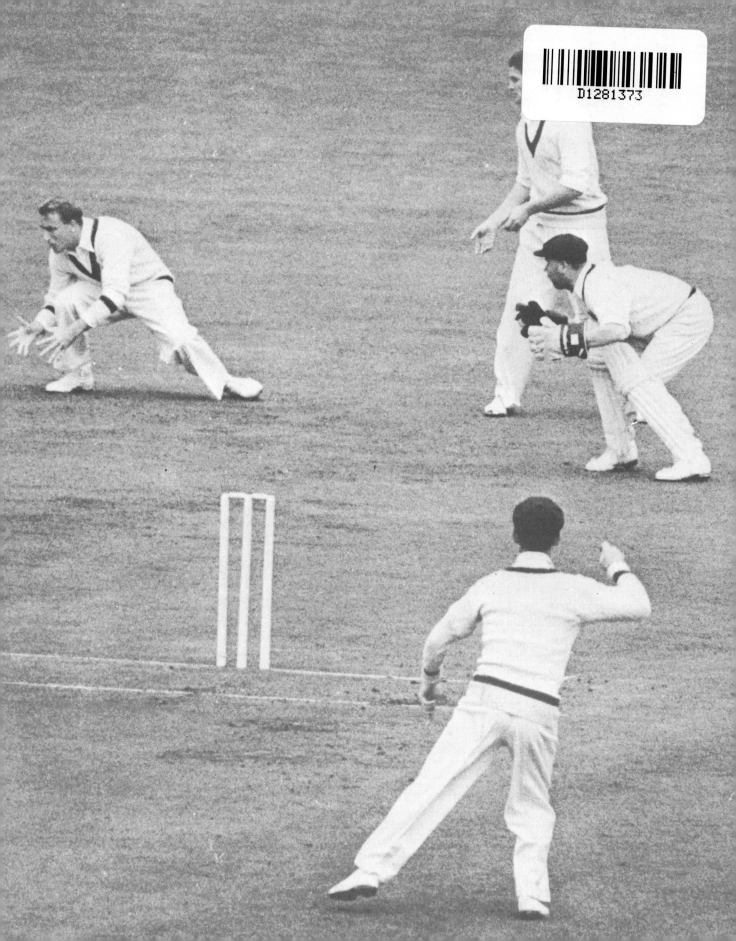

A HISTORY OF
CRICKET

A HISTORY OF CRICKET

Trevor Bailey

with a foreword by Sir Donald Bradman

and records compiled by Bill Frindall

London
GEORGE ALLEN & UNWIN
Boston   Sydney

See preceding page Worcestershire
v. Australia in 1930. For years the
first tourist match was always
played at Worcester, and it was
a particularly happy hunting
ground for Don Bradman, seen
on page 6 on his way out to
bat in the 1948 match

Author's Acknowledgments

I would like to express my sincere thanks to many people. First, to the veritable legion of writers on the sport, who have not only given me great pleasure, but have provided information which has made this leisurely saunter through more than three hundred years of cricket history possible.

Second, I am both honoured and delighted that Sir Donald Bradman has written the preface. He is the greatest batsman I have ever seen, with figures to substantiate the claim, and it is doubtful whether anyone possesses a greater knowledge about all aspects of the game.

Third, I must thank that human computer, Bill Frindall, for supplying the statistical section.

Finally, I am very grateful to Jim Coldham, who checked facts, corrected errors and made numerous helpful suggestions. He did all this with a speed and accuracy which left me both amazed and breathless. My indebtedness to him is enormous.

First published in Great Britain in 1979

British Library Cataloguing in Publication Data

Bailey, Trevor, b. 1923
 A history of cricket.
 1. Cricket - History
 I. Title
 796.358'09   GV913   78-40303

 ISBN 0-04-796049-3

This book was designed and produced by
London Editions Limited, 30 Uxbridge Road,
London W12 8ND

Printed in Great Britain
by Caledonian Graphics Ltd., London : Cumbernauld

CONTENTS

FOREWORD
by Sir Donald Bradman

Trevor Bailey has given me the privilege of seeing an outline of the history of cricket which he is in the process of writing.

My immediate impression was precisely what I would have expected—namely that it will be a well-researched and authentic publication bearing the typical Bailey hallmark.

We have recently celebrated a hundred years of Test cricket between England and Australia. That period has been blessed by such legendary figures as Grace, Hobbs, Rhodes and others.

Some players were so naturally gifted that they couldn't fail to achieve a measure of greatness and of these probably Sir Gary Sobers was pre-eminent for his incredible talents as batsman, bowler and fieldsman. Others whom nature endowed with priceless gifts were Jack Gregory, Keith Miller and Denis Compton. They all seemed to play with a relatively casual air—to approach their cricket with a 'laissez-faire' outlook, which I'm sure masked a more serious mental attitude.

Trevor Bailey was in a very different mould. He did not inherit their physical attributes but he made up for it by dedication, application, and a studious approach to the art of cricket which brought rewards of an unexpected nature.

Trevor Bailey did not set the turnstiles clicking. People did not rush to see him bat. In Brisbane in 1954, his first 38 took 160 minutes, whilst four years later, on the same ground, he batted slightly longer for 27.

His lengthy vigil at Lord's in 1953 with Watson is one of the classic defensive efforts of Test history. His batting was so often destined to occupy the role of saving rather than winning a match.

In his bowling there was also emphasis on economy, but so often his swing and cut succeeded where the more illustrious names failed.

I recall the 1953–4 series v. West Indies, when the triumvirate of Weekes, Worrell and Walcott were in their prime and our press announced West Indies all out for 139. I rushed to see who of Trueman, Lock or Laker had done the damage, only to find it was Trevor Bailey with 7 for 34 off 16 overs. That performance ranks high amongst the best of all medium-pace efforts under favourable batting conditions.

Performances like this kept cropping up to prove that his adherence to sound bowling principles paid dividends. And in the field took some of the greatest catches I've seen.

I'm sure his playing background has been of enormous benefit to Trevor in his development as one of the deepest thinkers and soundest critics amongst modern writers.

His ability to penetrate to the heart and core of events is quite outstanding and the defensive qualities which dominated his batting do not intrude in his writing, which is notable for aggressive and constructive comments.

I feel he is splendidly equipped to produce a history of great interest and authenticity and am sure readers of this volume will not be disappointed.

Donald Bradman

THE FIRST CENTURY

This engraving of a painting by Francis Hayman of a cricket match at the Artillery Ground, Finsbury, brilliantly portrays the game as it was played in the first half of the eighteenth century, with the curved bat, two stumps, underarm bowling, and the scorer busily notching away. Francis Hayman was a friend of Hogarth. They collaborated on several paintings, and the wicketkeeper is thought to be a portrait of Hogarth

There is something challenging and fascinating about trying to hit a ball that has been thrown, which has always appealed to man and still does. This is the basic attraction from which the game of cricket stems. The early origins of the game are obscure, as indeed is the name itself, which was probably derived from the Anglo-Saxon 'cricce', a staff or crutch.

In the Bodleian library there is a picture of one monk bowling to another, who is trying to hit the ball with a cricce, or staff, while other monks act as fielders. The striker stands before a hole, as there are no wickets. The object of the sport was to either get the ball into the hole or catch it.

There seems little doubt that club-ball, or cricce, was closely related to 'Handyn and Handoute', both popular in the fourteenth and fifteenth centuries, and the logical ancestors of the game we now know as cricket.

In the sixteenth century there were several references to cricket and by the seventeenth century it was firmly established as a pastime. Horace Walpole wrote in 1736, two years after he had left Eton: 'An expedition against bargemen, or a match at Cricket, may be pretty things to recollect but, thank my stars, I can remember things that are very near as pretty.'

The move from single to double wickets may well have originated in Scotland, where around 1700 they played a game called 'Cat and Dog', which was described as follows:

'Three play at this game, who are provided with clubs. They cut out two holes, each about a foot in diameter, and seven inches in length. The distance between them is about twenty-six feet. One stands at each hole with a club. These clubs are called dogs. A piece of wood, called a cat, is thrown from one hole towards the other by a third person. The object is to prevent the cat from getting into the hole. Every time that it enters the hole, he who has the club at the hole loses the club, and he who threw the cat gets possession of both the club and the hole, while the former possessor is obliged to take charge of the cat. If the cat be struck, he who strikes it changes places with the person who holds the other club; as often as these positions are changed, one is counted

as one in the game by the two who hold the clubs, and who are viewed as partners.'

This was really a double wicket version of the club-ball of the fourteenth century. It was when a single stump was placed in each hole, originally as a guide to the bowler and fieldsmen, that the modern game became really recognizable. By 1700 two stumps were used, twelve inches high and twenty-four inches apart with a bail on top.

The hole in the ground, which had been a target in club-ball and was replaced by two stumps, still had an important part to play in the early versions of the game, because in running the striker was required to put his bat into the hole to score a notch, or run, while the wicketkeeper was required to put the ball into the hole before he could run the striker out. Inevitably, both keeper and bowler received numerous painful knocks from the bat and eventually the present method of grounding the bat behind the crease was introduced.

In the first half of the eighteenth century, cricket became increasingly popular, with clubs springing up rapidly, mainly in the counties of Kent, Hampshire, Surrey, Sussex and Middlesex. It also gained in respectability, where previously it had been considered largely as a sport for common folk and schoolboys. Both these developments were to some extent due to the fact that the game attracted the big gamblers, who were also the aristocracy. They were not only prepared to wager large sums on the outcome of individual matches, but were also keen to take part in a game which many of them had learned either on their country estates or at school. Another reason for its development was the interest shown by the Prince of Wales, who became passionately fond of the game. He did much to assist Surrey and, appropriately, the county's emblem is the Prince of Wales's feathers.

Although the first recorded Laws of Cricket that have come down to us are dated 1744, there were obviously several earlier versions, which certainly varied from region to region. In these circumstances, and with big money at stake, it was hardly surprising that several of the matches finished in lawsuits and affrays. An early inter-county match between Kent

and London ended with the Kent players bringing a suit against their opponents for £100: the judge, showing characteristic wisdom, simply ordered that the match should be replayed. Anybody who imagines that there is anything new about gamesmanship should take note of what went on in those far distant days. There were plenty of genuine experts! The Laws of Cricket, which were to stand until 1774, really herald the start of cricket.

In this period a notch was the term for a run. Scorers normally lacked the education necessary to write down the runs, which were recorded by the primitive method of cutting a notch in a piece of wood, with a deeper notch for every tenth run. Individual innings were rarely recorded in other than big matches, and it was some time before the clubs began to keep complete and reliable results of their matches. The oldest known full card dates from 1744, when Kent beat All England by one wicket at the Artillery ground in London.

For the sake of convenience, and because it saw the formation of the Hambledon Club in Hampshire, which was to play such a large part in the development of the game, I have chosen 1750 to 1850 as the first century of cricket. In this period a comparatively simple and uncomplicated sport gradually developed into a national summer game.

The Hambledon Club has been immortalized in Nyren's *Young Cricketers' Tutor*, one of the most delightful books on cricket ever to have been written. No club has subsequently dominated the game to the same extent in the playing sense as Hambledon, whose home was first Broad-halfpenny Down, and later Windmill Down. Nyren had this to say about them at their peak: 'No eleven in England has any chance with these men, and I think they might have beaten any two-and-twenty.'

This club more than held its own against all comers until 1769, when it was nearly dissolved; but its many supporters refused to allow it to die and it found a new lease of life, and in the following decade the club made a regular habit of beating England!

The great men in this remarkably successful side were Beldham, the batsman, and Harris, the bowler. 'Silver Billy' Beldham was described by Nyren as possessing 'the beau ideal of grace, animation and concentrated energy',

Thomas Lord came from Yorkshire. His father had been a man of property, but he had chosen the wrong side in the '45 rebellion and had lost his money. A man of considerable charm and, as can be seen from this portrait by Morland, good looking, Thomas Lord was a keen cricketer. He showed foresight, determination and business acumen in making Lord's the home of cricket, and it remains the perfect memorial to him

Left The Grand Cricket Match played at Lord's in 1837. By this time, apart from the underarm bowling and the top hats of the players, the game was essentially the same as it is today

Fuller Pilch was the finest batsman in the land between 1825 and 1850. He was essentially a forward player, who used his height to good effect, and he scored at least ten centuries, which was rare in this period. Originally from Norfolk, he settled in Kent, where his batting had much to do with the considerable progress made by that county at the time

an assessment which could be said to apply equally to most of the truly outstanding players who were to follow him in the next two hundred years. He also, along with Lord Frederick Beauclerk, had the ability to play both off the front and the back foot, which was rare at that time.

Harris was probably the first bowler to appreciate the twin virtues of line and length. He also was able to turn the ball deliberately and did not rely entirely on the vagaries of the wickets, which were often considerable. One important effect of the introduction of good length bowling, instead of the usual fast daisy cutters, was that it led to the design of bats being changed from a hockey shape to a straight one. There was no law as to either the shape or the size of the bat until a man named White, from Reigate, obviously the possessor of a shrewd cricket brain, arrived at a match with a bat that was larger than the wicket, which resulted in a rule being immediately passed regulating the size. The Hambledon Club had an iron frame especially made, through which every bat had to be passed before it was allowed to be used.

In this era leg guards came into fashion, but as they were both uncomfortable and not very effective they did not become popular, being in effect no more than two wooden shin guards.

The most important year in the first century was undoubtedly 1774, because on 25 February of that year a committee of noblemen and gentlemen from Kent, Hampshire, Sussex, Surrey and Middlesex met at the Star and Garter in Pall Mall and drew up the new Laws, revising the old. It was an incredible and an historic meeting in every sense, because the results of their deliberations formed the fundamental basis of the game as it has been played for over two hundred years. When one considers the enormous amount of time that subsequent administrators have taken in their efforts to improve the game, the speed and the clarity of these early decisions become even more incredible. It was certainly one of the very few occasions that an authoritative group of cricketers have known exactly what they wanted, and have done it. I wonder what the chairman, Sir William Draper, would have made of a very high percentage of

modern meetings. You can almost hear him snorting 'Poppycock!', and he would be so very right.

The new Laws can be summarized as follows:

The Game of Cricket, as Settled by the Cricket Club at the Star and Garter in Pall Mall

The pitching the first wicket is to be determined by the cast of a piece of money when the first wicket is pitched and the popping crease cut, which must be exactly 3 Foot 10 inches from the wicket. The Other Wicket is to be pitched directly opposite, at 22 yards distance, and the other popping crease cut 3 Foot 10 inches before it. The Bowling Creases must be cut in a direct line from each Stump. The Stumps must be 22 inches long, and the Bail 6 inches. The Ball must weigh between 5 and 6 ounces. When the wickets are both pitched and all the Creases Cut, the party that wins the toss-up may order which side shall go in first at his option.

Laws for the Bowlers   4 Balls an Over

The Bowler must deliver the Ball with one foot behind the Crease even with the wicket, and when he has bowled one ball or more shall Bowl to the number 4 before he changes wickets, and he Shall Change but once in the same innings. He may order the Player that is at his wicket to Stand on which side of it he Pleases, at a reasonable distance. If he delivers the Ball with his hinder foot over the Bowling crease the Umpire shall call no Ball, though she be struck or the Player is Bowled out; which he shall do without being asked, and no Person shall have any right to ask him.

Laws for the Strikers, or Those that are In

If the wicket be bowled down its out. If he Strikes, or treads down, or falls upon the wicket in striking (but not in over running) its out. A Stroke or Nip over or under his Batt or upon his hands (but not arms), if the Ball be held before She touches the Ground, though She be hugged to the Body, its out. If in Striking both his feet are over the popping Crease and his Wicket put down, except his Batt is down within, its out. If a Ball is nipped up and he Strikes her again Wilfully before She comes to the Wicket, its out. If the Players have crossed each other, he that runs for the Wicket that is put down is out. If they are not Crossed, he that returns is

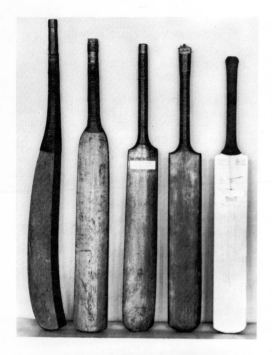

out. If in running a Notch the Wicket is struck down by a Throw before his Foot, Hand, or Batt is over the Popping Crease, or a Stump hit by the Ball, though the Bail was down, its out. But if the Bail is down before, he that catches the Ball must strike a Stump out of the Ground, Ball in Hand, then its out. If the Striker touches or takes up the Ball before she is lain quite still, unless asked by the Bowler or Wicket Keeper, its out.

Batt, Foot, or Hand over the Crease

When the Ball has been in Hand by one of the Keeper or Stopers and the Player has been at Home, He may go where he pleases till the next Ball is bowled. If Either of the Strikers is crossed in his running Ground designedly, which design must be determined by the Umpires. N.B.—The Umpires may order that notch to be scored. When the Ball is hit up either of the strikers may hinder the catch in his running ground, or if She is hit directly across the Wickets the Other Player may place his Body any where within the swing of his Batt so as to hinder the Bowler from catching her, but he must neither Strike at her nor touch her with his hands. If a striker nips up a Ball just before him he may fall before his Wicket, or pop down his Batt before She comes to it, to save it. The Bail hanging on one stump, though the Ball hit the Wicket, is not out.

Laws for Wicket Keepers

The Wicket Keeper shall stand at a reasonable distance behind the Wicket, and shall not move till the Ball is out of the Bowler's Hands, and shall not by any noise incommode the Striker; and if his knees, foot, or head be over or before his wicket, though the Ball strike it, it shall not be out.

Laws for the Umpires

To allow 2 minutes for each man to come in when one is out, and 10 minutes between Each Hand to mark the Ball, that it may not be changed. They are sole judges of all outs and ins, of all fair and unfair Play, of frivolous delays, of all hurts, whether real or pretended, and are discretionally to allow whatever time they think Proper before the Game goes on again. In case of a real hurt to a striker, they are to allow another to come in, and the Person hurt to come in again, but are not to allow a fresh Man to Play on either side on any Account. They are sole judges of all hindrances, crossing the Players in running, and Standing unfair to Strike; and in case of hindrance may order a notch to be scored. They are not to order any man out unless appealed to by one of the Players. These Laws are to the Umpires Jointly. Each Umpire is the Sole Judge of all Nips and Catches, Ins and Outs, good or bad runs at his own Wicket, and his determination shall be absolute; and he shall not be changed for another Umpire without the Consent of both Sides. When the 4 Balls are bowled he is to call over. These Laws are separately. When both Umpires shall call Play 3 Times 'tis at the Peril of giving the Game from them that refuse Play.

With the publication and acceptance of these Laws, cricket had achieved a genuine status, and was recognized as being suitable for both plebeians and patricians.

In the following summer the placing of the ball in the hole between the wickets was abolished, and the increase in the number of stumps from two to three was established. This was the outcome of a match between five of Hambledon and five of England, in which 'Lumpy' Stevens cleaned bowled John Small, the last batsman, on several occasions, only to see the ball pass through the stumps. The players, not surprisingly, deemed it unfair, and although Lumpy's comments at the time were not recorded, it did lead to the in-

Left Two fundamental pieces of cricket equipment, the bat and the ball, have changed little, certainly over the last hundred years. This can be clearly seen from the five bats which are on display at Lord's; a curved bat of 1750, a straight bat of 1793, Fuller Pilch's bat, W. G. Grace's bat and finally Don Bradman's bat of 1948. Recently, there have been various experiments with bats. These include a mandolin-shaped, or Jumbo bat, a two-faced, reversible bat and one from which part of the 'meat' at the back has been removed and the edges thickened. Different treatments are now given to the surface before use, so that it is no longer necessary to knock a bat in with an old ball or to oil it. Bats have also become more colourful, so that the make can be easily identified on television

troduction of a third stump.

Three stumps were in usage when James Aylward scored 167 for Hampshire CC out of their total of 403 against an All-England XI, an innings which was regarded as phenomenal and was thought to be a record individual score which would stand for a hundred years.

Several of the committee of noblemen and gentlemen who had drawn up the Laws in 1774 subsequently played together in the White Conduit Fields of Islington. This playing field was managed by the proprietor of the White Conduit Inn, and cricket had been played there since at least as early as 1719.

A year later, a group within the White Conduit Club decided that the easy access of the general public and the distinctly primitive conditions that existed at Islington were not good enough for them. They wanted somewhere private and much more exclusive. Two of the members, the Earl of Winchilsea and Charles Lennox, instructed Thomas Lord to look for somewhere suitable.

Lord was the son of a Yorkshire yeoman farmer who had lost his land as a result of supporting Prince Charlie in the '45 rebellion. He was an enthusiastic cricketer who acted as a bowler and a tactful general attendant for the White Conduit Club, and who would automatically have been a PRO in the 1970s. He obviously possessed considerable charm and business acumen, because his two patrons asked him to open a ground himself and guaranteed him both the money and their personal support, an offer which he could not refuse. He leased the land, now Dorset Square, from the Portman family, and in 1787 the first match was staged at Lord's between Middlesex and Essex. In that year the new club was christened the Marylebone Cricket Club and by 1800, having twice revised the Laws, was recognized as the game's supreme authority, a position that it has held ever since.

When the lease for the ground in Dorset Square expired, Thomas Lord rented two fields on the St John's Wood estate, and removed his sacred turf to the new home of the MCC in 1811, but it was not popular with the members, who never played there in either 1811 or 1812, and only made three appearances in 1813. When it became necessary to make the third and final move, because the Regent Canal was to be cut through the middle of the ground, Thomas Lord once again transferred his precious turf, this time to its present venue, and erected a pavilion, a tavern and a wall around the ground. The MCC and cricket had at last found their real and their spiritual home.

The rise of the MCC ended the domination of the Hambledon Club, as the former became the recognized authority for controlling the game. In 1788 the MCC issued their first edition of the Laws. These made life easier for the umpires by decreeing that a batsman was out l.b.w. even if his act was unintentional, and also cleared up a ruling which until then had allowed strikers to impede the fielding side in certain circumstances, and must have led to several distinctly unpleasant physical confrontations.

Cricket was designed for underarm bowling. Initially the majority of the bowlers largely relied on fast daisy cutters, whose effectiveness depended upon a combination of pace and the undulations in the pitch. Then, gradually, bowlers, with David Harris the outstanding example, discovered the advantages of length bowling in which the ball only bounced once. By the beginning of the nineteenth century bowlers were beginning to switch to the more suitable method of high underarm lobs. To counter these, batsmen were for the first time learning how to advance down the wicket to hit the ball on the full toss, by 'giving her the rush' as it was then called.

The marked improvement in both batting techniques and pitches was reflected in the ever increasing number of large totals and big individual scores. The bat was beginning to dominate the ball to an extent that was starting to upset the delicate balance that has to exist between the two. The solution was eventually provided by the round-arm revolution.

In the 1780s Tom Walker of Hambledon tried to introduce this new style, which was immediately condemned by his own club as throwing. However, it is generally agreed that the true innovator of round-arm bowling was John Willes of Sutton Valance. In 1807 his bowling in this style for XXIII of Kent against XIII of England proved so unpopular with

This picture by John Corbet Anderson shows William Lillywhite as he appeared in his Benefit Match at Lord's in 1853. Lillywhite was over thirty when he entered big time cricket, and it was the introduction of round-arm bowling which enabled him to become the finest bowler of his era. W. G. Grace wrote of him as follows: 'He was what we now call a "head bowler"; always on the look-out for a weak spot in the defence of the batsman, and trusting more to catches than to wickets bowled down.' He was a regular member of the All-England XI and Sussex. His sons and nephews, in addition to being fine cricketers, were to play a considerable part in developing the game through selling equipment, publishing cricket literature, and organizing tours to Australia

both players and spectators, because it made run-getting more difficult, that the game ended in a minor riot. Cricket history is full of rows.

Undeterred by this setback, Willes continued his campaign, and found imitators, although in 1816 the MCC decreed that all bowling must be underarm. His crusade eventually came to a dramatic end at Lord's in 1822, when he was playing for Kent against the MCC and was no-balled. Willes was so incensed that he threw down the ball, left the field in disgust and rode away on his horse, fading out of cricket history. This was rather sad because it was only a matter of time before his form of bowling not only became legal, but was to be the normal mode of attack.

He had, however, certainly sowed the seed, and his method was copied by immortal William Lillywhite and his bowling partner, James Broadbridge, whose combined success with the ball for Sussex transformed them into one of the most powerful teams in the land. The outcome was that Sussex were matched in three experimental games with the All-England XI. The county won the first two games and the English team, upset by these defeats, signed a manifesto that they would not play in the third unless 'the Sussex players bowl fair'.

The administrators ignored the threatened ban, and altered and strengthened the composition of the All-England XI, and the third

match took place, which Sussex lost by 24 runs largely because G. T. Knight produced an innings which showed that runs could be made against round-arm bowling.

The following year saw the round-arm advocates, with G. T. Knight at their head, launch a campaign to legalize the new style of bowling, and in May 1828 the MCC modified Law 10. Although this modification was not enough to allow either Lillywhite or Broadbridge to raise their hands to the height of their shoulders, they continued to do so with the tacit approval of the umpires and an ever increasing number of imitators. The outcome was that in 1835 the MCC gave way and altered the law to read: 'The ball must be bowled, and if it be thrown or jerked, or if the hand be above the shoulder in the delivery, the umpire must call "no-ball".'

The issue was nevertheless still not settled for bowlers, who, realizing that they would be even more effective if they raised their arms a shade higher, were soon transgressing without being penalized. Alfred Mynn introduced fast round-arm bowling and in 1845 the MCC were forced to modify Law 10 yet again, until in 1864 they at last gave bowlers complete freedom to bowl.

The many who feared that round-arm, and finally overarm, bowling would ruin the game were proved completely wrong, because batsmen quickly learned to cope with the greater pace and lift which occurred. Nevertheless, it

The famous Hambledon Club playing at Moulsey Hurst in 1790, by which time they had been overtaken by the MCC as the pre-eminent cricket club

was the most significant fundamental playing change to occur in the nineteenth century, because it revolutionized the art of both batting and bowling, so that towards the end of the century the game was not all that dissimilar to the cricket of the 1970s.

This law has continued to cause problems, because there has never been an entirely successful definition of bowling, covering all styles and all builds. The slight straightening of an arm can be difficult to discern even on a slow motion camera, and impossible for the human eye. Then there is the problem of the bowler with an abnormally flexible arm and wrist who will automatically become an object of suspicion.

In retrospect, one cannot help feeling that it might have been better if the eighteenth-century legislators had avoided definition and simply allowed bowlers to propel the ball any way they liked. This would have avoided numerous rows and witch hunts. It would have made batting more difficult, but speeded up the game, as the enormous run-ups which waste so much time would not have been necessary. Instead of great bowlers, there would simply have been great pitchers.

Before leaving the world of round-arm bowling, it is worth examining the contrasting methods of two of its greatest early practitioners, Lillywhite and Mynn.

Lillywhite, known as the 'Non Pareil', operated from round the wicket at slow-medium pace. He owed his success to his exceptional accuracy and capacity to 'think batsmen out'. It is significant that at fifty-five he was still able to bowl for the Players against the Gentlemen.

Mynn, the 'Lion of Kent', was a big man, over six feet tall, and weighing an impressive eighteen stones. He walked to the wicket 'like a soldier on parade' before delivering the ball at a pace which opposing batsmen found both fast and frightening. When one remembers that many of the wickets were still rough, that pads were decidedly fragile and often not used, and that gloves were seldom worn, this is hardly surprising. In addition, Mynn was a hard-hitting batsman and an immensely popular figure, as is illustrated by his epitaph, typically Victorian but completely sincere, when he died in 1861:

All were proud of him, all loved him . . .
As the changing seasons pass
As our champion lies a-sleeping underneath the
*   Kentish grass,*
Proudly, sadly, we will name him—to forget
*   him were a sin.*
Lightly lie the turf upon thee, kind and manly
*   Alfred Mynn.*

The first great county side was Hampshire at the turn of the nineteenth century. They were to be succeeded by Surrey, Sussex and then the Kent of Alfred Mynn, who so often defeated All-England.

Among the best players of this period was Fuller Pilch, who between 1820 and 1850 was easily the finest batsman in the land. He scored most of his runs, including ten centuries, off his front foot. His version of the drive was known as 'Pilch's poke' and he relied largely on placement. His opening partner on many occasions was another fine player, Felix, a left-hander with a pleasing style and undoubted character, who was also a musician and who invented both tubular batting gloves and a bowling machine.

At the start of the century Lambert was generally considered to be the most complete all-rounder and an outstanding single wicket expert. In addition to his batting and bowling, he was a capable wicketkeeper, while Lord Beauclerk was most consistent of the amateur batsmen.

Two of cricket's most interesting characters: Alfred Mynn and 'Felix' (Nicholas Wanostracht). The former was a massive man, weighing some eighteen stones, a hard hitting batsman, a very fast bowler and a much loved character. Felix was of Belgian extraction and extremely versatile. In addition to being the best amateur batsman of his time, he was also a musician, a painter, a headmaster and a writer. He wrote *Felix on the Bat*, an illustrated instructional book, and invented tubular batting gloves and a bowling machine

THE YEARS OF GRACE

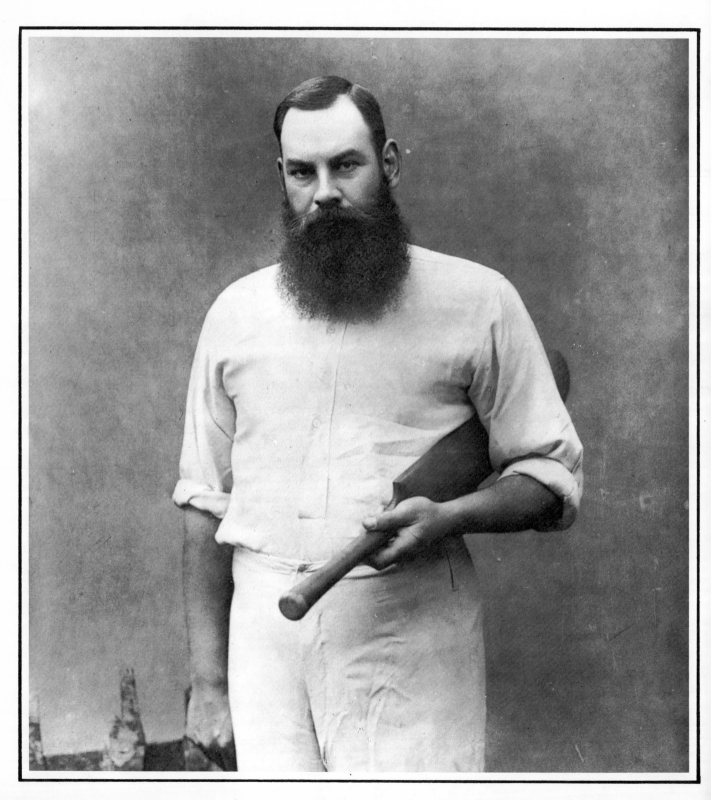

W. G. Grace was in every sense a big man, with a huge frame and the muscular strength to support sixteen stones and still move quickly. When over fifty, he was still a good enough cricketer to command a place in the England XI. Though he remained an amateur for more than forty years in First Class cricket, he was highly professional in his approach to the game and to making money. In addition to generous expenses, various testimonials brought him more than £10,000, a huge sum in those days. He needed the money as he was a General Practitioner in a poor country district and had to pay locums to stand in during the summer and occasionally the winter months. He was a good family doctor and especially sympathetic to his poorer patients. An absolute master of gamesmanship, Grace was not above bending the rules to suit his own requirements. The following sentence, taken from *The Book of Cricket* by C. B. Fry, sums him up perfectly: 'In the mythology of cricket, he is Jupiter, the king.' He was indeed a superb all-rounder, a born competitor, a very shrewd tactician and the greatest character the game has ever known. We shall not see his like again

Although W. G. Grace was not born until 1848, did not take part in his first county match against Devonshire until he was fourteen, and was still scoring runs in the twentieth century, I have no hesitation in calling this period the Years of Grace, because for the major part of the second half of the nineteenth century he dominated the game, both as a player and as a personality, to an infinitely greater extent than anyone before or since.

He was, in every sense, the Colossus of Cricket. His performances, which no other cricketer of his era even approached, combined with his striking physique and appearance, made him an irresistible attraction. Wherever he was playing crowds would flock to see him, the biggest single sporting box office attraction ever produced in England, and nobody did more than he to make cricket the number one summer sport of Victorian and Edwardian times.

In his very long reign W.G. broke all the existing records with figures which would be remarkable today, but which were quite unbelievable then. In First Class cricket he scored 54,896 runs, took 2,864 wickets, hit 126 centuries, and made 1,000 runs in May—thirty years after his first appearance at this level.

With international cricket in its infancy, the most testing matches were in the main those between Gentlemen and Players, which besides containing most of the finest cricketers, had that little extra bite resulting from a clash of class. W.G.'s performances in these games are probably the best illustration of his ability.

He first turned out for the Gentlemen in 1865, as a sixteen-year-old, and as the Players had won the last seventeen matches on the trot, the result was considered something of a formality. His skill with bat and ball was to change all that. The Gentlemen went on to win twenty-seven and lose only four of the next thirty-nine encounters. In three successive years at the start of the 1870s his personal scores were 217, 77, 112, 117, 163, 158 and 70, and this was against the best bowling in the land, because the Players, by the very nature of things, had always had the stronger attack and most of the fast bowlers. Before his playing career ended, the bearded doctor was to make 6,000 runs and take 270

wickets in these special contests.

Although in his later years the wickets were very good, in his early days he was regularly making centuries on indifferent tracks and on grounds where it was often necessary to run every run scored. He revolutionized the technique of batting and turned it into an art form on which the basic principles of modern batsmanship are based. Until his arrival batsmen tended to be either front or back foot players, but W.G. was equally adept off either foot, which automatically doubled his range of strokes.

D. J. Knight in Sir Pelham Warner's book *Cricket* also ascribed that hybrid defensive shot the half-cock to W.G., when he wrote:

'There is a stroke very often adopted by present-day batsmen—indeed we believe the king of batsmen, W. G. Grace, employed it a great deal—known by the name of the half-cock stroke. It is a cross between the forward stroke and the back stroke.'

In other words, W.G., besides being an expert off his front and back foot, discovered the usefulness of over-the-crease play against the quicker bowlers. Like all truly great batsmen, he had the time because he was in the correct position early. He had the defence, but he also possessed the ability to destroy good bowling by hitting it along the ground with a straight bat, and even as an old man he thrived against the quickies.

Although W. G. Grace was a natural games player and an outstanding athlete, batting is not a natural art, and he was lucky to have been well coached at an early age, to have had a talented family who were devoted to the game, and to have been able to practise as a very small boy on a good pitch in the garden, or rather orchard. W.G. wrote as follows:

'By the time I was nine years old I had got over the elementary stage of stopping the ball, and was slowly acquiring power in meeting it firmly and playing it away. Playing with a straight bat had become easy to me and my uncle [Alfred Pocock, who knew the game and was a very proficient player] told me that I was on the right track, and I patiently continued it ... "Do not allow the bowler to stick you up, or it is all over with you," he said. I could now play forward as well as back; but of course, had to be content with less firmness, quite satisfied if I could meet the ball with a straight bat.'

In other words, the success of W.G. owed much to a complete grounding in the game as a child, and he worked really hard at it. Incidentally, his elder brother E. M. Grace was also a fine batsman who played for England and was considered to be the most exciting and unorthodox hitter of his time.

Before 1850 cricket in England was largely confined to certain regions. It had long flourished in Kent, Hampshire, Surrey, Nottinghamshire, Middlesex and Sussex, but elsewhere it was mainly limited to certain country clubs and to several of the larger cities. What was to change all this was the formation in 1846 of the All-England XI, which proceeded to spread the gospel up and down the land and to make the game universally popular.

This club, founded by William Clarke, was conducted on business lines and contained the best professionals. Clarke was prepared to take his team anywhere, providing the price was right. The difficulty was finding strong enough opposition, with the result that his XI would normally play a local XXII, who were often reinforced by a couple of professional bowlers.

All aspiring cricket professionals wanted a place in this All-England XI, because of the money and the prestige that it provided. It soon became obvious that Clarke, a somewhat autocratic dictator, could not accommodate and please everyone, with the result that another professional side was formed, the United England XI, which included three of the All-England XI's best known players, Wisden, Grundy and Lillywhite. This trio were all dissatisfied with the remuneration they had received from Clarke.

Initially there was considerable bad feeling between the two teams, both of whom made money and found plenty of enthusiastic opponents. This animosity did not end until Parr had taken over the management of the All-England XI, after the death of Clarke, when a match was arranged between them for the benefit of the Cricketers' Fund.

The first English touring team, who undertook a highly successful trip to Canada and the United States in 1859

This drawing of John Wisden is by J. C. Anderson, who produced a series of portraits of cricketers in the 1850s. Wisden, who was a small man, played for Sussex and the All-England XI. He started as a fast round-arm bowler, and became the first man to clean-bowl all ten batsmen. Later, he switched to slow lobs, and throughout his career he was a dependable, rather unspectacular batsman. However, he will be remembered best for starting the 'cricketers' Bible', *Wisden Cricketers' Almanack*, first published in 1864 and still the game's main reference book

The United XI was eventually disbanded in 1869, largely because a splinter group had formed the United South of England XI, so that in effect there was then almost a split between southern and northern professionals, with the latter entirely making up the All-England XI. This seriously interfered with many inter-county matches and led to continual bickering, although the meetings between these two deadly rivals certainly provided the cricket highlights of the summer, and were fought in a spirit often not in keeping with the game.

The MCC and the administrators of the county clubs were not over-enthusiastic about these nomadic professional sides, but as the number of county matches was so limited they were unable to offer the best professional players sufficiently attractive contracts to lure them away, and were forced to tolerate them until, in the mid-1870s, there was enough support for county cricket.

However, it should not be forgotten that it was the efforts of these paid performers which really popularized the game and paved the way for the existing domestic system. The role of these great professional XIs was not dissimilar to that of the Rothman Cavaliers, who a hundred years later showed what could be achieved by forty-overs cricket on a Sunday afternoon, and having established the event were then replaced by the John Player League.

There will always be arguments as to when the County Championship commenced, because the oldest of cricket competitions did not start in a particular season and the first Championship table to be published by Wisden was in 1889. Today's Wisden dates the Championship back to 1864. A number of resolutions was passed by representatives of the First Class counties in December 1872, and the following summer at the Oval the basic rules for qualification were laid down, with the MCC appointed as the final arbitrator in any dispute.

What was not decided was how the Championship should be awarded, and in the early days it went to the county with fewest matches lost—an unsatisfactory arrangement, especially as the number of games played varied considerably. The nine original First Class counties were Derbyshire, Gloucestershire, Kent, Lancashire, Middlesex, Nottinghamshire, Surrey, Sussex and Yorkshire, with the bulk of the players in the north being professional, and in the south amateur.

In the 1880s Nottinghamshire was the outstanding team, thanks largely to two bowlers, Shaw and Morley, and the batting of Barnes, Gunn and Shrewsbury. The success of Shaw, round-arm, medium-paced, accurate and able to move the ball off the pitch either way, and Morley, very fast, left round-arm, who had the ability to pitch leg and hit off on certain wickets, illustrated the value—which has so often been rediscovered—of having a two-pronged, contrasting spearhead.

I like W. G. Grace's assessment of Morley in the two other departments, which underlines one of the ways the game has changed: 'He was a very poor bat, and a very indifferent fieldsman. His name was invariably last on the batting list, and when he made a run the crowd cheered him heartily'—shades of Bill Bowes, but this applies to very few modern bowlers. Morley's career suffered from an injury to his side, from which he never completely recovered. It occurred when the steamer taking him to Australia in 1882 collided with another.

A new system of points, one for a win and a half for a draw, was introduced in 1887, but the difference in the number of matches played made this also not entirely suitable or fair. It was to remain in force until 1895 and the period was dominated by an outstanding Surrey XI, which included George Lohmann, a fast-medium round-arm bowler with a beautiful action, who was able to change pace without any discernible alteration and was at that time considered the best bowler to have toured Australia; the big hearted Tom Richardson, a great fast bowler; a fine all-rounder Bill Lockwood; and the cheerful Robert Abel, a dependable batsman, brilliant field and useful change bowler.

Yorkshire, under the very autocratic Lord Hawke, won their first full Championship in 1893, a pointer to the future, while the next year Derbyshire (restored), Essex, Leicestershire and Warwickshire joined the First Class counties. Somerset had been admitted earlier, and Hampshire came in one year later. There was also another change in the points system,

Below The England XI which toured Australia in 1876–7 and lost by 45 runs the first Test ever to be played between the two countries, at Melbourne. The side, captained by James Lillywhite, had their revenge when they won the return by 4 wickets, also at Melbourne. This all-professional team was reasonably strong, but certainly not the most powerful side available

Below right The first Australian team to tour England, in 1878. It was captained by David Gregory, a member of a great cricketing family: three of his brothers represented New South Wales, and he was the uncle of the fast bowling all-rounder Jack Gregory and of Sydney Gregory, who played in fifty-two Tests, an audacious batsman and an ideal number six, because he could also defend. No Tests were played on the 1878 trip, but the tourists had a rigorous programme of forty matches, of which twenty-one were played against the odds. Their most memorable feat was to beat a powerful MCC XI in one day, thanks to some inspired bowling from Boyle and Spofforth, forcing the English to realize that Australian cricket had to be taken very seriously

Below The England XI of 1890, captained by W. G. Grace. England won two Tests against the Australians that summer, the first by 7 wickets and the second by 2 wickets, while the third, at Old Trafford, was completely washed out. Three players, Stoddart, Peel and Ulyett, opted out of the second match to play for their counties rather than their country

with one point being awarded for each victory and one point deducted for each defeat, the final order being decided by the proportion of points gained to matches completed.

The weakness was that it put a premium, in certain circumstances, on securing a draw. This, together with the improvement of batting among the counties and better wickets, inevitably led to a marked increase in the number of drawn games with seventy out of the 166 staged in 1900 ending in this way.

The Years of Grace saw the birth of overseas and international cricket. The first tour took place in 1859 and was, rather strangely in retrospect, to Canada and the United States. The twelve professionals chosen came in equal numbers from the All-England and the United England XIs, typical of the spirit of compromise which has been such a feature of English cricket and political life ever since. The opposition was far from strong and all the matches were won. This trip produced around £90 per head, which was very good pay (far better, indeed, than the remuneration players were to receive later) for a tour that only lasted two months, and included a couple of rather unpleasant boat trips lasting about fourteen days each.

Two years later the first tour to Australia took place. It was sponsored by Messrs Spiers and Pond, and although the northern professionals did not like the guaranteed terms of £150 for a lengthy trip, which was understandable after the easy money picked up in North America, H. H. Stephenson raised a reasonable side, certainly powerful enough for the task. The crowds Down Under were good and it is interesting to note that this was one of the very few times a sponsor has actually made a large profit from a sporting venture!

In the winter of 1863–4 another English touring party, under Parr and with E. M. Grace as the only amateur, visited Australia. They too, were undefeated. Although all the matches were against the odds, Australian cricket was steadily improving, so that when W. G. Grace took out the third English side nine years later on what was really his honeymoon, the opposition, although the games were still not on level terms, was much stronger, especially the bowling.

It was the fourth tour by an all-professional side under James Lillywhite that really caught the imagination of the Australian public. In 1877 England met for the first time a full Australian XI and, thanks very largely to an innings of 165 by Bannerman, were defeated by 45 runs in the first Test ever played between the two countries. It must surely have been more than fate that when the Centenary Test was played there in 1977 the outcome should have been identical. Lillywhite's team gained their revenge in the next encounter, but from that moment Australia had become a power to be reckoned with, though the point was not yet realized by England.

In 1878 the Australians made their first visit to England and W. G. Grace wrote:

'We were glad to see them, but not very much alarmed about being defeated by them. We had their victory against Lillywhite's team the previous year in Australia fresh in our memories, and inferred from it that the game had advanced rapidly in that country.'

What he did not believe, and nor did anyone else at that time, was that Australia was beginning to threaten England's supremacy, although he felt they *might* give some of the counties a close run for their money. This view was upheld when the tourists went down heavily in their first match against Nottinghamshire, but when they thrashed the MCC, one of the strongest all-round teams in the country, by 9 wickets in one day, the public began to sit up and take notice. In bowling and fielding the Aussies could hold their own, but their batting was not of the same class.

What surprised many people was that their bowlers, all amateurs, were the equal of the English bowlers, who were mainly professional. The growing strength of Australian cricket was further reflected when they won the only Test in Lord Harris's tour out there in 1878–9, though the English side was far from the best available.

The next Australian visit to England in 1880 was unusual in that nobody appeared to know for certain that they were coming, and the First Class Fixture List was completed without their inclusion. The outcome was that

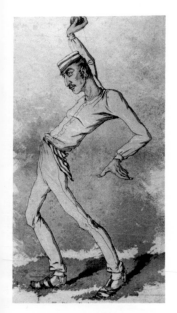

Between 1876 and 1886, F. R. Spofforth captured 94 wickets in eighteen Test matches against England, which more than justified his nickname—the Demon. The main secret of his success, apart from line and length, was his ability to change pace without this being perceptible to the batsman: with no change in run up or action, he could deliver a slow, a medium, or a genuinely quick ball, while he possessed a vicious break-back. The Demon was the most feared bowler of his age, and an all-time great

the tourists had to be content largely with matches with clubs against the odds, and they were even forced to advertise for fixtures! However, Lord Harris agreed to lead an England XI against them at the Oval on 6, 7 and 8 September. It was only appropriate that W. G. Grace should mark the occasion of the first Test in England, and his own first Test, by scoring 152. It was also to be the only Test played by his younger brother, Fred Grace, as within a month he fell sick and died.

The best Australian cricketers were Bannerman, with a redoubtable defence; Murdoch, a batsman of real quality; Blackham, who stood up to everything in all conditions and was to be the first of a long line of outstanding keepers from Down Under, and three bowlers, who on this tour secured a combined haul of 909 victims—the incomparable Spofforth, Boyle and Palmer.

Spofforth, so rightly called the Demon, was a right-hander with a good action, fairly fast, and able to move the ball either way off the wicket. He varied his pace with great skill, possessed a fast yorker, and his control was such that it was said at the time: 'If he were allowed to pour water on a space six inches square, he would bowl out the best XI in England for a very small score.'

Boyle was an accurate medium pacer, able to break the ball a little either way; while Palmer, close to being genuinely quick, relied on the 'nip-backer' but would include a genuine slow leg-break from time to time which, although occasionally successful, proved a rather expensive luxury in the long run.

The Ashes originated in 1882, when Australia dramatically defeated England, who, needing 85 to win in their second innings, were dismissed for 77, with Spofforth ensuring immortality 7 for 44. The mock epitaph the following day in the *Sporting Times* contained an N.B. which read: 'The body will be cremated and the ashes taken to Australia.'

The following winter, 1882–3, the Hon. Ivo Bligh took to Australia a team which won the rubber. At the end of the third match the stumps were burnt by some Australian ladies, who sealed up the ashes in an urn and presented them to the English captain. He bequeathed them in his will to the MCC, and they have remained at Lord's ever since.

Since then every series between England and Australia has been a 'Fight for the Ashes', which has both a romantic and a traditional appeal. It sounds far more dramatic to say that you have won the Ashes than to say that you have won the rubber. The snag has been that the country holding the Ashes retains them until beaten in another series, which has been known to make captains, at least in more recent times, over careful, for a drawn series can achieve the objective.

Tours to and from Australia continued for the remainder of the century, with fortunes zig-zagging backwards and forwards, as they have done ever since, with England on top for a spell and then Australia. There were, however, some intriguing incidents. In 1893, after the first day of their match against Oxford and Cambridge Universities Past and Present, the Australians found themselves 346 for 4, but the law as it stood at the time—it was to take a further seven years before it was altered—only allowed a declaration on the final day, so they went on batting throughout the second day and were finally all out on the third, by which time they had amassed 843. With much justification, Australian batsmen have ever been reluctant to throw their wickets away.

In 1887–8 two English touring teams went to Australia. This produced a substantial loss and highlighted the disadvantages of private individuals taking out sides. The need for controlling bodies to organize international cricket was obvious, and was eventually recognized. But not until the start of the twentieth century.

THE GOLDEN ERA

Left F. S. Jackson: talking to W. G. Grace in 1905, and a Spy cartoon of 1902. Jackson's year was 1905, when England won the Ashes under his command and he enjoyed a wonderful summer with both ball and bat. The season included a masterful 144 not out at Leeds and an over at Nottingham in which he dismissed Noble, Hill and Darling. He quite rightly acquired a reputation as 'the man for the big occasion'. A fine, orthodox batsman, he made 5 centuries against Australia as well as a number of scores of fifty or more, but unfortunately he was never able to tour. A medium-paced bowler with an easy action, he retired from First Class cricket in 1907, when he was still in his prime

Above C. B. Fry gained Blues at Oxford for cricket, athletics and soccer. He was also a fine performer at golf, swimming, rugby, tennis, rowing and throwing the javelin. He could run a hundred yards in evens, his high jumping was excellent, and he established a world record in the long jump which lasted for twenty-one years. At soccer, he was capped for England and played in an FA Cup Final. He started his cricket career as a predominantly front foot player, but later, no doubt influenced by his association with Ranji in the Sussex team, he also became a master off the back foot. A brilliant all-purpose fieldsman, he was also a useful fast bowler, until the legality of his action was questioned—probably the legacy of javelin throwing. An academic of real quality (he gained a First at university), a fine speaker, a good writer and above all a superb athlete— C. B. Fry was unique

There are various reasons why these fourteen years have become known as the Golden Era, although I rather fancy that the late Harry Altham and Jim Swanton, in their splendid *History of Cricket*, were more accurate when they termed it the 'Golden Age of Batting'.

In the first place, it was unquestionably an idyllic time to play cricket in England. The world was a settled and ordered place with Great Britain a rich and powerful country, supported by an empire upon which the sun never set. The realities of modern war were as yet unknown. The existing social structure was accepted by the vast majority of the population and the cricketers were able to concentrate on the game they loved without having to worry over-much about anything else.

Second, the game was very popular and did not have to compete with other sports, providing a reasonable standard of living for the professionals and enjoyment for the many amateurs who then had the money to play for fun. By this it should not be imagined that the counties did not have financial problems, despite good attendances and the receipts from membership. At the end of each season Essex, for example, would declare a loss at their AGM, but this would then be covered by a substantial donation from Mr Green, the President. The wealthy, who were not then taxed out of existence and moving to tax havens abroad, were generous to cricket, which to no small extent depended for its existence on patronage.

Third, the standards were high. It is doubtful whether England has ever had more outstanding players than in this period, certainly never so many high quality batsmen and genuine fast bowlers.

Fourth, there was an abundance of good batting, which has always attracted spectators. This was in no small measure due to the perfect pitches. Their excellence was the result of there being no shortage of labour to prepare them, which was also reflected in the high quality of the net wickets. In those days it was worthwhile, and usually possible, to have a net on a perfect pitch immediately before going out to bat.

It may have become a game for batsmen with the odds loaded against the unfortunate bowler, but as the amateurs who controlled the sport were mainly batsmen this was entirely understandable.

The ascendancy of amateur batsmen stemmed from the early coaching they had received on good wickets at school and university, where they learned to hit through the line of the ball without fear of it doing anything unnatural. The outcome was plenty of attractive shots played with the full swing of the bat. Unquestionably, cricket was a less complicated game, but must have been enormous fun to play and watch.

I remember asking Kortright, a legendary fast bowler from Essex, if he ever deliberately bowled a bouncer. His answer was revealing. 'No', he said, 'I simply bowled as fast as I could at the off stump and they tried to hit me as hard as possible through the off-side.'

This emphasis on hitting the ball to the off was borne out by that fine Australian all-rounder, George Giffen, when he wrote: 'Leg-hitting during recent years has become almost an extinct art.' He went on to extol the virtues of the leg glance:

'The fact that usually two men only are placed on the on-side of the field by most bowlers makes this a stroke which ought to be specially cultivated, for even if you make a mis-hit there is seldom anyone at hand to catch it.'

With batsmen thirsting to drive the ball through the covers and most of the bowlers trying to make the ball leave the bat, a good in-swinger had to prove successful. In 1901 George Hirst, a lively fast-medium, discovered how to swing the ball into the right-handed batsman and proceeded to cause havoc with his late in-swing through the 'gate'. What was especially impressive about his large haul of wickets was the high percentage which came from the first five in the order. It should be remembered that only one new ball was allowed per innings.

To substantiate the claim that England has never produced quite so many high quality cricketers as in the Golden Era, I have simply picked out some of the star performers. Cricket, like all sports, has changed and in certain aspects improved, but I have always believed that the outstanding performer of any age would be able to adapt himself to the new requirements.

I thought I would start with the amateur batsmen who graced the cricket grounds and who, although they were very keen to score and were often successful, did not have the pressure of knowing that failure could lead to the non-payment of the mortgage.

The Australians of this period considered that Archie MacLaren was the best batsman England had sent out there. He played in a grand, almost disdainful manner, convinced that he could dominate any attack and equally determined that no bowler should be allowed to dictate to him. He captained England and although an interesting, if sometimes rather naive, theorist and a reasonable tactician, lacked tact. More Victorian than Edwardian in outlook, he never really came to terms with the post-war world.

C. B. Fry was not only a superb all-round athlete, but also possessed an academic brain which he used to very good effect in cricket. He studied the game and turned himself from a highly competent player into one of the best, and probably the most consistent batsmen in the country. He would have been even more successful (and a career average of almost fifty is an indication of his skill) if he had not been so sensitive and highly strung, and therefore susceptible to the criticism which occurred whenever he failed with the bat.

The Hon. F. S. Jackson, although never able to tour Australia, made five centuries against the Australians, as well as numerous fifties. A thoughtful, studious bat, he realized the importance of playing himself in, which considering his Yorkshire background was hardly surprising. He was also a good medium-paced bowler, and like another great Yorkshire cricketer many years later, Maurice Leyland, he was very definitely a man for the big match occasion. He proved himself to be a good captain of England, tactful and considerate, so that he was both liked and respected by his team.

Gilbert Jessop was probably the most exciting cricketer that this country has ever produced, a genuine hitter, who scored runs at the highest level and at a pace which made him both a unique entertainer and a match-winner. In addition, he was a very fine fast bowler and a superb fielder. His closest modern equivalent was probably Sir Learie Constantine, but he never matched Jessop's batting feats at Test level. A Philadelphian newspaper described Jessop as 'the human catapult who wrecks the roofs of distant towns when set in his assault.'

He crouched at the wicket and relied largely on the power of his driving, his pulling and his ability to cut fiercely anything remotely short. His feats of fast scoring are a legend. His highest innings was 286 against Sussex, which took under three hours. In the Lord's Test against South Africa, never having faced their googly bowlers before, he made 93 out of 145 from the 63 balls he received, and a century in an hour was a score he achieved on numerous occasions. If it were possible to reincarnate one player from the past, my choice would be Gilbert Jessop—the 'Croucher' would pack any ground.

The incomparable Ranjitsinhji will be dealt with in the Indian section, but he was unquestionably the most exciting stroke-maker in country cricket at the turn of the century.

R. E. Foster, who made 287 in his first Test at Sydney, was an exceptionally graceful player, who, like Fry, also represented England at soccer and indeed excelled at all games, while Reggie Spooner was a supreme stroker of the ball, whose timing was so good that he would reach the boundary without appearing to have put any power behind the shot.

It must not be imagined that all the star batsmen were to be found in the amateur ranks. Tom Hayward, who scored 3,518 runs in the 1906 season, was not only a great and consistently successful opener, but being completely imperturbable, was ideally suited to the role. Very sound and strong off his back foot, he was the sheet anchor which every side requires.

Johnny Tyldesley was a magnificent batsman and, as might have been said earlier about Arthur Shrewsbury, he was supreme on a really bad wicket. In England these can be difficult, but in Australia they can be nearly impossible. On a Melbourne 'sticky' in 1904 the Lancastrian made 62 out of a total of 103, and anyone who has ever tried to bat under those conditions will know exactly what that

Below The Master. Jack Hobbs was born in Cambridgeshire and recommended to Surrey by Hayward. From the moment he appeared for the county XI in 1905 it was obvious that a player of genius had arrived. Jack Hobbs is generally considered to have been the most complete batsman of all time: he had all the strokes, together with a wonderful defence; he was equally at home against pace or spin, and he excelled on every sort of wicket. His most spectacular period was before World War I, when he was England's leading batsman and it was by no means unusual for him to start a match with three fours in the opening over. When he eventually retired from the game in 1934, he had made 61,237 runs and hit 197 First Class centuries **Below right** Frank Woolley, a tall, graceful man, in his early days before World War I, when he was a world class all-rounder. As a batsman, he was a glorious left-hander, with flowing strokes and the ability to hit the ball over the top with elegance and certainty. He was also a very good slow left-arm bowler, slightly quicker through the air than Blythe and devastating on a sticky. In addition, he was an excellent slip or short leg. I had the good fortune to see him score a half century against Essex in the

The 1911–12 MCC team to Australia was one of the finest ever sent there. Sir Pelham Warner, who led the party, fell ill after the first match, and J. W. H. T. Douglas captained all five Tests. Australia won the first Test by 146 runs, thanks very largely to a Trumper century and to 12 wickets taken by leg-break and googly bowler H. V. Hordern. The remaining Tests were won easily by England. The decisive factor was the bowling of S. F. Barnes and F. R. Foster, who formed a deadly spearhead. They received excellent support, especially from J. W. H. T. Douglas and W. Rhodes. J. B. Hobbs was also in wonderful form with the bat, and there were plenty of runs from G. Gunn, F. E. Woolley, J. W. Hearne, F. R. Foster and W. Rhodes

late 1930s on a green wicket against a very accomplished pace attack. He was then about fifty years old, but he had no difficulty in driving the fast bowlers back over their heads, or hooking them to the boundary. His runs came in under the hour, and I have seldom seen anything more beautiful

represents in terms of skill and determination.

Then, of course, there was Sir Jack Hobbs, the most complete batsman England has ever produced, the acknowledged master, and the greatest opener the world has ever seen. Although he was to go on breaking records and scoring centuries after World War I, it is generally agreed that he was at his most brilliant and exciting in this halcyon period.

Since the end of World War II, England has produced only a handful of all-rounders of international calibre, of whom two, Tony Greig and Basil d'Oliveira, learned the game in South Africa. But there was certainly no shortage in the Golden Era. Frank Foster was only twenty-two when Warwickshire, with a far from exceptional side, carried off the County Championship under his captaincy. This was in the main due to his deeds with both bat and ball. He was for his age the most brilliant all-rounder England has ever produced. It was his bowling with Barnes which was mainly responsible for England's success in the 1911–12 tour to Australia. Unfortunately, a motor-cycle accident cut short his career before he had even reached his prime. Another great amateur all-rounder of the period was J. W. H. T. Douglas, who was mentally and physically tougher than the volatile Foster, but had less natural ability. Jack Hobbs rated him as one of the finest new ball bowlers he had ever encountered, while he invariably had to be dug out when batting.

Wilfred Rhodes and George Hirst were surely the finest pair of all-rounders any county has ever possessed, the former doing the 'double' on sixteen, and the latter on fourteen occasions: the mind boggles. In 1906 Hirst achieved what I consider the most remarkable all-round feat ever, scoring more than 2,000 runs and capturing over 200 wickets, a performance that required not only outstanding ability, but also immense stamina. Hirst was to be the backbone of England and Yorkshire for many years, a born fighter, yet liked and respected by everyone because, as Sir Pelham Warner wrote: 'In many ways he is the ideal cricketer, so straight, so strong, so honest.'

Middlesex also had two brilliant all-rounders, the Australian, Frank Tarrant and 'Young Jack' Hearne, who after he had established himself as a brilliant batsman developed into a fine leg-break and googly bowler.

Frank Woolley, that graceful left-hander,

was yet another of the superb all-rounders of this era; while one must not forget Gilbert Jessop, nor the arrival of J. N. Crawford, possibly the best schoolboy cricketer of all time, who went straight into the Surrey side and immediately established himself as a top-class performer with bat and ball.

Every team needs a good slow left-armer who is both a match winner and a stock bowler, and England have never again had three of the same stature as the supreme classical artist 'Charlie' Blythe, Wilfred Rhodes and Frank Woolley, all available at the same time. Nor was there any shortage of wrist-spinners. This form of attack became very popular after the 1907 visit by South Africa, who included no fewer than four leg-break and googly bowlers in their team: Schwarz, White, Vogler and Faulkner.

Writing in the early 1920s, A. C. MacLaren had this to say about googly bowling, which again indicates how the game has changed technically: 'The unfortunate effect of googly bowling has been to drive the batsman back on his wicket in order to get time to see which way the ball would break.' Because the batsman was unsure of which way it would turn, he considered these tactics sensible. This is interesting, as from the 1930s to the 1960s to play back to a wrist-spinner was to invite disaster: out l.b.w. to the top-spinner. However, MacLaren's complaint was that more and more batsmen were moving back and

across the wicket before the ball had been delivered for *all types of bowling*, which automatically put them on the defensive. This is precisely the initial movement which most of the great batsmen of the world were to employ against pace, not wrist-spin, in the years that lay ahead.

The googly, a wrist-spun off-break which gives the appearance of being a leg-break, was the brain child of Bernard Bosanquet, father of the British newscaster. He discovered the principle by tossing a spun tennis ball over a table with the object of making it difficult for the receiver to make a clean catch. He noted that he could often deceive the catcher as to which way the ball would turn after landing. His next task was to see if it were possible to achieve the same effect when the ball was actually bowled. It took five years of constant practice, starting with a rubber ball in a net, before Bosanquet introduced this new type of delivery, the 'Bosie', into First Class cricket. At first he was laughed at, but he was soon to have his revenge, because batsmen, especially the ordinary players, were worried and disconcerted at having to play a ball whose break they were unable to determine until after it had pitched.

Clem Hill believed that England would not have won the Ashes on the 1903–4 tour without Bosanquet. 'There were five or six in the side who were practically certain to be got out by Bosanquet . . . Those men would have

Above and top right Sydney Barnes bowls his way to another victory: England v. South Africa at the Oval in 1912. The tourists were dismissed for 95 and 93, Barnes capturing 5 for 23 and 8 for 29, and clean-bowling 6 of his 13 victims. He was born in 1873 and played his first First Class match for Warwickshire in 1895, when he was twenty-two. He only took part in two seasons of First Class cricket, both for Lancashire. Most of his career as a professional cricketer, which spanned forty-five years, was spent in League and Minor County cricket. He captured 1,441 wickets at 8.15 apiece for Staffordshire—unbelievable figures. Barnes was highly dangerous on the best pitches, and a killer on anything which gave him the slightest assistance

Right George Hirst was originally a fast left-arm bowler, who learned to harness swerve and who used it to great effect. A squat, chunky figure, he scored a great many runs and held a large number of catches for both Yorkshire and England; but above all else this magnificent all-rounder was a fighter in the very best traditions of a county which has produced more than most

BARNES (LANCASHIRE)

made their thirties and forties against Rhodes, Hirst, Arnold and Braund.'

The inventor, however, like so many of his subsequent imitators had his off days when he found he could not drop his googly and the batsmen took their sweet revenge.

Since World War II, genuine fast bowlers, as distinct from the fast-medium seam brigade, have been in short supply, but this was not the case in the Golden Era, which produced Mold and Brearley of Lancashire, Richardson and Lockwood and later Knox for Surrey, Kortright of Essex, Warren and Bestwick of Derbyshire, Jessop of Gloucestershire, Bland of Sussex, Wilson of Worcestershire, and Fielder and Bradley of Kent, to name but a few.

If the Golden Era provided some of the finest batsmen the world has ever seen and certainly the best wickets, it also produced many great bowlers. It had to, because good pitches and batting will inevitably beget quality bowling. There is no place on plumb tracks, where the shine quickly departs and the outfields are not slowed down by a thick carpet of grass, for the 'phantom seamer', who 'does a little' on a grassy pitch. It was therefore not surprising that probably the greatest of all attacking bowlers should have been at his peak in this period, Sydney Barnes, a difficult, frequently irritable character, a loner who did not suffer fools gladly, but what a beautiful bowler!

His speed was akin to that of Alec Bedser, with a high classical action and immaculate control. He swung the new ball, varied his pace, and detested batsmen, but his greatest asset lay in his ability to make the ball deviate after pitching, both from the off and from the leg. Because the spin, or cut, was derived from the fingers, the batsman could not judge from his hand.

His First Class career was brief, as he was to play most of his cricket in the Lancashire League and for Staffordshire, because Lancashire were not prepared to pay him what he considered to be his worth. If A. C. MacLaren had not appreciated his outstanding ability and taken him to Australia as a comparative unknown, his most outstanding feats for England in Australia, South Africa and at home would never have occurred.

Between 1911 and 1914 in three consecutive series he took 122 wickets in fifteen Tests against Australia and South Africa, in one of which he did not bowl because of rain—at Manchester, naturally. However, I am inclined to believe that the greatest example of his unique skill occurred in 1928, when, at the age of fifty-four, he played for Wales against the West Indies and took 7 for 51 and 5 for 67 in 48 overs. In the circumstances, it is not surprising that the West Indies, who encountered all the top bowlers in this country, rated him the best. George Challenor, one of the finest players to come out of the Caribbean, summed it all up when he confessed: 'I simply couldn't guess as the ball floated fairly quickly to the pitch what it was going to do— leg or off spin.' Imagine, therefore, what it must have been like facing him in his prime, when his pace was nearer to fast than medium!

If England had a large number of outstanding cricketers in the Golden Age, this was equally true of Australia, who won the series four times in six years prior to the visit by the MCC under Sir Pelham Warner in 1903-4. England retained their supremacy with F. S. Jackson as captain, in 1905, when he not only spun the coin with diabolical skill, but proceeded to head both the batting and bowling averages.

Australia came again in 1909, when the English Selectors showed panic by choosing no fewer than twenty-five players. This unsuccessful move was to be copied in like circumstances on so many occasions in the future. England ended the era on top by winning the Ashes in 1911-12, after losing the first Test and then taking four on the trot, thanks very largely to the bowling of Barnes, Foster and Douglas, and the batting of Hobbs, Rhodes, Woolley and Foster.

Among a galaxy of Australian batting and bowling stars, one name, Victor Trumper, shines brightest of all and, strangely, not so much for his deeds, though they were remarkable enough, but rather for the manner in which they were achieved. Sir Pelham Warner's description, 'Batting just seemed part of himself', perhaps goes closest to expressing the special charm he possessed. Another example is to talk about batsmanship with anyone who actually saw Trumper in action: immediately his face will light up and he will say, 'Ah, but you should have seen Trumper', because he is convinced that this was the supreme cricketing experience.

Trumper had that rare gift of being able to make batting look both graceful and simple even on difficult wickets, as he so eloquently demonstrated in the very wet summer of 1902 in England, when he made 2,570 runs and hit 11 centuries.

The value of left-handers is obvious and Australia were lucky to find three during this period, all fine players and excellent competitors, Darling, Hill and Bardsley. Joe Darling came first into prominence as a fifteen-year-old, when he made 252 in a school match. He would inevitably have been playing for his state and Australia at an early age if his father had not sent him off to manage a farm in the outback. As a result, he did not have the opportunity to play First Class cricket until he was twenty-three, but immediately showed his ability with a century in his first encounter with English bowling. His defence was obdurate, but George Giffen wrote: 'I have seen him make the biggest hit recorded on the Adelaide Oval.' He was a fluent driver. He was also an expert cutter, not usually a speciality of left-handers, and was to captain Australia with the practical sense to be expected from a farmer.

Although Clem Hill possessed an immaculate defence, he was at his happiest attacking the bowling. Like most left-handers he was very strong on the leg side, a flowing driver through the covers, and used his feet well against slow bowlers.

Warren Bardsley lacked some of the sparkle of the other two. He was more of a utilitarian run-getter, dour and effective, who always sold his wicket dearly. He once put on 224 with Clem Hill against the South African attack in 1910–11, an early indication that left-handers would often prove the best antidote against high class wrist-spin bowling.

Charles Macartney, like Sir Donald Bradman after him, was a natural destroyer of bowlers. Every time he strode to the crease the bars would empty, because he was never dull, never uninteresting, a man who was to score a century before lunch at Leeds after the Australians had been put into bat. A positive

If it were possible to bring back players of the past, there are few whom I would rather see in the modern county game than G. L. Jessop. He was a real hitter, and quick—his 53 centuries in First Class cricket were scored at an average of 82.7 runs an hour. Jessop was also a fast bowler and an outstanding field, and would have been a natural for the limited overs game. It was said that he 'reduced rustic batting to a science.' He differed from other hitters in that he did not rely solely on front foot drive for his effectiveness. If the bowler pitched slightly short, he was a devastating cutter

Wilfred Rhodes made his first Test appearance in 1899, and in 1926, by which time he was a Selector, he was persuaded by his colleagues to play in the final Test. England's victory owed much to this incomparable all-rounder. Rhodes started his international career as an orthodox slow bowler, who went in at number eleven, and developed into a wonderful all-rounder. By 1912 he opened the innings with Jack Hobbs, and was seldom called on to bowl. As a slow left-arm bowler, he was deadly on a nasty wicket, and would think them out on a plumb one with a combination of flight, control and spin. As a batsman, he was a watchful and business-like acquirer of runs, unworried and unhurried by the events around him

batsman and a positive person: it would have been interesting to see his reactions had the opposing side adopted entirely negative tactics. He certainly would not have liked them, nor would he have approved; even Fred Root's in-swingers irritated him.

Neville Cardus once wrote: 'Macartney's batting gave the impression that it was perpetually creative throughout an innings, with several strokes for the same kind of ball.' He regarded a maiden as an insult, and his repertoire of strokes meant that length and line were not sufficient to keep him quiet. If the bowlers failed to dismiss him, then he made every minute he spent at the wicket count. After the Don, he was almost certainly the greatest match-winning batsman the Australians have ever produced.

It should also be remembered that in his early days he was a well above average slow-medium bowler, who took 11 wickets for 85 in a Test against a strong England in 1909. He, along with Hobbs, Armstrong, Barnes, Bardsley and Woolley, was to emphasize by his performances after World War I just how good cricket was in that Golden Age.

There has never been any shortage of Australian all-rounders, so it is hardly surprising to find an impressive quota in those days. One important reason is that they do not play so much cricket. It is not a strain to score runs and take wickets once a week, but it is a different matter when cricket is played every day.

George Giffen was at his peak in the 1880s and 1890s, but was still playing after the turn of the century. He had an insatiable thirst for bowling, and when he eventually became captain he often forgot to take himself off. Although he was essentially an all-purpose bowler, rather than a specialist, in 1893 he gave an indication of things to come by bowling off-breaks round the wicket to four short legs. He was certainly the finest all-rounder in Australia for a long period, and was known as the 'Grace of Australia'. His mantle was to be assumed by M. A. Noble, who was a better batsman, second only to Trumper in the national XI, a great fieldsman anywhere and a fine medium-pace bowler, who swung the ball.

The massive Warwick Armstrong made four tours of England and in 1905, before he put on weight, showed his remarkable all-round ability by scoring over 2,000 runs and taking more than 100 wickets. He drove fiercely and bowled leg breaks of great accuracy, often to a packed leg-side field.

Right from the very beginning, when their batting was inexperienced, the Australian attacks, almost invariably backed up by high class fielding, have been powerful. They have bred good bowlers, because their hard, true, often mat-on-concrete pitches make them essential. In England, the weather and the wickets are usually more sympathetic to bowlers and give them some encouragement. The outcome has been that the Aussies have usually enjoyed bowling in Britain, and have been successful. The one exception to this generalization in recent years has been the wrist-spinner; but the player who can move the ball off the seam, swing it or make it break in Australia will automatically find he gets a shade more movement, swerve or turn in England.

Another advantage which many Australian bowlers have possessed is that they have often been far better than they have looked. In recent times one thinks of Neil Hawke and Max Walker, while in the Golden Age there was the ambling camel, the redoubtable Hugh Trumble. His height enabled him to achieve lift, and to his outstanding control he added change of pace and cut. A. C. MacLaren, who did not praise lightly, or often, reckoned him to be the 'most consistently excellent bowler' he ever encountered, and he encountered a great many fine bowlers.

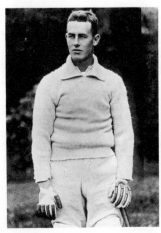

Few batsmen have ever approached the grace and style of Victor Trumper. He scored many runs, but it was the way he made them which qualified him as an immortal. In 1902, when runs were in short supply, he still managed to conjure up 11 centuries—the rest of Darling's side managed 13 between them— and one was made before lunch, despite a rain-sodden outfield and a far from easy pitch

BETWEEN THE WARS

Above Herbert Sutcliffe going out to bat. He was a superb judge of what to play and what to leave alone, and this was one of the main reasons for the introduction of the new l.b.w. Law. His technique on all types of pitch was masterful. Invariably immaculate, he did much to give to the professional cricketer the prestige and recognition he deserved

Left The Champions: the Yorkshire XI of the 1930s, led by Brian Sellers. The team contained Sutcliffe, who, after Hobbs had retired, was the finest opener in the world, and a young Hutton, who would eventually inherit the title. This side had plenty of batting and a strong and varied attack which was splendidly supported in the field. They did not just play cricket: they lived it. They won with an ease and a regularity which was to prove something of a handicap to successors who lacked their flair

English cricket took several years to settle down after a war which had not only cost so much in terms of death and suffering, but had also extinguished so many of the dreams, standards and beliefs which had been part of the game.

Probably 1919 was too early to restart the County Championship, while the experiment of two-day matches proved to be an entirely predictable disaster. This was not surprising, for it is very difficult to achieve a clear-cut result in that time on good pitches without declarations, and when both teams have reasonable batting line-ups. It was not helped by a fine summer; while the very unequal number of matches played by the contestants made something of a nonsense of the Championship. Yorkshire, for instance, took part in twenty-six and were taken to the last game before finishing ahead of Kent, who had only played fourteen matches.

The following year three-day matches were resumed and Worcestershire rejoined the fold (they were prevented by financial difficulties in 1919). Middlesex finished as Champions by dramatically beating Surrey in the last game at Lord's. It was during this summer that P. G. H. Fender struck the fastest century, in 35 minutes, against Northants. Fender was a brilliant all-rounder, a consistent hitter, a flamboyant wrist-spinner, who was always prepared to buy his wickets, and a fine slip. He also captained Surrey with imagination and flair, ever prepared to risk defeat in the pursuit of victory.

In 1921 Middlesex retained the title and Glamorgan brought up the number of First Class counties to the present seventeen. Middlesex's success owed much to the batting of the old master, Hearne, and their new star, 'Patsy' Hendren. Normally the decisive figures in a Championship side are the bowlers, but not this time, and it is interesting that when Middlesex repeated their triumph in the 1940s, it was mainly due to the brilliance of the next pair of 'Middlesex twins', Compton and Edrich, well supported by Robertson and Brown.

The outstanding county in the period between the wars was Yorkshire, Champions on no fewer than twelve occasions and invariably finishing up near the leaders. Their success was built round five basic ingredients. First and foremost, four frontline bowlers who could be relied upon to pick up a large number of wickets both cheaply and quickly. Second, a minimum of five quality batsmen to provide the bulk of the runs, to adjust their game to suit the situation, and who would each score well over 1,000 a season. Third, fine fielding to support their attack, and a reliable keeper. Fourth, a tough, positive approach and a certain arrogance: they knew they were better than other sides and they played to win, not for fun. Their fun stemmed from winning. Fifth, pride in being Yorkshiremen and playing for Yorkshire, which enabled them to pull out that little extra when in difficulties. Yorkshire's strength was such that they could afford to carry a captain who often would not have made the side in terms of playing ability.

Although they took the title in 1919, Yorkshire's first great sequence began in 1922 and lasted until 1925, in which period they won eighty-six matches and suffered only seven defeats. Most of the runs were supplied by Sutcliffe, Oldroyd, Rhodes, Holmes, Kilner and later Leyland, but the main reason why they won so many games was the bowling of Rhodes, Macaulay, Kilner and Waddington, splendidly backed up in the field. Every member of this varied quartet expected to capture over a hundred wickets a season, gave precious little away, and exploited to the full any help in the pitch or weakness in the opposing batsmen. Waddington was fast; Macaulay, like his successors, Smailes and Appleyard, was a dual purpose operator, a fast-medium seamer and an off-cutter, and Rhodes and Kilner were both slow left-armers and outstanding batsmen. They were to be joined by Emmott Robinson, a medium-paced swing bowler who always remembered to keep the ball up to the batsman and so regularly trapped them in the slips when attempting to drive.

Yorkshire's highly professional approach to the game was reflected in the systematic way they invariably trampled upon their weaker opponents. They were not above a little gamesmanship if it suited their purpose, and this did not always please their opponents.

The climax occurred in the second match

against Middlesex in 1924 at Sheffield, when the barracking of the crowd so incensed the Middlesex team—I wonder what they would have thought of modern day spectators—that they announced they would not meet Yorkshire again, a decision which was later rescinded.

Yorkshire, although always there or thereabouts, lost the top spot four times to Lancashire, the club on the other side of the Pennines, and once to Nottinghamshire, before they took control again in 1931 for the start of their greatest era, in which they were Champions for every year, apart from 1934 and 1936. This was the golden age of Yorkshire cricket. Their reign started dramatically. With nearly a third of the season gone, the 'Tykes' were not even serious contenders, but then proceeded to beat Middlesex, Hampshire, Kent, Somerset and Surrey—all by an innings! After one drawn contest, they produced another winning sequence in which they annihilated Essex, Nottinghamshire, Glamorgan, Gloucestershire and Somerset. Their eventual record was that they won thirteen out of their last fifteen games to finish undisputed Champions in every sense. The three key figures were Herbert Sutcliffe, who scored more than 2,000 runs for an average of over 97, and the two bowlers, Hedley Verity and Bill Bowes, who both captured over a hundred wickets at very small cost. This trio, who were to play such a big part in the ensuing success saga of their county, were not only different as players and individuals, but also far removed from the usual Yorkshire cricketer.

Herbert was a great opening batsman with a superb technique and an imperturbable temperament. His judgment, when he moved back and across his wicket, on what to play and what to leave alone was so precise that he was one of the main causes for the introduction of the new l.b.w. law, which was eventually to have such a profound effect on the game. With Hobbs, he formed the best opening partnership England has ever possessed, and with Holmes he formed the best opening partnership his county ever had. Although he thought and wrote that the l.b.w. law would reduce his own effectiveness, it did not, because he was essentially a master

Hedley Verity was the prince of slow left-arm spinners. Here, he is bowling against Surrey, backed by a typically attacking field. Over the years the Tykes have produced a large number of great slow left-handers, and Verity was arguably the best. He could be used either as a match winner or as a stock bowler. His height enabled him to achieve more lift than most bowlers of his kind, and he was also rather quicker through the air

craftsman. His partiality for the hook cost him his wicket on occasions, just as it did Cyril Washbrook, but it brought him a vast number of runs, as Essex once found to their cost, when Ken Farnes employed fast leg theory against him at Scarborough and the ball kept being picked out of the crowd.

However, apart from his cricketing ability, Herbert raised the status of the professional cricketer in rather the same way Henry Cotton did that of golf professionals. He was invariably immaculate and well groomed, not a speck of dirt to be seen, not a hair out of place. He was able to combine his cricket and business interests, making money with the same skill as he made his runs. His demeanour was essentially aristocratic—the first truly amateur professional! Once in the West Indies, when the Yorkshire captain, not a natural speaker, was unable to make the expected response, Herbert moved naturally into the breach. One has the feeling that if being an amateur had not been at that time considered an essential requisite for the captaincy, Herbert would have made a successful skipper, for although rather remote he possessed greater knowledge, as well as far more presence and authority, than most amateurs. Jack Hobbs and Wilfred Rhodes were universally admired, but Herbert did more than any other person to make the professional socially acceptable.

Hedley Verity was the type of bowler every captain wants, an orthodox left-hander, a match-winner on a helpful pitch, where his height and pace through the air made him nearly unplayable, and the perfect stock bowler on a placid track, because of his command of line and length, combined with subtle nuances of pace and flight. Yorkshire bowlers over the years, both fast and slow, have tended to be intolerant, frequently bad tempered, and often difficult to handle, but none of these characteristics was to be found in Hedley, or indeed his immediate predecessor, Wilfred Rhodes. Hedley was a quiet, rather studious person who liked reading and serious discussions. He was intensely patriotic, and was to die of wounds received fighting for the country he loved so much.

In his early days, Bill Bowes was a genuine fast bowler and, like Fred Trueman, he was to become an even better one when he reduced his pace and relied more on movement off the pitch. His height, allied to his high arm action, enabled him to secure lift, while he also studied and worked at his trade with a devotion few have equalled. A tall, gangling individual, he was not a natural athlete, only a natural bowler with a rather awkward looking, but very effective action. Underneath a basically shy exterior lurked a pronounced sense of humour; a man who was liked and respected by all who knew him, both as a cricketer and later as a distinguished cricket writer.

Other outstanding performers in what was easily the best organized team in the country included Maurice Leyland, a left-hander who bubbled with laughter, but was also a born fighter, which was the main reason why he was so very effective in Test cricket, revelling in the big occasion, or a difficult pitch.

From 1933 Brian Sellers ruled the side with the despotic efficiency of a dictator. Later, when the chairman of the county, he found it difficult to understand the social revolution which had occurred, or that what the professional of the 1930s would accept, the professional of the 1960s would not.

Although their run was not as long or as spectacular as the White Rose of Yorkshire, the Red Rose of Lancaster had three years of glory—1925, 1926, 1927—and then came back to take the title twice more in 1930 and 1934. Their success was based on an all-round solidarity. Their batting was well above average, with Watson and Hallows an outstanding opening pair, who in one season put on over a hundred for the first wicket no fewer than twelve times! Ernest Tyldesley was one of those players who never received the international recognition his ability warranted. This is perhaps best reflected by the fact that, when he toured South Africa in 1927-8, he succeeded in every Test, comfortably heading the batting averages, outscoring both Sutcliffe and Hammond. Nor should it be forgotten that he achieved one of the most spectacular purple patches of all time—1,128 runs in nine innings, including 7 centuries in consecutive matches. In support, there was the stubborn Makepiece and later Eddie Paynter.

The Lancashire bowling was less im-

The great Australian side of 1921, which destroyed England with the pace of Gregory and McDonald and the spin of Mailey and Armstrong. The tourists also possessed an exceptionally strong batting line up, including high class players like Macartney, Armstrong and Bardsley, plus real depth in the middle and lower orders

pressive, especially as the incorrigible Cecil Parkin, always at odds with authority, departed in 1926. 'Plum' Warner reckoned that, on all wickets, Parkin was for a period the best bowler in England, always trying something different, so that setting a field for him became quite a problem. However, in their Australian import, Ted McDonald, they had one of the greatest fast bowlers ever, a match-winner with a beautiful action, control, a vicious bouncer and enormous stamina. Dick Tyldesley was on hand to winkle out the opposition with his leg-breaks, with two reasonable slow-arm all-rounders, Iddon and Hopwood, in support; while behind the stumps was the inspiration of George Duckworth, full of infectious enthusiasm and loud joyous appeals.

The only two clubs to break the Yorkshire-Lancashire domination between 1922 and 1939 were Nottinghamshire in 1929 and Derbyshire in 1936. Both owed much to their respective pace attacks. Of the two, Notts were a much better all-round side, as there were some very good batsmen and bowlers backing up Larwood and Voce, whereas Derbyshire could muster only three players with a batting average of more than 30 and achieved their success by bowling out the opposition, largely through the bowling of

Copson, the two Popes and Tommy Mitchell.

The decline in English cricket after World War I, which was to repeat itself after World War II, is best illustrated by the heavy defeats inflicted by Australia. In 1920 J. W. H. T. Douglas took out what was initially considered to be a powerful MCC party, but the English team lost all five Tests—a humiliation without parallel in English cricket history.

The MCC side did well in the state games, but were outclassed in the internationals. The harsh truth was that the batsmen, apart from Hobbs, were not good enough, though the absence of Hearne through injury made a considerable difference. England fell before the blistering pace of Gregory and the persistent guile of Mailey. Their own bowling lacked penetration, and their fielding was distinctly substandard, largely because too many of the side were past their peak.

The hope that these disasters would be remedied in the summer of 1921 on English wickets was not fulfilled. The Australians, under Warwick Armstrong, proceeded to win the first three Tests, all of three-day duration, by 10 wickets, 8 wickets and 219 runs. The fourth and fifth were left drawn, and in the final one Armstrong expressed his understandable dislike of hard-to-finish three-day Tests by reading a newspaper in the outfield, a

The Wally Hammond cover drive was one of the most exciting sights in cricket between the wars. It had both beauty and power. Here, Wally is seen playing a cover drive in a Test trial at Old Trafford

gesture not entirely appreciated by the Establishment. England's batting, without the services of Hobbs, found itself either mown down by the speed of Gregory and McDonald, or hypnotized by Mailey and Armstrong, although there were two vintage innings by Woolley at Lord's, and a brave one-handed effort by the Hon. Lionel Tennyson, who had replaced Douglas as captain. In contrast, the Australian batsmen were seldom in trouble. The consistent Bardsley, the dashing Macartney, Collins, Andrews and Ryder, plus runs from the two all-rounders, Armstrong and Gregory, did all that was required.

Predictably, the English Selectors panicked and called upon no fewer than thirty players. They even tried to bring back C. B. Fry at the age of forty-nine—shades of Brian Close—but Fry wisely declined, although, as they wanted someone who was an acknowledged master against great pace, it was odd that they ignored Gunn entirely.

A. C. Russell scored a century in both the drawn matches. The second meant little, as it was acquired against non-bowlers and un-interested opponents; while the value of his first was to some extent reduced because the game had been shortened to two days by the weather. Nevertheless, he must have been a shade unlucky to have been selected for only

ten Tests. A lack of mobility in the field, plus a poor arm, had something to do with this. For Essex he would stand in the slips, but this was a luxury England could not afford.

The 1921 Australian touring side was certainly one of the strongest to visit England, and they looked like going through the tour undefeated until they went down later on to A. C. MacLaren's Amateur XI at Eastbourne and C. I. Thornton's XI at Scarborough. Inevitably, there is something of an anti-climax for any visiting team after the final Test. I have always maintained that this is when their tour should end, but it has taken a long time for this point to be appreciated by the powers-that-be.

The next fight for the Ashes was in 1924–5, by which time, it was felt, English cricket had recovered sufficiently to get them back. There were good reasons for this optimism. Hobbs and Sutcliffe proved to be the ideal opening pair, four times putting on over a hundred for the first wicket—three times in succession—and, above all, there was their all-day stand of 283 facing an Australian total of more than 600.

Maurice Tate was the most feared new ball bowler in the world, and certainly justified this rating by capturing 38 wickets in the series. His run-up was short, while his pace, lively fast-medium, was derived from a fine, powerful body action. A batsman always knew that if he stayed long against Tate his right hand would be automatically jarred. Tate moved the ball either way, often without design. This had much to recommend it, since if a bowler is not certain, the batsman can have no idea. Strudwick kept wicket beautifully—small, neat and undemonstrative, but very efficient; while Woolley and Hendren were two genuine international batsmen.

Despite this nucleus, Australia proceeded to win a very high scoring home series by four Tests to one, a margin which rather flattered them, as there was not all that amount of difference between the sides. England lost largely because their lower order failed to provide nearly as many runs as their counter-parts. This was especially important when it is remembered that the first three Tests all went on into the seventh day. Second, the English attack failed to provide Tate with sufficient support. The fast bowlers, Gilligan and Howell, were neither good enough nor fast enough for Australian conditions. Third, there were too many wrist-spinners in the party: Freeman, Hearne and Tyldesley, like so many of their kind, were to find the conditions in Australia far less helpful than at home. Fourth, in the third Test, with their opponents reduced to 119 for 6 in their first innings, they had to do without the services of Tate, Gilligan and Freeman, whose absence must have been largely responsible for the last 4 Australian wickets putting on 370 runs. As England only lost by 11 runs, these three injuries might be said, in all fairness, to have settled the issue. Finally, Arthur Gilligan, though a delightful person and an inspiring leader, was a naive tactician.

From the Australian angle, the series marked the arrival of Ponsford and Grimmett, Ryder, Collins and Richardson, all of whom scored heavily. Mailey and Gregory bowled consistently well, and Oldfield kept superbly.

The following summer England at long last regained the Ashes by winning the final Test which, as all four previous ones had been drawn and were of three-day duration, was played to a finish. It was a memorable occasion in many ways: Wilfred Rhodes was recalled to the side at the age of forty-nine, and exploited a worn patch in the Australian second innings; Percy Chapham was entrusted with the captaincy, and Harold Larwood made a most impressive debut.

However, it was not until the 1928–9 tour to Australia that England won in the grand manner and could justifiably claim to be the top cricket nation. They were one of the most powerful sides ever to visit Australia and were ideally suited to the perfect pitches and timeless Tests of the period.

Although the attack is usually the deciding factor in a series when the games have to be finished within a set period, this is not nearly so true in timeless Tests on shirt-front wickets. To win in these conditions it is essential to have high scoring batsmen, and in Wally Hammond the MCC had the ideal person. He proceeded to make 905 runs in the Tests with a flawless technique, in which he disciplined himself to eradicate risk. He was admirably supported by Hobbs, Sutcliffe; Hendren,

Leyland and Jardine, so that totals of 500 and more became the accepted norm.

The English bowling revolved mainly around the tireless Tate, the pace of Larwood, the dependable Geary and the steadiness of that very accurate orthodox slow left-armer, J. C. White. The success of White came as something of a revelation. He was never a big spinner, even in England, but he proved to be the perfect stock bowler on the faster Australian wickets, as he wheeled away over after over, relying mainly on flight and human frailties for his considerable haul. Throughout the tour the English fielding, with their captain Percy Chapman always setting a fine example, was of a very high standard.

Although the visitors took the first four Tests, they lost the last, a warning that a new look Australian team was about to emerge. Don Bradman appeared in the first, was dropped for the second, returned for the third, and from that moment remained an automatic choice until his retirement twenty years later. This tour also saw the arrival of Archie Jackson, who celebrated with a beautiful century on his first appearance as a slightly built nineteen-year-old. If he had not died of tuberculosis within four years, he must have become one of the greatest of all Australian batsmen. There was an elegance about his style which made older spectators think back to Trumper.

The Australian Selectors decided to overlook the claims of Ryder and Richardson, and picked Woodfull to lead the next side to England. He proved an inspired choice, a solid dependable batsman, a perfect foil for Ponsford, an exceptionally shrewd tactician who believed in gambling only on certainties, and with a personal charm which made him liked by all who met him.

After their comfortable win in Australia, England started firm favourites and their victory in the first Test, helped by a rain-affected pitch, confirmed this view; but it failed to take into account that this was the start of the Bradman era. The Don brought a new dimension to batting with his ruthless efficiency. Hundreds, double hundreds and one treble hundred flowed from his bat, all scored with a proficiency and at a pace that nobody else has ever approached. His 254 at

Lord's had much to do with his side levelling accounts. His 334 at Leeds was responsible for England following on, but bad weather came to her rescue and also made sure no decision was possible in the fourth.

With the Ashes at stake, the fifth Test at the Oval was scheduled to be timeless and did not end until the sixth day. Rather surprisingly, Percy Chapman, the hero of England's recent triumph overseas was dropped and replaced as skipper by Bob Wyatt, who knew far more about the game, but lacked his flamboyant appeal. A Roundhead had taken over from a Cavalier.

Percy Chapman epitomized the ideal captain of the 1920s, straight out of the *Boy's Own Paper*. His background was perfect—Public School and Cambridge University. A tall, handsome blond and a natural athlete who fielded superbly, he was a dashing, impetuous left-hand bat. He hit the ball very hard and had the world at his feet, but eventually threw it all up, a victim of the bottle, which eventually transformed a once splendid young man, a cricketing god, into a pathetic wreck.

As captain, Chapman was a 'doer'. He relied largely on instinct and personal example rather than deep thinking. Walter Robbins related to me how, when he was being hammered all over Lord's by the Australians in full cry, the only time he was not forced to have a silly mid-off was when Chapman was off the field with a bruised ankle. But in general the field placing of this era was less scientific. Although I am absolutely sure the Bradman of 1930 would have scored plenty of runs in the 1950s, I am equally sure they would have taken him longer.

Interest in the final Test was enormous. The big question was whether the Bradman run-machine would continue to churn them out. He had scored well over a hundred in the first three Tests and, although he had failed in the fourth, he had gone to the crease only once. He proceeded to take his aggregate for the series to 974 with an average of 139.14 by making 232—Australia won by an innings, and regained the Ashes.

The powerful MCC party which set out for Australia in 1932 was led by Douglas Jardine, a hard, autocratic, thinking captain. He was not interested in such incidentals as being a good ambassador. He considered that his job was to beat the Australians and if in the process people were upset or offended, it was just too bad.

Jardine had seen Bradman mutilate the English bowling in 1930 and everything indicated that, with assistance from the likes of Ponsford, Woodfull and McCabe, he would repeat this performance on the Australian wickets, which at that time were even more unsympathetic to bowlers, once the initial shine had departed in about six overs. He had been given a battery of fast bowlers— Larwood, Voce, Allen and Bowes—and there had been signs at the Oval, although he had gone on to make a double century, that the Don had not been entirely happy when the ball was lifting and flying, which is hardly surprising.

The problem for Jardine was to ensure that his fast bowlers made conditions unpleasant for Bradman on good wickets. The occasional bouncer was of little use, as he had the knack of hitting these with a cross bat along the ground to mid-wicket. The answer was fast leg theory, or as it became known 'body-line'.

It had been tried out in England, although not extensively, and was devised to reduce the effectiveness of the Australian batsmen, particularly their run-machine, Don Bradman, and thereby regain the Ashes. It was a technically well conceived plan, brilliantly executed by Larwood and Voce under the direction of Douglas Jardine, and it achieved its objective. But the cost was high. It did not break the laws, which were subsequently changed, but it offended against the ethics of sportsmanship.

Once the shine had departed Larwood and Voce would revert to bowling short into the unfortunate recipient. The ideal delivery would hit the batsman, if he failed to take any action, around his chest—a painful experience. If he played either a defensive back-stroke or a leg glance, he was in danger of being caught out by an encircling group of close short legs; if he hooked, there was a chance of holing out to fielders stationed on the boundary for that shot.

It must also be remembered that the wickets were usually quicker than those in England and that both Larwood and Voce were

Body-line, or fast leg theory: an Australian ducks to avoid a short-pitched delivery from Harold Larwood, during the fourth Test at Brisbane in 1933. A catch was likely to occur when the batsman was forced to defend his body, and six short legs are waiting for their chance

Left It did not happen often! Bradman is bowled for a duck by Bowes in the second Test of the 1932–3 tour, at Melbourne. He attempted to pull the Yorkshire fast bowler and dragged the ball into his stumps; but he had his revenge in the second innings, when he made an undefeated century and Australia went on to record their only victory of the series. Would Bradman have played that stroke so early in his innings had it not been for body-line, which was specially devised to cut down his run-getting?

A solitary spectator on the famous Hill at Sydney sees England win the first Test of the 1932–3 tour. Could he have been a Pommie?

genuinely fast and accurate bowlers. With the batsman worried about his personal safety and afraid of losing his wicket, they would vary the short ball with the yorker, so that it was hardly surprising that many of their victims were clean bowled. They also made sure that they did not send anything down outside the off stump, which would have given the batsman the opportunity of scoring in a largely unpopulated area of the field.

As a tactical exercise it was an unqualified success, even though Gubby Allen, the third fast bowler in the side, would not bowl leg theory, because he did not approve. The Australians, not surprisingly, were incensed by what they considered to be an offence against the spirit of the game, the more so as it was producing dividends.

The relationship between the two teams became distinctly cool, and was not helped by Jardine's aloof manner. The Australian press, never noted for its sophistication, made the

most of the opportunity, while the enormous crowds showed their disapproval as their players and the stumps were regularly knocked over.

Cables were exchanged between the Australian Board and the MCC who even went so far as to offer to cancel the tour. All this hostility automatically welded the English side into a very close-knit unit, and they even worked out a drill as to who should seize which stump should the crowd invade the ground. Had the same situation arisen in the less disciplined world of today, there would certainly have been a serious riot.

Stan McCabe showed that body-line could be conquered by courage, fierce hooking and a little luck, with a memorable 187 not out. Bradman, the prime target, by brilliant improvisation, including cutting balls from outside his leg stump into gaps on the off, managed to average over fifty, but there were no double and treble hundreds. This leg theory reduced his effectiveness and England took the series by four Tests to one. They failed in the second Test on a slow turning pitch, after omitting Verity.

The 1932–3 MCC party was a very powerful and well balanced team. They might have won, but not by nearly such a large margin, without resorting to body-line. Although they lacked a high quality partner for Sutcliffe to open the innings, there was the masterful Hammond and the indomitable Leyland, plus the depth of batting which was so essential in Australia during this period of timeless Tests. Every player was prepared to sell his wicket dearly, an attitude which was perhaps best epitomized by Eddie Paynter rising from his sick bed in Brisbane to play a crucial innings.

The sad outcome of the body-line tour, apart from the rift it caused between the two countries, which was bigger and took longer to heal than many appreciate, was that Harold Larwood, who had been branded a hero by most Englishmen and a villain by most Australians, became a victim of circumstances. He felt, and still feels with justification, that he was let down by the authorities. To make matters worse, he had splintered a bone in a toe towards the end of the tour, and although he remained a very fine fast bowler he was never quite so quick again. Nevertheless, there was reason to suppose that he would be picked against the 1934 Australians for the first Test on his own ground at Trent Bridge, but he was not.

This was the final straw. He decided, understandably, to sell his story and wrote just prior to the second Test that he would not play against the Australians any more. He never did. A great bowler gradually faded from the scene, eventually settling in Australia, where he received far more recognition than in his own country.

Harold is now a charming, rather shy man in his seventies, who smiles when he says: 'You know that I am now an older Australian than Dennis Lillee.' It is difficult to believe that he was once the central figure in one of the biggest of all cricket rows.

His partner, Bill Voce, was to make two further Australian tours but, strangely, was not once picked to play against them in England. One of the most moving of the many

The MCC team which toured Australia and New Zealand in 1932–3 was one of the strongest ever selected. It was led with ruthless efficiency by Jardine and contained four genuine fast bowlers, Larwood, Voce, Allen and Bowes; two fast medium bowlers, Tate and Hammond, and three spinners, Verity, Mitchell and Brown. The batting was also powerful, as it included Hammond, Sutcliffe, Pataudi, Leyland, Paynter, Ames and Wyatt, while the tail was virtually non-existent

Bill Voce was an excellent left-arm fast bowler, with a powerful body action, who was much feared by batsmen because he had the knack of tickling them in the ribs from round the wicket. Unlike most modern bowlers of his kind, he usually bowled round, rather than over the wicket, which was ideal for leg theory, when the ball had to come in to the batsman

nostalgic moments conjured up by the Centenary Test of 1977 was the sight of Harold and Bill walking on to the Melbourne ground, where they had once been barracked so bitterly, to an immense reception. Time heals.

The Australian downfall, plotted with so much care by Douglas Jardine, marked the high spot of one of the most dedicated, ruthless and autocratic of all England captains. He retired from the First Class game shortly afterwards. The Iron Duke of Cricket had abdicated.

Body-line was eventually banned in England because batsmen, including many who had rather enjoyed seeing the Australians suffer, were noticeably less enthusiastic when on the receiving end. The West Indies tried it against England, and it clearly did not assist in creating a happy relationship between the countries. In 1934 the Australians had a most unhappy match against Nottinghamshire in which Voce employed a largely leg-side field and, spurred on by an enthusiastic and noisy home crowd—they resented seeing their two finest bowlers excluded from international cricket—overdid the number of short deliveries. This eventually led to an apology from the offending county and Voce himself did not take the field on the last day of this acrimonious encounter.

The eventual outcome of the body-line dispute was the following instruction issued to First Class cricket umpires:

'The type of bowling which has been defined by the MCC Committee as "persistent and systematic bowling of fast short-pitched balls at the batsman standing clear of his wicket" has always been considered unfair and it must be eliminated from the game. Umpires are the sole judges of fair and unfair play (vide Law 43) and are therefore empowered to deal with "direct attack".'

This was followed by the action that umpires should take if any bowler offended. It did the job for which it was intended— outlawing body-line. What was not taken into account was the deluge of bouncers without the leg theory field which subsequently occurred. The problem has been in the following wording: 'As soon as he decides that such bowling is *persistent*.'

Umpires' interpretation of *persistent* has been, and still is, varied. Most cricketers would not like the bouncer prohibited, as apart from anything else it would mean the end of the hook, one of the game's more exciting strokes, but one would have thought that more than one bouncer per six-ball over could, and should, be termed excessive.

Since the war, numerous fast bowlers from many countries have unquestionably offended against the spirit of the game by sending down too many bouncers. Their intention is to soften up the opposition and this has often proved a most effective ploy. Brian Close may stand there and be hit without giving an inch and revelling in the physical danger, but many others are noticeably less keen.

There was the classic case of one talented batsman from overseas who scored heavily in country cricket, but invariably failed against Yorkshire when Fred Trueman was playing.

In addition to the fact that generous doses of fast pitched and short deliveries often upset the concentration of the timid, the bouncer has also become a highly lucrative wicket-taker, because batsmen have been caught mis-hooking, lofting to a fieldsman on the boundary, or employing a poorly executed defensive stroke. The practical success of this delivery has not gone unnoticed by the fast-medium brigade who now regard it as an essential part of their repertoire.

The hook is both a rewarding and exhilarating stroke, but whether it should be attempted by anyone who is not an expert must be open to considerable doubt, as it is also a dangerous shot. A batsman has to hit and control a ball that has risen about shoulder high and is travelling quickly. It follows that the faster the bowling the more difficult it is to hook well, but it is noticeable that even bowlers of little more than medium pace are regularly employing the bumper and being rewarded with a wicket as a result of an indifferently executed shot.

The most effective hookers are usually small, quick moving men like the Don, or Everton Weekes, who are sometimes able to get into position early enough to hit the ball along the ground in front of square. The best hookers tend to have an initial movement back and across, although Tom Graveney was

Bradman and McCabe going out to bat in 1934. McCabe was a glorious attacking batsman, and like so many small men he was a wonderful hooker. The 187 not out which he made in the first Test of the body-line tour was certainly one of the finest and bravest innings ever played, while the 232 which he scored in the first Test in 1938 is still talked about with justifiable awe at Trent Bridge. His second hundred took only 84 minutes and, with number eleven as his partner, he hit 72 out of the last 77 runs

able to play the shot off his front foot.

The fast bowler regards the bouncer not only as an intimidatory but also as a wicket-taking weapon, because so many batsmen are unable to resist the challenge and will hook instinctively, even when the ball has flown far too high for it to be an acceptable risk.

In recent years it has been increasingly evident that the bouncer is no longer reserved for recognized batsmen, but is also directed at tail-enders, who are less able to protect themselves. At one time there used to be almost a fast bowlers' union, whose main purpose was to make sure that they always pitched the ball well up to each other. One of the more amusing sights in the game would be to see a fast bowler playing contentedly forward at his opposite number, while at the opposite end the ball was whistling around the other batsman's earholes.

What was far less acceptable and far more lethal than the genuine bouncer was the deliberate head-high full toss, or beamer. Fortunately it is far more difficult to bowl with any accuracy and has, by tacit agreement of the players themselves, more or less disappeared from the game.

In 1934, under Bill Woodfull, one of the finest of all captains, Australia regained the Ashes, thanks very largely to the batting of Bradman and Ponsford and the bowling of O'Reilly and Grimmett. They lost on a wet wicket at Lord's which Verity exploited to the full, but comfortably won the first, drew the third, had much the better of the drawn fourth and clinched the series with a victory in the fifth Test by a little matter of 562 runs.

The visit in 1936–7 was not only important in the cricketing sense. It was necessary to heal the rancour that remained from the body-line trip. In all respects it proved an outstanding success with England taking the first two Tests and eventually going down 2–3. It could easily have been a different story had England, on a very difficult wet wicket, not delayed their declaration until they were 76 for 9. This did not give them enough time to bowl at their opponents before the wicket dried out on the following day, when Bradman, well supported by Fingleton, went on to register yet another double century.

The Australian side under Bradman which visited England for their last tour before the war contained plenty of batsmen in addition to their captain, but their attack was thin, with L. B. Fleetwood Smith unable to provide the great O'Reilly with the same support as Grimmett had done in the past. The first two Tests were high scoring draws; the third was abandoned without a ball being bowled because of rain; Australia won the fourth on a turner, and England levelled the series, although Australia retained the Ashes, in the Oval massacre. This last illustrated both the danger of the over-prepared wicket and the timeless Test. Against what was virtually a three-man attack, England put together 903 for 7, of which Len Hutton scored 364 runs— a world record which was to stand for a long time. With both Bradman and Fingleton incapacitated, the tourists, not unexpectedly, quietly capitulated.

THE FUN FORTIES

One of the less rewarding occupations: bowling for Essex against Don Bradman at Southchurch Park in 1948. Essex dismissed the Australians in one day, which was unusual, but the Aussies scored some 721 runs, which was even more so. The tourists never really accelerated: they just kept the score moving steadily along at nearly 250 runs per session!

Although blue birds were not circling the white cliffs of Dover in 1945, the Third Reich had been expunged and the dropping of the atom bomb had hastened the end of Japan's resistance. World War II was at last over and England, with more than a little help from her friends, had won.

It was a time to think of building and re-building, rather than destroying. It was a time for living and laughter, as there had been too much dying and too many tears. It was time for optimism. Little did we then realize that through our inability to control our destiny we would eventually lose the peace. It was time to enjoy good things like sport, which had been severely rationed, and in 1946 First Class cricket resumed after a break of six years. Civilization had returned.

When the war had started in September 1939 I was fifteen. I had spent two years in the Dulwich College 1st XI, played for the Young Amateurs of Essex, Essex Club and Ground, under the cheerful dictatorship of Brian Castor, and Westcliff CC, a strong club side. At that time the odds were that I would be given the opportunity of some matches with the county in the next year or so, but there was no more county cricket until 1946.

Fortunately there was a certain amount of cricket of varying standards to be had during the intervening period, and I was lucky enough to play rather more than most, first as a schoolboy and later as a Royal Marine. Cricket lovers throughout the country over-came innumerable problems to keep the game alive and flourishing, part-time groundsmen worked wonders, and the armed forces col-laborated whenever possible, especially in those unreal days before the collapse of the Allies.

In particular the British Empire XI and the London Counties took teams of First Class and near First Class standard to play clubs and associations throughout the country, and Lord's, undeterred by the bombs, still staged several prestige matches containing named players, who were either on leave, or con-veniently stationed, or not in the armed forces.

The presence of troops from the Common-wealth in England also helped to provide good cricket and cricketers. It was in one such wartime game that I first encountered Keith Miller, who was serving with the RAAF. I was playing for the Royal Navy at Hove and Keith, who had already acquired a reputation for his batsmanship but not his bowling, was a member of the opposition. He arrived at the ground with gear consisting of a shirt and a pair of rather battered boots draped round his shoulders.

The pitch was good, the bowling friendly and I was rather enjoying myself, until the fielding captain had an inspiration. He tossed the ball to Keith, who casually ambled up from a few paces. I am still not sure whether the wicketkeeper, who was standing up to the stumps, or myself was the more surprised, when the first delivery sped through to the boundary for four byes. Keith was un-questionably the fastest fifth change bowler that either of us had ever encountered!

Throughout this difficult period the county clubs, sometimes without a ground—the Oval was turned into a caged area for prisoners of war—did their best to support cricket with occasional matches and were greatly indebted to those members who continued to pay part or all of their subscriptions. It was easier for the leagues, whose clubs were structured round weekend matches and within easy reach of each other. As a result they were able to maintain good fixture lists and were often strengthened by those county players who were available.

After years of impromptu make-and-mend cricket, the war in Europe shuddered to its end in May 1945 and allowed a partial resumption of First Class cricket with the playing of eleven First Class matches. The highlights were provided by five 'Victory' Tests against the Australian Services, which caught the public imagination and rekindled the flame. The series was appropriately undecided, with two victories apiece and the fourth Test drawn.

The debt owed by English cricket to the Australian Services team was considerable. In addition to the Tests, they played nearly fifty matches with a zest which provided enormous pleasure to lovers of the game, who had just completed five dillusioning years of total war. The so-called Tests were fought with a friendliness which Wisden said it would like to

47

see when the real Tests were resumed; but of course this never happened. That summer the players were really taking part in a series of exhibition games, after a rainbow had replaced the clouds of war. They wanted to win—I never met an Australian who did not!—but for two of the visitors, R. G. Williams and D. G. Carmody, who was later to do so much for Western Australia, both of whom had been prisoners of war, the sheer joy of playing transcended all else. Most of the players chosen for the various England teams had had previous Test match experience. They were thankful and grateful to be back in action again, playing in matches with big crowds and atmosphere. Others, like Ken Farnes and Hedley Verity, would never have the opportunity.

On paper England, except when D. B. Carr, J. G. Dewes, and the Hon. L. R. White were thrown in the deep end before they were ready to swim, looked more formidable than their understandably makeshift opponents, who in typically Aussie fashion gave such a good account of themselves. The Australian Services side was better than many county teams and about as strong as a reasonable, but not exceptional, state side. A. L. Hassett, K. R. Miller and C. G. Pepper were all of genuine international calibre and probably six of the others were capable of holding their own in good First Class cricket. In retrospect it is easy to understand why Australia crushed England in the first two proper series. On their way home the Australian Services side stopped off to make a short tour of India, which provided plenty of runs and entertainment, even if most of the matches were drawn.

However, it was not only the Australians who helped to restart serious cricket in England; players from all over the Commonwealth rallied to the call: M. P. Donnelly, C. S. Dempster, and R. C. Blunt from New Zealand, Learie Constantine and C. B. Clarke from the West Indies are merely some of the names.

The resumption of Test and county cricket in 1946 brought a joyous, happy time for everyone, with large, cricket-hungry crowds, laughter and plenty of entertainment. It was not just another season, but a reunion of old friends and foes spanning an entire summer.

Wally Hammond and Sir Learie Constantine at Lord's in 1944. I had the good fortune to play with both of them in this war-time period. In my not unfamiliar role of non-striker, I watched in fascination as Learie cut two sixes for the British Empire XI. I also took part in a century stand with Wally: although my contribution was about 11, it provided a wonderful lesson in the art of batsmanship

For most of the players it represented a return to a way of life which they loved, and had been forced to give up six years earlier. In the interim they must often have wondered whether it would ever come back, and their pleasure was reflected in a very sporting approach. The cricket was keen, but never mean, fun to watch and fun to play.

Although during the war years I had played against and alongside most of the leading cricketers in the country, this was my first opportunity to take part in the County Championship, and it would be difficult to imagine a better introductory season, because everybody wanted to play, humour abounded, the approach was positive and spectators were prepared to applaud the opposition.

A classic example of this occurred in the Essex match against Lancashire at Old Trafford. We had set them a target of 299 which, after Washbrook and Place had made 120 in 45 minutes, seemed insufficient. It was the first time that I experienced two fine batsmen flaying my bowling to all quarters of the field: the faster I bowled, the faster the ball seemed to travel off their bats. However, the combination of some fine leg-break bowling from Peter Smith and the excitement of the chase proved too much for Lancashire who even-

Keith Miller, the golden boy of Australian cricket, bowling in the nets at Lord's. This was never his favourite pastime, and he was often a reluctant bowler for the Don, with whom he did not see eye to eye. Keith was a world class all-rounder and a naturally gifted sportsman, who did everything exceptionally well and without apparent effort. Handsome, with a superb physique, he had a presence and a personal magnetism which few have equalled. He would probably have made a good captain in his later days, but his constant battles with authority in his early years and his unconventional approach to life were held against him

tually failed by 15 runs. The result is of no importance, but what I shall always cherish was the way the whole pavilion, and it was packed on the third day of a county game, rose to applaud Essex off the field for beating their team in a splendid contest.

In sharp contrast, a decade or so later, a considerable section of the Lancashire Members booed as their captain came out to bat against Essex. That type of behaviour could never have occurred in 1946, when pre-war standards prevailed and chivalry was still very much alive.

Superficially the summer of 1946 was so like 1939 that it was almost as if there had been no gap. The touring side, India, under the captaincy of the Nawab of Pataudi, were as expected beaten by England in a three-Test series, each match of only three days' duration (only the major cricketing countries, Australia and South Africa, were allotted longer playing time). The tourists were also defeated by three counties and their party included probably only four players of genuine international calibre—Merchant, Hazare, Amarnath, and that superb all-rounder Mankad—while the Nawab of Pataudi was past his peak.

Yorkshire won the twenty-six-match County Championship under Brian Sellers, with the strongest challenges coming from those two traditionally powerful sides, Middlesex and Lancashire. Leicestershire began the trend of importing overseas mercenaries, which was to cause so many problems later, by including those two fine Australians Jack Walsh and Vic Jackson, who were to be largely responsible for turning a rather mundane outfit into a middle-of-the-table combination. Jack Walsh was one of that comparatively rare breed, a left-arm wrist-spinner, who turned the ball consistently more than any bowler after the war. Few players were able to pick his googly with any degree of certainty, including his own keeper. I discovered this when I attempted a neat leg glance which the wicketkeeper was trying to catch and the ball nipped over the top of my stumps for four byes!

One person this master magician of spin could not deceive was his fellow Australian, Vic Jackson, who frequently moved from first to leg slip, thereby not only preventing byes, but also taking the occasional catch.

All the counties, apart from Leicestershire who gave the job to L. G. Berry, were captained by amateurs, as the belief still persisted that this task was beyond the capabilities of a professional, even if the idea of the value of an officer elite class, preferably with a Public School background, had not always been substantiated in the war. It will be remembered that W. G. Hammond, who skippered both England and Gloucestershire, would have done neither, if he had not turned amateur. When Bill Edrich, who at the time looked his most likely successor, followed suit, the decision cost him a Benefit which would have been in excess of £10,000, without securing the most coveted role in the game.

Amateurs in 1946 still stayed in separate hotels, changed in different dressing rooms, and had their initials printed in front of their names, while Gentlemen versus Players was probably the most important match of the season, outside the Tests. It was an odd system which I did not question at the time and merely accepted, even though I was amused by some of the more peculiar happenings. There was the county captain, not even a reasonable club player, who had been entrusted with the job because he happened to have the same name as the amateur the committee really wanted. The invitation had been inadvertently sent to the wrong man. In innocence and delight he accepted with the result that the country found themselves landed with a liability, but were much too polite to correct the mistake.

My own county also made an amateur captain for half a season because he was able to take the time off. When Tom Pearce was able to resume command the stand-in was thanked, capped and sent on his way. It did not make much sense, as in the Essex team was Ray Smith, under whom I had often played for the British Empire XI. He was not only available but was tactically better suited to the job.

Essex was fortunately a democratic and easygoing club, but there were still some counties where an amateur, irrespective of age, was addressed as Sir by the professional staff, who almost stood to attention.

Behaviour was essentially pre-war. Nobody would ever have considered having breakfast without wearing a tie and jacket, or failing to wear a blazer for lunch on the ground.

Although 1946 was in so many ways like 1939 there were many differences. Beneath the surface the social revolution which eventually was to change the whole face of the game had begun, while the standard of the actual play had inevitably fallen. Every county team contained two or three players who would not have commanded a regular place before the war.

The pre-war players were rusty, many of them past their prime, and there was an acute shortage of young cricketers because the intervening years had denied them the normal apprenticeship. In addition, many were still in the forces, as I would have been myself if it had not been for an emergency release as a schoolmaster.

It is difficult to estimate the effect of such a long lay-off on a cricketer, but I remember how missing one season of football as the result of an overseas tour affected me when I resumed, and six years is a very long time. There were still some quality batsmen around, and a healthy sprinkling of spinners, who so often, like wine, improve with age, but no

really fast bowlers, a deficiency which the Australians were to exploit dramatically in the next few years.

As the majority of the players were pre-war, the outlook and the tactics were straight out of the 1930s, especially the rather standardized field placings and the handling of the attacks. At this stage of my career I was more concerned with playing than thinking, but I do recall being slightly surprised to have on one occasion taken 5 for about 20 in two brief spells, while the opposition made nearly 300 and the two Smith cousins sent down some 100 overs between them. It did not make much sense at the time, but makes even less now.

After that happy, fun summer of 1946 England sent a team, under Wally Hammond, to do battle for the Ashes. The Selectors immediately showed the same cautious attitude which was to govern so many future teams, a preference for backing the form horse, judged by domestic cricket, rather than taking a gamble on the unknown with potential. The party included only three members with no basic experience of pre-war conditions, and was defeated by an Australia that was better, younger, fitter and included two fast bowlers, Lindwall and Miller.

The team sailed out on a dry ship, with the compensating factor that the majority of the passengers were female, fiancées and brides *en route* for Australia. It is generally agreed that the MCC were more successful on the first part of the trip than they were in Australia. The unfit, legendary Don Bradman was enticed out of premature retirement to captain Australia, and with the aid of one rather dubious decision and the fact that he was still a world-class batsman re-established himself as the game's number one personality.

It soon became obvious that not only were Australia far stronger than had been anticipated, but the English attack was almost certainly the weakest ever sent on a major tour Down Under, containing only two true international class bowlers, Alec Bedser and Doug Wright. To make matters worse, the fielding never rose above the mundane and the main strength, the batting, took time to settle down to the different conditions and the first serious confrontation with genuine pace since the war.

Cyril Washbrook and Joe Hardstaff, two batsmen with very different styles, who scored heavily both before and after World War II. A dapper opener and very quick on his feet, Cyril was strong off his legs with plenty of bottom hand. He invariably wore a cap at a jaunty angle. Joe was a more classical player, with an upright stance and a top-of-the-handle grip, who used the full swing of the bat when driving. Handsome sums up both the man and his batting

Sir Len Hutton strokes the ball to the boundary with a perfectly timed and placed off-drive. Len scored a higher percentage of his runs off his front foot than the majority of the great modern batsmen

Wally Hammond, aloof and rather with-drawn, was unable to establish the type of relationship with his opposite number, Donald Bradman, which might have made it the friendly, 'the war's over, let's have a jar' type of tour which had been envisaged. His own failure with the bat contrasted sharply with Bradman's success: the Don rattled up the little matter of 187 in an innings in the first Test, although judged not out at 28, a bitterly controversial decision. On his next appear-ance he scored 234, both matches being won by an innings and plenty.

Although England were outclassed and outgunned throughout the tour there were some outstanding moments, including a breathtaking exhibition of strokes against the new ball by Len Hutton, which is still recalled with delight by all those lucky to have wit-nessed some forty minutes of pure magic; Bill Edrich, battling it out on an Australian 'sticky', which has to be experienced to be fully understood; the success that came to Denis Compton, when ignoring his captain's instructions he used his feet against the spin-ners, and the determination of Alec Bedser, who with Doug Wright simply went on bowl-ing over after over. From the Australian angle the most important feature was the return of the Don, a psychological, as well as a practical advantage. Also noteworthy were the sheer pace of Ray Lindwall and Keith Miller, the teasing flight of Colin McCool, the authority of Sidney Barnes and the arrival of Arthur Morris as an opening bat.

The loss of the Ashes by an enormous margin was, however, soon forgotten in the golden summer of 1947, which contained the run-getting feats of Denis Compton and Bill Edrich, an exceptionally close fight for the County Championship and a visit from the South Africans, who, like the MCC in the previous winter, suffered from not having had any international competition for a long period of time.

It was roses, roses all the way for the Middlesex twins, Denis Compton and Bill Edrich, who conjured runs with a regularity and in a profusion which will never be sur-passed. Denis made 3,816 runs for an average of 90, which included 18 centuries, the most ever recorded in one season. I happened to be his partner when he made his seventeenth against the South Africans (he had an absolute passion for their bowling, not entirely without cause) at Hastings. It was one of the few occasions when I felt nervous, because it suddenly struck me while he was in the 80s and 90s how infuriated the crowd and the news cameras would be if I managed to run him out. This was a distinct hazard, as his running between the wickets was so erratic—it has been suggested that his first call, if he bothered to make one, was merely a prelude to further negotiations. Many years later I was to fall victim in a match against Pakistan to the Golden Boy's three-call trick, a 'yes', a 'wait', which left me stranded in mid wicket, and a 'no' as he passed me running hard.

Bill Edrich was scarcely less successful with 3,539 runs for an average of 80, while two more Middlesex players, the elegant Jack Robertson and the more functional Sid Brown, both climbed aboard the gravy train, the former with 2,760 and the latter 2,078.

The most interesting feature of Middlesex's Championship victory was that it was not achieved by the usual recipe for success—a powerful, varied and penetrating attack, supported by good catching and adequate batting—but stemmed from some of the most exciting, and attractive batsmanship ever seen in the competition. If R. W. V. Robins won the toss he simply informed his team that he wanted 400 runs by teatime on the first day. They seldom failed to achieve this, which provided him with both the time and the runs to dismiss the opposition twice, and if he looked like failing, he was prepared to talk or bamboozle the opposition out. However, they also had to beat (and did) their chief rivals Gloucestershire at Cheltenham on a 'turner' in a low scoring game played during the final Test, without Compton and Roberston.

The South Africans began badly, losing the five-Test series three nil with two drawn, and did not do themselves justice until the later stages of the tour. Alan Melville, Dudley Nourse and Bruce Mitchell were all fine batsmen; Tuckett was as good, possibly better, than any of the English opening bowlers; Athol Rowan was at the time the finest off-spinner in the world, and Tufty Mann proved a tight and effective slow left-armer.

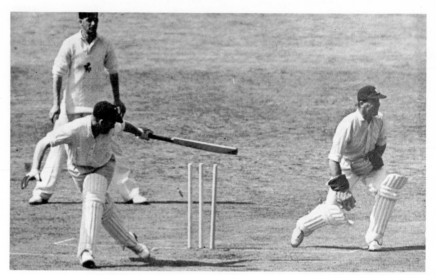

The ambition of every wicketkeeper—a leg-side stumping. Here, Godfrey Evans, showing his customary skill and pace, dismisses Jack Parker with a lightning movement from outside the leg stump

The Middlesex Twins, Compton and Edrich, going out to bat in that unbelievable summer of 1947. Between them they were to score 7,355 runs, despite the fact that Denis had a tendency to become bored with the proceedings after he had reached a hundred, and frequently gave it away

Big Al, Alec Bedser, was a big man with a heart to match. He was the best fast-medium bowler since the war and one of the truly great bowlers of all time

Having gone up to Cambridge in 1946, I had the good fortune to spend the early part of the summer gaining confidence on the perfect pitches at Fenners and after the University Match joined Essex for the remainder of the season.

It was not only an exhilarating, uncomplicated period in which to play First Class cricket, but it was also the start of a vintage era for both universities. Oxford and Cambridge have always been an ideal nursery for a future international player and in the 1940s and 1950s the sides were stronger than usual because the undergraduates were, in the main, older. The Freshman, instead of coming straight from school, had several years in the services behind him and was therefore tougher, both mentally and physically. The selection boards at that time were also less obsessed with pure scholastic achievement and believed that a sportsman who eventually gained a Second or even a Third Class Honours Degree had something to offer to the university, and eventually to the world.

In the winter of 1948 the MCC undertook what must surely have been one of the most disastrous and unintentionally funny tours of all time, in which they failed to win a game, lost the four-Test series easily and were outplayed in every department, even though the selection of the opposition's teams and captains depended more upon inter-island politics than ability.

The first mistake was the failure to realize that whereas English cricket had gone back, West Indian cricket had improved. The second was to select too many senior cricketers, including Gubby Allen (as captain and manager at forty-five), when it was known that it needed at least half a mile of elastoplast and a personal masseur to see him comfortably through one First Class match. The outcome was a daily sick parade which frequently resembled a casualty clearing station. The third was the timing, as many of England's most accomplished players were unwilling to tour in successive winters.

Of the four comparative youngsters who went to that Caribbean massacre, Jim Laker and Johnny Wardle both learned much about the difficult art of slow bowling against class players on good wickets; but Maurice Trem-

lett and Gerry Smithson experienced a very depressing time. On the other hand, the West Indies' future looked ominously bright. Frank Worrell and Everton Weekes were palpably batsmen of great talent, and there was no shortage of very good support with the bat; there were also several distinctly hostile bowlers; a jolly leg-spinner, Ferguson, and a couple of tough, capable all-rounders, John Goddard and Gerry Gomez.

Like the great Julius Caesar, Donald Bradman in 1948 could say *veni, vidi, vici*. He, and his outstanding Australian side stormed their way through the country, winning twenty-three of the thirty-four matches and drawing nine. Their record in the five-Test series (they won four and drew one) is an impressive testament to their strength, but it does not do full justice to their superiority, or show the completeness of their victories. They were a great combination by any standards and in any era, made all the more formidable by the weakness of the opposition.

First, in Don Bradman they had one of the most astute tactical brains the game has ever seen, expert at discerning weaknesses and exploiting them to the full. He handled his formidable attack in a masterly fashion and possessed that killer streak which is always to be found in the finest Australian sportsmen.

Under his command he had almost certainly the strongest batting side ever to have toured Britain. Bradman, Morris, Barnes, Hassett and Brown were all established world class players; young Harvey was destined to become one, and Miller was the most devastating all-rounder Australia has produced. The fact that Bill Brown, who made 8 centuries on the tour, was unable to claim a regular Test place is just another indication of their run-getting capabilities, which were still further enhanced with members in the later order, such as Sam Loxton, Ray Lindwall, Ian Johnson and Don Tallon.

With batsmen like that it was inevitable that not only would the tourists score a great many runs, but that they would also gather them quickly.

In addition to their splendid run-machine, Don was given a penetrating and varied attack, with the perfect spearhead, two outstanding fast bowlers, Ray Lindwall and

Keith Miller, and two distinctly lively fast-medium bowlers, the left-hander Bill Johnston, with Sam Loxton in close support. The menace of this quartet was made the more formidable by the ruling that a new ball became available after fifty-five overs. There may have been finer or faster bowlers than Ray Lindwall, but nobody of real pace has moved the ball in the air as much or as late. One of my abiding memories of Ray is seeing Reg Simpson attempt to force a ball, which had started well outside his leg stump, through the on side, only to be caught by Richie Benaud in the gully!

While the pacemen rested, Bradman relied on the nagging persistency of Ernie Toshack, a left-arm medium pacer who was difficult to collar, a negative rather than an attacking bowler, and the slow, flighted off-breaks of Ian Johnson. It is interesting to note that the two leg-spinners, Doug Ring and Colin McCool, although they took plenty of wickets against the counties, only appeared in one Test each—an early and possibly the first indication that the wrist-spinner was on the way out in England.

Backing up his bowlers, Don had a fine fielding side, with safe hands and strong arms. All in all it proved too much for England and the counties, who were sunk without any trace, the ultimate humiliation occurring at the Oval, when a panic-inspired national team was shot out for 52 and lost by an innings.

The Australians dominated the First Class cricket scene to a greater extent than any subsequent touring party. They caught the imagination of the public, who swarmed to see them whenever or wherever they appeared. Nevertheless, on the domestic front there was one interesting and unusual feature. Glamorgan carried off the County Championship for the first time in the club's history, and in so doing illustrated a new trend that was creeping into the game. Whereas Middlesex's triumph of the previous summer had been due largely to the majesty of their batting, Glamorgan's win owed an enormous debt to their fielding, and especially their close catching, because neither their batting nor their bowling could be termed exceptional.

The rather standardized field placings of the 1930s were giving way to the close-to-the-wicket specialist, who was to make such a difference to the success of the off-spinner. Captains were beginning to appreciate that first slip for an away-swing bowler was a vital wicket-taking position, rather than a convenient place to push one of the less active fielders.

In many respects 1948 was the most important year in my cricket career, because although it was a rather disappointing one, it made me think about the game and analyse it in some depth, rather than superficially. This change was largely due to my experiences against the Australians. My first meeting was at Fenners, where I made the elementary mistake of running hard to the same end with Doug Insole. My second error was to bowl, although not fully fit, against high class batsmen. I did have the satisfaction of scoring some runs in the second innings, but the vital lesson learned was that I would never be a fast bowler. (I had seen Lindwall and Miller in action.) Incidentally over 25,000 people watched the Australians beat us by an innings.

Showing considerable naivety, I travelled by coach with the Australians to play for Essex against them at Southend, where we bowled them out in a day, while they scored 721. It was a revelation. They never bothered to accelerate, they simply ambled along at just over 200 runs per session. In the first quarter of an hour a finger on my left hand was broken attempting to stop a hook at short leg off Ray Smith. It did not prevent my bowling for the first time against the Don. I even had the satisfaction of dismissing Keith Miller first ball not, I regret to say, because it was a good delivery, but merely because he had lost interest in the proceedings and it happened to be straight.

After being forcefully struck for five runs an over throughout that remarkable day, I had to ask myself what on earth I was doing bowling with basically the same attacking field at the close as I had used at the outset. Something was clearly wrong and gradually the penny dropped. There are times to attack and there are times to defend.

My next encounter against the tourists was for the Gentlemen at Lord's, Bradman's last appearance at the game's headquarters, which he celebrated with 150. My two wickets cost over a hundred, but were relatively less expensive than on the previous outing. R. W. V. Robins captained the Gentlemen. Some newspapers, not fully appreciating the near impossible task of Norman Yardley as skipper of England, thought Robins was the man needed to revitalize the national side against the Australians.

In the course of his innings Lindwall let go a very fast, playful bouncer which had Robins, much to everyone's amusement, flat on his back taking evasive action. At the end of the day Don, who was a close friend of Robins with much in common, poked his head round our dressing room and remarked in his dry, laconic way: 'Good thing you didn't attempt a comeback, Robbie, we'd have dropped you.' I have no doubt he was right.

My final meeting in 1948 was for the South of England at Hastings—the third successive occasion I had bowled Bradman and his third successive century. I trapped him with a long hop when he was 143, leaving me rather grateful that he was now well past his prime. It made me appreciate just how fine a batsman he had been in the 1930s.

After the disasters of the summer the MCC set sail for South Africa with a much stronger side than the one which had fared so badly in the West Indies. It included three high class batsmen; Len Hutton, Cyril Washbrook and Denis Compton, with useful support. Their attack was less formidable and one can imagine the heavy toll that the Australians would have taken off two medium-pacers and two leg-spinners who were to be the main wicket-takers, but fortunately the South African batting was competent rather than exceptional, and also timid. As a result England, under the leadership of George Mann, deservedly won a series, even though the South Africans possessed the more penetrating bowling.

Of all the countries with Test Match status, the New Zealanders were considered the weakest—one reason being the lack of practical assistance from their nearest neighbour, Australia. Imagine the impetus it would have given to the game if Don Bradman and company had paid them an extended visit in the 1930s! It was therefore expected that England, having beaten the South Africans,

would prove too much for Walter Hadlee and his men, but it turned out differently. There was no way that England were going to dismiss them twice on good wickets in a dry summer and in three days. The batting line-up included two outstanding left-handers, Martin Donnelly and Bert Sutcliffe; the classy Wallace and Hadlee, though both were disappointing in the Tests; the stubborn Scott, and the promising Reid, with the rest of the side determined not to lose. They wanted to show the authorities the absurdity of Tests of this duration—and they did.

The inability of the home cricket authorities to recognize that England in the 1940s was no longer the dominating force in world cricket and had worsened while the other countries had improved is one of the mysteries of the game. The result of this blindness was that New Zealand travelled across the globe to take part in four draws, of which three are best described as bore draws, with the outcome a foregone conclusion long before stumps were drawn. Four four-day Tests, or four five-day Tests would have produced a fascinating series, which England with greater depth in batting and variety in bowling would in all probability have won. It would also have meant that this exceptionally popular New Zealand team would not have had to take part in so many rather pointless minor games.

However, the visitors certainly made good their point and we have never again had to put up with the futility of three-day Tests in the post-war cricket world.

The English Selectors, in a desperate effort to win the final Test at the Oval, succeeded in picking a gloriously unbalanced team. It contained no fewer than four wrist-spinners, an off-spinner and three seamers. There are problems about giving adequate bowling to two leg-break bowlers in Britain and eight bowlers in a three-day encounter is simply an embarrassment for the captain. It also meant that our eventual batting line-up was painfully thin.

RENAISSANCE IN THE FIFTIES

One of the famous ten wickets: Jim Laker and Godfrey Evans successfully appeal against Ian Craig during Australia's second innings of the Old Trafford Test in 1956. On a difficult pitch, which had originally crumbled and was then further enlivened by rain, Jim went on to capture all 10 wickets, having taken 9 wickets in the first innings. This gave him a match analysis of 19 wickets for 90 runs, figures which have never been approached before or since, and which are not likely to be bettered. Jim naturally bowled round the wicket, because the ball turned sharply

The renaissance of British cricket which took place during the 1950s did not suddenly occur, but gradually developed over a number of years and stemmed from several different factors. First and foremost, it was due to the emergence of a number of high class post-war cricketers, batsmen, fast bowlers and spinners. Until these arrived England had had to rely largely on the pre-war cricketers, plus Alec Bedser and Godfrey Evans, the two players of international calibre who had firmly established themselves in the 1940s. This had been sufficient to beat off the challenge of South Africa and India, but was not strong enough for Australia, or the rapidly improving West Indies.

Secondly, a new, and meaner thinking began to creep into the game. The ideas and the tactics of the pre-war years were being questioned and queried. Was it right to take a leg-spinner to Australia simply because he was a leg-spinner, and to ignore an off-spinner, because it was assumed that he would not be successful? It was an intriguing question, made all the more logical by the fact that English leg-spinners had over the years seldom done well out there.

There was also the strange belief that to take wickets abroad, bowlers needed either to be very fast, or to rely largely on flight and spin, though this was not borne out by facts or figures, as it overlooked the feats of S. Barnes, M. Tate and A. Bedser, for a start.

Field placing became more elastic and subtle. The idea that bowlers had set fields which seldom changed gave way to bowlers employing different fields, not only for different batsmen and situations but also depending upon which stump was being attacked.

Captains began to appreciate that if two stroke-makers were well set and scoring quickly, the most effective counter might well be to try deliberately to shut the game up. This move, if executed properly, meant that the batsmen would have to take some risks if they were to maintain the tempo, and therefore increase the chances of securing a wicket. If they did not adopt this policy, then the runs would take longer to score.

Field placing, in general, became far more defensive, except at the commencement of an innings, for a new batsman, or when the fielding side were on top. In these circumstances the batsman would be encircled by close fielders, because it was well worth conceding a few boundaries if this automatically increased the chances of securing a wicket.

It became normal for even a genuine fast bowler with an old ball to reduce the number of attacking fielders to a mere two when he was confronted by a well set batsman, which automatically reduced the run rate.

When on top, the fielding captain naturally encouraged his bowlers to send down as many deliveries as possible, because this would increase the chances of winning; conversely, if Walcott and Weekes were in full cry, then a deliberate slowing down of the over rate lessened the number of runs and the chances of losing.

There was nothing new about leg theory. Fred Root had used it most effectively in conjunction with his in-swingers long before the war, but the 1950s saw a different form in which the principal aim was to put an effective brake on the scoring, rather than to have batsmen caught by the leg slips. For this purpose, the accurate fast to fast-medium seamer switched his attack to on, and just outside, the leg stump, which effectively reduced by fifty per cent the scoring arc, as few batsmen had either the ingenuity or the skill to hit good length quick bowling from on or outside the leg to the off. Even if they were able to improvise effectively for a short period, the odds were against them succeeding for long and on them eventually losing their wicket.

In the leg theory of the 1950s, the scoring area was restricted to the leg-side, heavily populated with fielders, specially stationed to make both the glance and the pick-up off the legs risky. It was, of course, essential that the bowling was good length, so that the batsman never had the opportunity to hook or pull a short delivery, or to drive the over-pitched. Although it is possible to hoick a good length, quick ball off the pads to the boundary, even the greatest players will find difficulty in doing it with regularity and assurance, particularly against bowlers with the ability to alternate the ball that is intended to miss the stumps, with the one that can knock out the leg peg. It will be appreciated that a top class seamer should possess sufficient control to enable him to nominate and hit an unguarded stump three times out of six.

This essentially negative though often effective leg theory meant that bowlers had found a method of closing down the game on good wickets when it suited them. I never encountered any batsman capable of scoring fast for any length of time against this particular form of bowling, and first employed it when the strategic situation demanded in Australia in 1950–1. However, the most famous, or infamous, occasion was in the Headingley Test of 1953.

England had to all intents and purposes saved the match when Australia commenced their second innings, but Len Hutton was still remembering the way they had crumbled before Wardle's spin at Old Trafford, and as the pitch was a little damp he opened with Bedser and Lock, supported by ultra-attacking fields. The outcome was that the Australians suddenly found themselves in a winning position which they themselves had never envisaged.

It was then I suggested to Len that I could stop them with leg theory, and so it proved, though it would never have been necessary if Len had not, for once, misread the situation.

Although this form of bowling had been designed primarily for use in Test matches, I did on one occasion employ it against Denis Compton in a county game. He was in superb form and threatening to score a century before lunch. These tactics did not please Denis, as he was unable to maintain the tempo, and because I was bowling normally at the other batsmen. It also achieved its objective when a frustrated Denis was eventually bowled round his legs by a genuine round-arm delivery.

There can be no doubt that this type of leg theory made the game less exciting for the spectator, because it reduced the effectiveness of the finest strokemakers in the world. The players themselves recognized this fact and tacitly abandoned an interesting tactical ploy in the overall interest of the game. The last time that persistent leg theory in this form was used was in the first Test of the MCC's West Indian tour of 1953–4.

Not unnaturally the authorities had never

Len Hutton tosses the coin in the 1953 Test at Headingley and Hassett calls correctly for the fourth time in succession. England were sent in to bat on a damp pitch with an outfield slowed by heavy pre-match rain. When Hutton was bowled by Lindwall second ball for 0, a deathly silence enveloped the Yorkshire crowd, who simply could not believe this personal tragedy

approved of the tactical containment and decided to make it more difficult by legislation. This permitted only five fieldsmen on the leg-side, of whom only two could be stationed behind the bat.

As always the intention was admirable, but the outcome rather less satisfactory. For one thing the new ruling did not penalize to the same extent the left-arm seamer from over the wicket who repeatedly pitched outside the leg stump, as Trevor Goddard, for one, was to demonstrate from time to time at little above medium pace. On the other hand, it penalized both the attacking off-spinner, and the genuine in-swinger.

The renaissance of English cricket might be said to have begun at the Oval in 1953, when, under Sir Len Hutton, England regained the Ashes, which had been in Australia's possession since 1934. It was the climax of what had been a close, absorbing battle between two evenly matched sides, in which the fortunes of both had continually fluctuated, and which had caught the imagination of a British public starved of success.

England followed this by beating Australia convincingly in the next two series. The first victory owed much to the pace of Frank Tyson with back-up from a well above average attack. On the second occasion the Surrey spinners, Laker and Lock, proved too much for the Aussies on pitches which were not ideal for international cricket, ruthlessly exposing the limitations of their batting in conditions which were testing, but not as impossible as they were made to appear.

In addition, England came back from being 2–0 down in the Caribbean to square the rubber and then beat the West Indies very comfortably at home, while South Africa were defeated in England and the series tied out there. As a result by the mid-1950s England could with justification claim to have the strongest team in the world.

The decline began in 1958, when the Australians thrashed what on paper appeared to be a very powerful MCC party under Peter May because it failed dismally to play to its true potential. The outcome was that the Selectors decided to dismantle and to rebuild. They were not noticeably successful, as for the next two decades England were not again able

to claim to be the unofficial world champions. This honour was shared between Australia, the West Indies and, until excluded from international cricket, South Africa.

The 1958–9 tour was also directly responsible for a tightening up of the law defining a throw. It was noticeable that every state, apart from Queensland, included at least one bowler, usually of the quick variety, who had what could only be described as a suspect arm action. These are not easy for an umpire, who must rely entirely on his eye and is naturally unwilling to become embroiled in unpleasant incidents, but are only too obvious when shown on slow motion film. The MCC were in no position to criticize as the basic actions of two of their own party were certainly open to doubt.

The majority of the Australian offenders could be best described as 'throw-draggers'. They opened up in their delivery stride so that their front foot was pointing towards the slips in the case of a right-hander, and released the ball rather like a javelin thrower. It enabled the bowler to send down the ball more quickly than his run up suggested, and also allowed him to produce one that was either faster, or slower, without any noticeable change. The latter was especially revealing because it takes years for a fast bowler with a full arm action to learn to camouflage a slow ball successfully, yet Ian Meckiff possessed a very well concealed one from the outset of his international career.

Over the years Australia, even more than England, had shown very little concern about the occasional bowler with the suspicious action. What upset them on this occasion was that they were producing a breed of throw-draggers, as their youngsters inevitably copied what they saw in First Class cricket and it was spreading fast.

I discussed the problem with Alan Davidson, who had a perfect action and was therefore not a supporter of the bent-arm brigade. We were discussing Jim Burke, the Australians' opening bat, who was an occasional 'dart-throwing' off-spinner. He told me about one of his friends, who had injured his back and could no longer bowl quickly. When he saw his Grade team dismissed cheaply by Jim, he immediately appreciated the possibilities

Overleaf Almost, but not quite! Tom Graveney does well to keep down a lifting ball during his innings of 55, which saved England from collapse against Australia at Leeds in the fourth Test of 1953

and took up throwing off-breaks with considerable success.

It should be stressed that the players were not to blame. Ian Meckiff, one of the nicest Australians I have ever encountered, sincerely believed that there was nothing wrong with his action. The blame rested firmly on the clubs and the authorities for allowing him to start. If they had stopped him all the unpleasantness of being ultimately no-balled would never have happened to this charming man.

Another threat that some of the throw-draggers posed to batsmen was the extent of the drag. This was epitomized by O'Rourke, who for a short period was perhaps the quickest through the air of all the Australian bowlers. The reason for this was that umpires were prepared to allow him to drop behind the bowling crease yet break the batting crease with his right foot before releasing the ball off his left foot from way in front of it.

The Australians quickly and effectively purged their own game of all throwers, but this has tended to make them hyper-sensitive to anything that has the slightest resemblance to a throw.

England's success in the 1950s stemmed from a powerful and well balanced attack which enabled them to bowl out the opposition on all types of pitches. Although their batting contained several outstanding players, it really ended at number five, leaving four main bowlers and the wicketkeeper, who were all capable of chipping in with the odd thirty, but were not dependable. As a result I found a niche for myself at number six as the all-rounder and tried to drop anchor until the arrival of number eleven. These periods of crease occupation were to become almost second nature. Possibly, this approach, assisted by a personal distaste for losing my wicket, had always been lurking beneath the surface, as I remember P. G. Wodehouse writing in the Dulwich College Magazine—he was an Old Alleynian—when I was fifteen, 'Bailey awoke from an apparent coma to strike a four.'

Fast bowlers are frequently the decisive figures in an international series, especially abroad, and England in the 1950s was very well equipped in this department. Fred Trueman and Brian Statham formed one of the finest opening pairs the country has ever possessed. Not only were they both great bowlers in their own right, but they were complementary. How did they compare? Personally, I preferred to bat against Fred rather than Brian, because he did occasionally produce the bad ball, whereas with Brian one could wait several months for a long hop, and a whole season for a full toss. On the other hand, great batsmen, such as Graveney and May, thought differently, because Fred moved the ball more and sent down a high proportion of unplayable deliveries.

Fred was fast, volatile, with a natural away swing and a vivid imagination which allowed him to convince himself that there was something special about every ball he bowled, even a straight half volley that knocked out the stump of some wretched tail-ender as he trod on the square leg umpire's toe. Like good wine, he improved with the years and was more dangerous when he had become a complete master of his trade and was less dependent upon sheer pace. His record of 307 wickets in only sixty-seven Tests speaks for itself, but, as he will be only too happy to tell you at length, his vast haul and his number of appearances would have been considerably higher if the Test Selectors had known more about the game, though he would put it more pungently!

Brian's philosophy of bowling could be summed up by the words: 'If the batsman misses the ball, then I hit the stumps.' He was very accurate, moved the ball off the seam, rather than in the air, and was prepared to bowl for long spells uphill and into the wind. Unlike most fast bowlers, he had an equable, quiet temperament, and was even willing to tolerate batsmen.

Frank Tyson was the fastest bowler England has produced since the war. He blew in like the typhoon to which he has so often been likened, leaving a trail of destruction behind him before swiftly disappearing from the scene. His secret was excessive pace, and with this he destroyed the Australians in 1954–5 and played a major part in winning the series Down Under.

How quick was Frank at his peak? I once posed this question to Arthur Morris, who had the doubtful privilege of opening the Australian batting against him. Arthur

Frank Tyson was the fastest bowler produced by England since the last war. Like a slugger who depends upon the power of his punch, Frank relied upon sheer speed for his wickets. He did not do much with the ball, but he was so quick through the air that a bad delivery would often go unpunished. In his great tour to Australia of 1954–5, when he played a major part in winning the Ashes, it was by no means unusual for him to clean-bowl a batsman with a full toss while he was still on his down swing. Originally he used a long, ugly and rather clumsy run up, but he found in Australia that he was just as quick, and a good deal more accurate, off a short one. His First Class career was all too brief, but though very strongly built, with magnificent shoulders, his action, effective rather than flowing, put too much strain on his body for him to have lasted very long in domestic cricket. He was not helped by the pitches in Northampton, which at that time tended to be dead

reckoned—and I believe this to be one of the best assessments—that the difference in speed between Frank and Brian Statham, who was a genuine fast bowler, was about the same as between Brian and myself, and that was considerable.

Another indication of his exceptional pace for those few brief years was the number of Australians who were bowled out with straight, over-pitched deliveries, when they attempted to drive but failed to bring their bat down in time. On occasions, they were still on the upswing.

Standing in the slips against Frank was an experience, as there were times, despite being over thirty yards from the batsman, that one was too close for comfort!

Although Peter Loader was not as fast as the other three, he could swing the ball more and possessed a particularly vicious bouncer and a slower ball, which I never learned to pick. This was, in fact, so well disguised that he often had to employ a signal to his keeper.

Alec Bedser was at his peak in 1953, when Fred Trueman and Brian Statham were still establishing themselves as world class performers. His pace was fast-medium, rather than fast, but, like Maurice Tate before him, he hit the bat hard enough to make sure that it jarred the hand of any batsman who had the good fortune to last long against him. He preferred the wicketkeeper to stand up, and was lucky in having behind the stumps Godfrey Evans for England and Arthur McIntyre for Surrey, both of whom could cope. His pace was about the same as that of Geoff Arnold, and this, combined with his swing, lift and bounce, made keeping difficult. It would certainly have been sufficient to have had any keeper of the 1970s automatically standing well back.

Alec, massively built, had an economical approach with a powerful body action. Rather strangely, as he was essentially a sideways-on bowler, his natural ball tended to dip in very late to a right-hand batsman. The outcome was often an inside edge and catch to leg slip, as Sir Donald Bradman will testify. His control was excellent, and if a batsman missed the ball it would almost inevitably hit the stumps or bounce over the top. However, what made Alec into a truly great bowler was that he eventually perfected the best leg-cutter

the game has ever seen. His hands and fingers were so big and strong that he was able to 'spin-cut' this delivery so that it would bite even on good pitches, while on a wet wicket he could dip and pitch leg and hit the top of the off, which made life (for the batsman) difficult.

A match winner with the new ball, or in helpful conditions, he was in addition a splendid stock bowler who never seemed to tire or to break down.

Alec possessed a dry, somewhat laconic sense of humour, as he showed on one occasion at Sydney in a high temperature in his twenty-first eight-ball over with the Australians on top, when he informed the world at large that he had just received a cable from the Surrey Secretary telling him to keep fit for the following summer. He was a craftsman and a true professional.

Alec later became a Selector and eventually chairman of the Selection Committee, sound and sensible, but not very imaginative.

When Jim Laker took nineteen wickets in the Old Trafford Test of 1956, he became an instant legend, as this performance will surely never be equalled. However, if Jim had never accomplished that unique feat, he would still go down as one of the greatest—arguably in all conditions the greatest—off-spinners in history. He had all the classic requirements: a beautiful action, control, spin, flight and the ability to drift the ball away from the bat. Unlike Lance Gibbs and Hughie Tayfield, he was equally at home either round or over the wicket. It is strange that he should have only once been invited to tour Australia.

Bob Appleyard burst into the First Class scene comparatively late in life, and was forced to retire through ill-health after only a brief stay, but in his few short seasons for England and Yorkshire he proved to be a wonderful wicket-taker, even managing to secure 200 one summer.

Although Bob was used by Yorkshire as both an in-swing, opening bowler and as a quick off-spinner, or cutter, he will be remembered chiefly in the latter role. He sent down his off-breaks at a brisk medium pace, considerably faster than Underwood. With his height and high arm action he made the ball bounce, and on a pitch giving some assistance he was close to being unplayable.

He was happier bowling over the wicket. His control was such that I have seen him perform with only two supporting fielders on the off-side and take eight for next to nothing.

Although Bob was quick through the air, he also possessed a most deceptive loop when he was spinning the ball. I batted against him frequently in the nets in Australia and he would convince me that he had sent down a half volley, only for me to discover at the last moment that it was not quite there to drive. Because his career was so short there is a tendency to underestimate Bob, but for a few years he was one of the best, and most feared bowlers anywhere. I never saw him collared.

The two England left-arm spinners, Johnny Wardle and Tony Lock, were very different in technique and temperament. Johnny was a very good and, like all Yorkshiremen, a very mean slow bowler, who spun the ball enough to beat the bat and could be employed either as a match-winner or as a stock bowler. Being a slow left-hander in Yorkshire has its disadvantages, in that one is automatically and unfavourably compared with either Hedley Verity, or Wilfred Rhodes, and purely as an orthodox left-armer Johnny did not rate as high. What made Johnny special was that he learned to bowl chinamen and googlies so well that for a period he was probably the best wrist-spinner in the world, despite the fact that he was very seldom called upon to bowl them for Yorkshire.

On the less responsive pitches abroad this extra ability proved a big boon and made him rather more dangerous than Tony Lock, who in those conditions could often be played as a seamer. Although Johnny was a well above average cricket comedian, and consequently very popular with the crowds throughout the world, he was not naturally a funny man, and took life very seriously.

Tony began his first Class career as a flighty left-armer with classical action and pleasing flight, but who did not impart overmuch spin. One winter, which he spent coaching in an indoor school, he discovered that by bending his left arm and pushing the ball through faster and flatter he could turn the ball on most surfaces. The new-style Lock immediately began to take a large crop of wickets in county games. He became the first,

and the most successful, of a whole brigade of bent-arm spinners who really should have been no-balled for throwing. They were allowed to continue because the umpires, the counties and the authories were prepared to overlook bowlers with very suspect actions, and my own immediate reaction was to start looking for a thrower.

Why were Lock and a host of imitators allowed to go unchallenged until the throw-draggers of Australia appeared in the 1958-9 tour to Australia? The simple answer was that an umpire likes a peaceful life and naturally does not want to be responsible for jeopardizing a man's livelihood, especially as in this case the clubs for whom the offenders were taking their wickets were selfishly satisfied.

Wardle, who had an entirely legitimate action, not surprisingly resented being kept out of the England team by a bowler who was blatantly transgressing the laws of the game.

Tony, in his bent-arm, or second period, was not a subtle bowler. His aim was to pitch the ball around about middle stump at medium pace and hit the top of the off. And with a little encouragement from the pitch— there were plenty of suitable pitches around— he was able to do this with some regularity and consistently turned in fine figures. Tony also had a faster ball for which he was once no-balled in the West Indies, and which was close to Trueman's pace.

The most intriguing feature of Tony Lock's career was to occur after he had seen himself on slow motion film, following the 1958-9 tour. He changed his action once more and became an outstanding slow bowler in both England and Australia. In fact, he was more effective in his third phase on overseas pitches than he had been in his middle era.

Sir Len Hutton batted with so much grace and style that even when scoring slowly he was always worth watching. He favoured the front foot more than most great players and consequently was never an outstanding hooker. His defence was superb and he was especially good on a bad wicket. His off drive was beautiful, while his ability to take, almost at will, a single by careful placement or ride a 'lifter' were object lessons.

As a skipper, Len was a splendid tactician, quick to spot weaknesses in the opposition

Doug Insole and I going out to bat for Essex. In a twenty-year partnership, we batted in the middle order for Cambridge University, Essex, the Gents and England. Possibly our most remarkable stand was when we both scored centuries before lunch against Notts. When I first bowled against Doug in the nets at Fenners, I wondered what he was doing there, because he was just about the worst net player I had seen. However, it was a very different story in the middle, where he had the happy knack of consistently scoring runs in his own highly individual way on all types of wicket and against all kinds of bowling. I believe he would have played more often for England if his style had been smoother, and if the Selectors had realized that his habit of hitting good length bowling to midwicket off his stumps was an asset rather than a handicap. This view is substantiated by his most unusual international career. He was picked five times at home, but all in different series. On his one overseas tour, to South Africa, he played in all five Tests and headed the averages. It is normally stupid to bring in a player for one game, but to do this five times is criminal

and to exploit them to the full. His record as captain was very impressive, but he did have a strong side of experienced players. By nature rather remote and retiring, he would probably have struggled if he had had to lead, shall we say, the 1948 team against the Australians, when he would have needed to extract the best out of the limited and demoralized material. He was respected both for his ability as a player and for his deep knowledge of the game, but he lacked the charisma of a born leader.

Denis Compton, handicapped by a bad knee—a legacy from his footballing days— was never the same mercurial force in the 1950s as he had been in the 1940s, but he was still a fine batsman, with all the shots, plus some with his own individual mark upon them. Although his Middlesex partner, Bill Edrich, had lost the flair and the dash of his earlier years, he still remained a dependable fighter, and if he had been included in the party to Australia in 1950–1 England might well have won the Ashes three years earlier.

From the moment I first bowled at Peter May, when he was a Freshman at Cambridge, there was no doubt in my mind that he had the quality which divides the true international from the accomplished batsman. This included the ability to hit a good length delivery for four off his back foot with a straight bat. Like many tall players he discarded the hook from his considerable repertoire of elegant and powerful strokes.

Peter made a popular and astute captain, as a result of his considerable charm and his tactical appreciation. He was also much tougher than many realized. A combination of illness and a disenchantment with certain sections of the press after the disastrous 1958–9 Australian tour made him retire from the game while he was still among the four finest batsmen in the world, and many would have said that he was the best. If he had been entrusted with the England captaincy later in his career, he might well have stayed longer. The same could also be said to apply to Ted Dexter.

Colin Cowdrey looked like a mature professional, even when he was still a schoolboy, and he went on to score more runs in Test cricket than any other Englishman. His de-

fensive technique, concentration and wide range of strokes ensured that he would become one of the greatest players of the world. What was so impressive about Colin's batting was the amount of time he seemed to have and the way that he would caress the ball to the boundary. One felt that with his ability it should have been impossible to get him out and he should have been even more successful. His problem was that in some respects he was too nice a person for professional sport, and never fully realized just how good he was. It was his lack of self confidence, or perhaps it was humility, which was responsible for him so often being second, instead of first choice captain of England, and prevented him from achieving his ambition of taking the MCC to Australia, where he made more tours than anybody else in history.

Although he was a professional, Tom Graveney played with the casual elegance of an Edwardian amateur. In his early days, Len Hutton found him too easy going, and he certainly became a more effective player when he joined Worcester, following a row with his native Gloucestershire after they had replaced him as captain. This took some of the laughter out of his bat, but increased the run output.

Very few of the great players have been so predominantly front foot as Tom. He would even paddle-hook a genuine fast bowler off his front foot, and it naturally followed that he was a superb driver with a high backlift and a full follow-through, while his height enabled him to ride the lifting ball using the half-cock shot with his weight on his left foot.

It would be difficult to imagine Ted Dexter playing any game less than very well. He was a natural athlete, with a wonderful eye and an impressive physique, and he was a fine mover. In addition to the ability which enabled him on occasions to destroy a top class international attack, and to strike a ball much harder than most, 'Lord Edward' had a presence. If he had possessed just part of Geoff Boycott's dedication he would not have been just a fine, very exciting batsman and a useful, slightly unpredictable bowler; he could well have become a cricketing god, or at the very least a cricketing king. From time to time he became bored with the proceedings, especially during county games, and would drift off into a world of his own.

Ted held numerous theories, some distinctly unusual, and he sometimes found it difficult to understand anyone else's view. A tendency to be dogmatic plus an entirely unconscious lack of warmth proved a handicap as captain.

The cricket of the past is inclined to appear more attractive than the cricket of the present, and it was ever so. Quite apart from natural nostalgia for the heroes of one's youth, the careers of so many have stretched over long periods.

The late 1920s, the 1930s and the 1950s were all vintage times for England and full of the game's outstanding performers. When looking back one always tends to remember them in their prime and to forget that at that time some were actually past their peak and others had not fully arrived. Although Ken Barrington first played for England in the mid-1950s, his most successful years belong to the following decade, before a heart complaint caused an all-too-early retirement.

Ken originally appeared on the international scene as a fluent strokemaker and like so many others failed to establish himself immediately. When he was eventually recalled, he had drastically changed his style and turned himself into one of the most consistent of all the run-accumulators, complete with a two-eyed stance, a rock-like defence and a utilitarian approach to his job of churning out the figures. Although the charm of his early days had gone, he virtually eliminated risk and was therefore far more successful.

Ken provided England with the solidarity which is so important to any team, but he did not attract the hum of excitement when he walked out to bat. He was once, quite illogically, dropped by the England Selectors for a very slow century he had grafted against New Zealand. On this occasion the Selectors were themselves to blame because they had picked him in the middle of one of his few bad patches and in spite of this he gave them a hundred, albeit a leisurely one, which was more than they had any right to expect in those circumstances.

The importance of a brilliant wicketkeeper to any team is enormous. Not only does he have more opportunities to effect a dismissal than anyone else, but he is the hub around which the rest of the fielding revolves. England have been wonderfully served in this department by a succession of great Kent keepers—Leslie Ames, also a high quality batsman, Godfrey Evans and Alan Knott.

Leslie was a very safe, quiet and unassuming wicketkeeper, who missed very little. Many believed that in the late 1920s and early 1930s the more flamboyant and far noisier George Duckworth was superior but Les was also a fine batsman, good enough indeed to have earned his place in many international XIs solely in that capacity. Later, as the administrative supremo of Kent, Les was to play a big part developing and fostering the game in his native country. He was also a most congenial and efficient manager.

Before Alan Knott had established himself as the Kent keeper, and long before he became an ever-present member of the England team, he came as the second keeper for the International Cavaliers which I captained on an unofficial tour to the West Indies. What impressed me at the time, apart from his natural ability, was his determination to succeed and his willingness to learn, which has been largely responsible for his developing into a world class wicketkeeping all-rounder.

He used that trip to gain experience, not only by keeping to Jim Laker and Fred Trueman, but by willingly going in as nightwatchman against Wes Hall. One did not need to be a prophet to say at the end of the trip that the next time Alan came to the Caribbean it would be with an MCC blazer.

Small, neat, agile, and a fitness fanatic, for ever doing exercises, Alan can have had few superiors standing back, where he snaps up the catchable and the nearly uncatchable with remarkable consistency. Standing up to the stumps, which is the biggest test for any keeper, he was not quite as impressive as Godfrey Evans, except when taking his colleague Derek Underwood, who because of his pace must rate as something of a nightmare to any keeper. On the other hand, he has far fewer opportunities, as standing back to medium pacers has become standard practice. This has the obvious advantage of making the catches easier to hold for both the wicketkeeper and the attendant fieldsmen. It

Brian Statham was double jointed, which helps to account for his very 'whippy' action. Lithe and lean, Brian was known as the Greyhound, a bowler who invariably gave of his best on all wickets and on all occasions—a true professional, very popular with everyone in the game, and an outstanding tourist, whose favourite party piece was to make pancakes

is surprising that more batsmen do not take advantage of this situation by batting well outside the crease.

Alan's efforts for England in the lower middle order have been outstanding, because he is a born fighter with an excellent temperament and is also a very good player in his own right, able to defend and attack. In many respects, the greatest attribute of his batting is that it is unconventional and he produces shots which have his own trade mark. These tend to upset opposing bowlers. A left-armer does not appreciate being swept to square leg from outside the off stump, fast bowlers resent being chopped over the top of the slips and the seamers are never happy at being squirted with a straight bat to mid wicket off the middle stump.

Godfrey Evans and Alan Knott had three things in common. They both came from Kent, they both were world class wicket-keepers and they both possessed remarkable stamina, but as characters they were entirely different. Godfrey was always a flamboyant extrovert forever on the look out for excitement and big parties, while Alan after the labours of the day will sip a glass of milk and settle for quiet relaxation.

Godfrey exuded vitality and bounce, which remained throughout the trials and tribulations of a five-day Test. He acted as perpetual tonic to his side, while his optimism was indestructable. His battle cry, 'We'll get 'em tonight, lads', was infectious even though, with two hours remaining, seven wickets down, a difficult pitch and 350 runs required, this might seem somewhat improbable.

How good was Godfrey behind the stumps? The following two instances, although neither occurred in a Test, which always served to bring out the best in him, illustrate both his skill and extraordinary mobility.

The first was in the near farce of the Test trial at Bradford, where Jim Laker took 8 wickets for 2 runs on a 'sticky', figures which might well have been rather impressive if he had not decided to give Eric Bedser, his county colleague, one off the mark. Don Kenyon played back to one that turned and lifted sharply. The ball, on the way down off Don's bat, flicked his pad and Godfrey took the catch full length one-handed in front of the

astonished batsman, and an equally bemused gaggle of short legs.

The second took place during the Scarborough Festival. Billy Sutcliffe, who was both a better batsman and captain then he is often given credit for, played a full leg glance off Alec Bedser, which should have gone too square for fine leg to have stopped the boundary, but Godfrey took off and caught it left-handed, airborne and horizontal.

The number one county of the 1950s, standing head and shoulders above everyone else, was Surrey. They acquired a taste for the title in 1950 under M. R. Barton when they shared the championship with Lancashire. They were then a good rather than an exceptional team, and one rather doubts if they would have been so effective if the beautiful pitches of the 1940s had still been in existence. This is what Wisden had to say about that season.

'In 1949 the pitches at the Oval gave evidence of favouring batsmen much less than hitherto, and last year they afforded increased help to bowlers. Men of pace frequently found it possible to make the ball get up awkwardly from a good length, and, particularly following rain, those able to apply spin could make their deliveries turn considerably.'

The trend to encourage groundsmen to produce wickets which gave assistance to bowlers and therefore provided more definite results, without recourse to declarations, was to be copied by many clubs. It was one of the features of the 1950s and was partially responsible for the shortage of real stroke-makers and the considerable increase in the number of seamers produced by the county clubs in the next decade.

In 1951 Warwickshire, who were rank outsiders, sneaked in to take the County Championship, the first time it had ever been achieved by an all professional side. It was essentially a team effort, in which the key figures were Tom Dollery, who captained in masterly fashion, as well as providing many of the runs when they were most needed, and Eric Hollies who picked up nearly 150 wickets at small cost with his leg-breaks.

Surrey's remarkable run began in 1952,

Jim Laker leaving the field to the applause of his colleagues and the crowd, having taken 19 wickets against the Australians. Sitting in the dressing room immediately afterwards, I said that I could not believe it had happened, and I still find it difficult! The amazing thing was not so much that Jim should have secured 19 wickets on a difficult, but not impossible pitch, as that Tony Lock, normally such a deadly exploiter of conditions which gave him just a modicum of assistance, should only have picked up one wicket as he toiled away at the other end. The reason was that Tony had become so furious with himself and with his lack of success that he had bowled faster and faster, while the Australians surrendered to Jim at the other end. There was never any suggestion that Tony, in order to help Jim to his record, had stopped trying: the Surrey Spin Twins did not operate like that. They were a deadly pair, but they were just as deadly rivals

when they won twenty out of their twenty-eight Championship matches and went on to retain the Championship for seven consecutive seasons. They dominated domestic cricket to a larger degree than the great Yorkshire side of the 1930s and were even more impressive because the overall standard of the opposition was stronger. It is doubtful whether there has ever been a more formidable county XI.

What was their secret? First and foremost, they had an outstanding attack with four bowlers of international calibre—Alec Bedser, Peter Loader, Jim Laker and Tony Lock—while in reserve there was Eric Bedser, who would have been number one off-spinner in most sides, and reasonable reserve cover. On a pitch that gave an attack only a little encouragement this quartet were capable of bowling out most teams twice. On a bad wicket they were virtually unbeatable, while taking a century off their bowlers even on a feather bed was considerably more difficult than making a hundred against many Test XIs!

Second, this deadly quartet of match winning bowlers was superbly supported by the close catching of Lock, Stewart and Surridge in particular, and the keeping of McIntyre.

Third, although their batting was not as impressive as their bowling it did contain Peter May, who in the mid-1950s was the best player in the land, and over the years plenty of support and runs were provided by the likes of Subba Row, Barrington, Fletcher, Constable, Clark, Stewart, Eric Bedser and Whittaker, plus a distinctly formidable tail. However, it will be appreciated that the side very seldom needed to put together large totals, because they knew they could bowl out their opponents for less.

Fourth, in Stuart Surridge they had an enthusiastic, highly competitive and forceful captain, who was later succeeded by Peter May. Although even an indifferent skipper would have been pushed to do badly with that amount of talent at his disposal, Stuart succeeded in getting the most out of what was not the easiest of sides to handle.

It has always been a sporting belief that crowds will follow a winning team but strangely this did not prove to be the case with Surrey, possibly because their success lasted too long and stemmed from great bowlers, rather than exciting batsmen, who apart from genuine fast bowlers are the game's biggest draw.

In their constant pursuit of victory Surrey naturally became an aggressive team, but there were occasions when this aggression spilled over into the type of verbal abuse which was to become such an unpleasant and common feature of the game in the 1970s. Certainly, the West Indies were taken aback by the language they encountered from the Surrey XI. From time to time one gained the impression that the Surrey players enjoyed winning, but in the process had lost some of the enjoyment which stems simply from playing cricket.

The county's long run was eventually ended in 1959 by Yorkshire after a close and exciting race for the Championship, in which Gloucestershire, Warwickshire and Surrey were all well placed in the closing stages. Yorkshire eventually took the title on 1 September when they chased 251 in 105 minutes to beat Sussex. The surprising thing about their success was this was achieved by a Yorkshire XI which was far weaker than many of the teams they had fielded in the mid-1950s, when they had possessed an outstanding attack and well above average batting support. It was only the power of Surrey at their peak which had prevented Yorkshire from winning then. After all, their bowling line up, Trueman, Appleyard, Wardle and Illingworth, with Close on hand to provide additional support, was strong enough to have carried off the Championship in most other eras. To some certain extent they were handicapped by playing on a number of different home grounds, many with pitches that were less helpful to bowlers than the Oval.

THE SAD SIXTIES

This picture, taken near the end of Fred Trueman's long career, captures the perfect, powerful body action which was one of the main reasons why, unlike so many of his kind, he rarely broke down, although he expected to bowl more than a thousand overs per summer, pick up well over a hundred wickets, and do a six-month winter tour. It was this splendid action which enabled him to remain a world class bowler for so long: he was, in fact, more effective in his early thirties than in his early twenties, when he was over dependent on sheer speed. But Fred was far more than a fast bowler, hard hitting batsman and outstanding field: he was and still is a personality. There are more stories, mostly untrue, about Fred than any other player, except perhaps W.G., and certainly many of my happiest memories concern him. I shall always remember the disbelief on his face as he surfaced fully clothed from a swimming pool at a party given by John Mills in Australia. I had discreetly retired into the background by the time Fred emerged looking for the culprit. He picked the wrong one; but the following summer he reminded me of the incident with a lively bouncer

Despite some splendid cricket, some great players and a massive increase in the number of Test matches, the 1960s were a period of depression for the game in England which was reflected in various ways. The most serious was the marked decline in both cash and interest. More and more of the general public were turning to other forms of recreation, or simply switching on the television, which had become for so many the god of leisure, providing a permanent passport to the land of the Lotus Eaters.

The outcome was that attendances dropped at all levels, but especially at the County Championship matches. The fall off in the number of spectators for anything but the big occasion was to be found in most sports, including soccer and tennis, while the cinemas of the country were closing rapidly. Nevertheless, this was little consolation for cricket's administrators who were faced with rising costs, and a rapidly falling revenue.

The situation was not helped by much of the Test and county cricket being dull, professionally grey and lacking in character, with both the over, and the scoring rate slowing down. There were various reasons for the reduction in excitement. High on the list was the big increase in seamers and a corresponding decrease in spinners, for which artificial fertilizers must take much of the blame.

The great improvement in artificial fertilizers enabled groundsmen to produce lush, green outfields, which were beautiful to look at and to field upon, and which prevented the ball from becoming ragged. The outcome was that there would often be shine left when the next new ball became available. This situation was further helped by the technically improved finish that the manufacturers put on the ball. With the outfield acting as a polisher, rather than as the abrasive it had so often been in the past, the seamers and the swing bowlers were able to keep moving and swerving the ball for long periods and the spinners, particularly the wrist-spinner, became less essential.

In conditions when the ball tends to move about, the grafter, rather than the dashing strokemaker who draws the crowd, is more likely to succeed. The English professional, whose livelihood depends upon the consist-

ency with which he scores his runs, appreciated the point and acted accordingly, though there were some notable exceptions, like Colin Milburn.

What is revealing about Colin is that his career record in First Class cricket is no more impressive than that of Roger Prideaux, who was not nearly such a talented batsman, but took fewer chances.

Most of the English players who came forward in the 1960s had been brought up on the indifferent county pitches of the 1950s. Consequently, few had the confidence to hit through the rise on the up in the manner of their overseas counterparts. When they were struggling to establish themselves in the county team, they had understandably become more concerned with what the ball might do, than with what they intended to do to the ball!

The amateur now departed from the game and everyone became a player. Although by this time he had become something of an anachronism in a world which had undergone a social revolution, the amateur had enjoyed one considerable practical advantage. Because he was not paid by his county, he could afford to be far more blunt with the committee than if he had been a salaried employee. This was especially beneficial in the case of a captain, because county committees are often filled by people who know little or nothing about First Class cricket, but imagine that they do.

In addition to the obvious plus of having a captain who could afford to be independent, it meant that a county could pick a man whom they would not have chosen, because of his lack of technical qualifications, if they had been restricted to a small professional pool. Colin Ingleby-Mackenzie, who led Hampshire to their first Championship victory, provided a perfect example. Colin was not a great cricketer, though better than many appreciated, and not an outstanding tactician, though shrewder and meaner than many realized, but he brought fun and laughter to the game, a couple of ingredients which were becoming increasingly rare. He also played a vital part in Hampshire's Championship victory.

The decision to do away with the amateur

was also to cost money which the counties could ill afford, because employers who had been prepared to pay salaries, which were often merely an early form of indirect sponsorship, were no longer prepared to do so under the new conditions.

The abolition of the maximum wage for footballers and increased length of the soccer season virtually ended the cricket-footballer and meant that many potentially fine cricketers were lost to the summer game. Even more important, many boys who possessed the ability to become good cricketers turned to football because the financial rewards had become so much greater.

Another worry was that the schools, especially government schools, who were the main source of supply, were playing less and less cricket. It must be admitted that as a game it has serious disadvantages at school, because it takes up too much time and space and is technically rather demanding on the master in charge.

Oxford and Cambridge, which had been such a prolific breeding ground for the First Class game, were no longer as strong. The days when an undergraduate could afford to concentrate more on his cricket than on his books had gone for ever.

These were just some of the reasons why county cricket was speeding towards financial disaster. It was saved by the introduction of limited overs cricket, plus a vast injection of sponsored cash which eventually turned the Sad Sixties into the Sunny Seventies.

However, it would be entirely wrong to assume that this was just a sick era, as it contained one of the greatest, and almost certainly the most romantic tour in history. This was the West Indian visit, under Sir Frank Worrell, to Australia in 1960–1, which caught the imagination of the cricket public and made something of a mockery of much that had gone before and that was to come after.

The West Indians arrived comparatively unknown and departed from Melbourne four months later to the largest and most affectionate send-off ever given to a cricket team. Why was this tour such an outstanding success, both from the playing and financial angles?

First, the West Indian team contained not only some of the finest strokemakers in the world, such as Gary Sobers, Rohan Kanhai, Seymour Nurse, Conrad Hunte, C. Smith and Frank Worrell, who were still prepared to attack the opposition, and, in Wes Hall, a spectacular fast bowler, but also they were essentially entertaining cricketers, whose approach had not at that stage become over-professionalized. They enjoyed their cricket and it showed.

Secondly, the two captains, the charming Frankie and the erudite Richie Benaud with his appreciation of the importance of public relations, were prepared to adopt a positive and an open attitude. Their joint contributions added greatly to the overall enjoyment of the series.

Third, the Australian team also included more than the normal quota of attacking batsmen, a great opening bowler, Alan Davidson, and used plenty of wrist-spin, with Benaud himself collecting 23 wickets altogether and Simpson, Martin and Kline all having long spells.

Finally and most important of all, the ever-changing fortunes of both teams continued throughout the five Tests and built up to a tremendous climax at Melbourne, which was watched by more than 274,000 spectators.

The series began with a dream start at Brisbane, a wonderful game of cricket which ended as a tie. Australia then proceeded to win the second, lose the third, the fourth was drawn and the final Test was won by two wickets by Australia, but for once the game proved greater than the result. The West Indians may have lost, but they won the hearts of the Australian people and in so doing rekindled an interest and an enthusiasm which had begun to dwindle.

The popularity of the West Indies under Frank Worrell in Australia continued when they toured England in 1963 with Frankie in charge for his last major tour. Although his own powers as a player had declined his team was stronger and more mature than the one that had done so well Down Under. Gary Sobers had reached his peak, the finest all-rounder the world had ever seen, Charlie Griffith proved the ideal partner for Wes Hall, Butcher had improved enormously and Hunte

Although Ken Barrington will be remembered chiefly for his consistency, concentration and rocklike defence, he could hit the ball very hard and was distinctly partial to the lofted drive for six, completing Test hundreds in this fashion on more than one occasion. In this photograph, he has gone for the big hit using plenty of right hand, which accounts for the open finish

Two of the game's outstanding personalities, Sir Donald Bradman and Ted Dexter (Lord Ted) going out to toss before the start of a friendly match between the Prime Minister's XI and the MCC at Canberra in 1963

had a marvellous summer with the bat.

Unlike their predecessors, no fewer than nine of the team had extensive knowledge of English conditions and therefore took less time to settle down, while Worrell was not only tactically wise, but proved again to be the right man to extract the utmost from this highly talented group of individuals and mould them into a very formidable combination. They took the Test series by three games to one, and only lost one other First Class match, when Fred Trueman destroyed their batting on a helpful pitch, just as he was to do in England's only win at Edgbaston in the third Test, when he captured 12 wickets.

Not only were the West Indians warmly welcomed by the normal home crowd, but they were rapturously received by the many emigrants from the Caribbean, who turned out in vast numbers to support them.

The tourists' attack of Hall and Griffith, Sobers doubling as third seamer and wrist-spinner, and the off-spin of Gibbs, with Worrell as stand-by, proved too much for the English batting, who never found an opening pair able to cope with the threat of the new ball, though John Edrich in his first series gave signs that he had the determination and the ability to stand up to extreme pace. The outcome was that despite the occasional spectacular counter-attack by Dexter, watchful defence from Barrington and the typical, over-my-dead-body approach from Close there were seldom enough runs for the English bowlers, of whom Trueman with 34 wickets at just over 17 apiece was way ahead of everyone. The absence of Cowdrey, who had his wrist broken by Wes Hall in the most dramatic of the Tests at Lord's which ended in a nail-biting draw, was a serious loss.

The one fundamental weakness of this West Indian team who had now taken over from the Australians as the best team in the world was the lack of an adequate partner for Hunte. They continued to dominate under the captaincy of Sobers, who led from the front by personal ability, but had also acquired considerable knowledge of tactics as first lieutenant to Worrell. They defeated Australia for the first time in the West Indies and beat England again in England. Then inevitably they began to decline, as Hall and Griffith lost their edge, Sobers himself was troubled by a damaged knee and shoulder, and some of their best batsmen started to fade.

There were five series against Australia during the 1960s, three at home and two away. In the fifteen Tests England only achieved four wins, though they did manage to draw three rather unsatisfactory series, losing the other two series. Both those in England, in 1961 and 1964, were won by Australia, who retained the Ashes throughout a period which contained rather too much that by international standards could only be termed mediocre.

Although the high proportion of drawn games was to some extent due to excessive caution by the captains, the main trouble was that neither team was able to field a high quality balanced attack. At the start Australia had Davidson and Benaud, and later McKenzie, Gleeson, and Connolly, while England had Trueman and Statham in the early part, three good off-spinners at different times in Allen, Titmus and Illingworth, and later both Snow and Underwood came on to the scene.

However, much of the support bowling was unexceptional, so that there were plenty of runs to be had and the batsmen of both teams were able to enjoy themselves, especially as there was no really fast bowling. In this situation inevitably some fine batsmen emerged and some others who in another era would probably have not made the national XI. In the 1960s, however, they returned most impressive figures. A classic case was Peter Parfitt, who averaged over 40 in thirty-seven Tests. Yet it is difficult to think of Peter as anything more than a very good county batsman. By no stretch of the imagination did he measure up to another former Middlesex batsman, Jack Robertson, who was only capped eleven times.

The finest batsman England produced in this era was unquestionably Geoff Boycott, whose appetite for runs and consistency in procuring his staple diet has seldom been surpassed. He turned himself into a run-making machine by acquiring a defensive technique which was really special, eliminating strokes which contained any element of risk and punishing any bad ball.

For a great player it could be said that Geoff was hit rather too often by fast bowling, and has seldom dominated high calibre bowling, although he has repeatedly churned out large scores over a period of time against it.

The reason for his vulnerability, one suspects, is that there is a certain puppet-like jerkiness in some of his movements. He lacked the feline grace of Sobers, who could safely sway out of the way and allow the ball to fly harmlessly by or hook it savagely. Incidentally, Gary never bothered with a thigh pad and reckoned that he only ducked once in his career. That was against Wes Hall, when they were both playing for Australian states and he claims that it was intended as a gesture of courtesy, which is strongly refuted by Wes.

Geoff was never a natural mover and he had to work hard to turn himself into a competent fieldsman, because it was not an instinctive gift.

He did not dominate, as he mathematically restricted himself to comparatively few shots against good length bowling; the push, the discreet nudge and a handsome square drive off his back foot. Confident in the security provided by his near impregnable defence, he was prepared to wait for the bad ball and liked nothing better than taking on the role of sheet anchor, when he could afford to take all the time he wanted.

For personal reasons, and resenting the appointment of Denness as captain of England, Geoff decided to declare himself unavailable for his country and concentrated on continuing to captain and score runs for Yorkshire. This meant that during his self-imposed exile from international cricket far less talented batsmen than himself were finding themselves blitzed by Lillee, Thomson, Roberts and Holding.

The Yorkshire captain eventually returned to the Test scene in the third match against the Australians in 1977, and immediately proceeded to frustrate them by occupying the crease for hour after hour of intense concentration. This comeback culminated in his appointment as England captain on tour after Brearley's injury.

His utter absorption in the main objective of his life, the acquisition of runs, made the scoring of his hundredth century in front of a Yorkshire crowd in an Australian Test, almost a racing certainty.

The other outstanding batsman to come to the fore in the 1960s was John Edrich. Like Boycott, he was an opener and a gatherer of runs, rather than a spectacular stylist, but there the similarity ended. The Surrey player was a short, stocky left-hander with a rough-hewn style that was backed up by the determination which has always been such a characteristic of that remarkable cricketing family.

John has never been a pretty player to watch, but only Boycott of the same era has been more consistent with the bat in both Test and county cricket. His lack of height, plus a tendency to play from over the crease rather than right back on the stumps, has brought problems against the sharply lifting ball from the very fast bowlers, especially as he has never been a really effective hooker. As a result he has received more than his share of painful knocks, but these have had little effect on him. He has simply continued to shuffle across into line.

It was significant that when the West Indies pace trio were knocking over the England batsmen with distressing regularity in 1976, the Selectors should have turned to John and Brian Close, both past their peak, and at Old Trafford this pair proceeded to withstand without flinching the most unpleasantly physical bombardment of the entire series.

Although John will be remembered more for the runs he made, including a hundred hundreds, than the way he made the most of them, he did unexpectedly abandon his usual restrained and careful role in the 1960s for a period of biff, bang and wallop, when he startled everyone, not least the opposing bowlers, by regularly driving them over the top with a power and a regularity which suggested that if he had been brought up on overseas cricket he might well have developed into an exciting, attacking batsman, rather than a dependable grafter, especially adept at running the ball down through the gully with an angled bat, and strong off his legs.

The most controversial figure to emerge in the 1960s was John Snow, who throughout his career has had the knack of being involved in incidents. This is chiefly because he has been

Above M. J. K. Smith, a master
of on-side placement, who
devoured off-spinners and was
one of the game's most prolific
run-getters, puts one away through
the leg field for Warwickshire
against the MCC. Mike was a
good captain of both his county
and his country, and in addition
there can have been few more
popular leaders

Right Ray Illingworth tossing up
with Gary Sobers at the start of
the second Test against the West
Indies at Lord's in 1969. This was
Ray's second game as captain of
England and he was to establish
himself both as a player and as a
leader. His century in the first
innings saved his side and he also
captured 3 wickets. This game was
a Yorkshire triumph, as two
other Yorkshiremen, John
Hampshire, on his debut in
international cricket, and Geoff
Boycott also hit centuries

One of the greatest of all cricket photographs: J. Inverarity l.b.w. to Underwood, giving England the victory in the final Test at the Oval in 1968, just as time was running out. A remarkable feature of this picture is that every member of the fielding team is in view. A very heavy shower had threatened to put an end to the proceedings, and without the assistance of hundreds of spectators, who helped to remove the water from the pitch and square, the game would never have been completed

perpetually at war with authority, a natural rebel, frequently without a cause but always willing to find one. He was never easy for a captain to handle, but at his best and when he was really interested in the proceedings, which was by no means always, he was an outstanding fast bowler with a fine action and lovely easy approach, who could make the ball rear unpleasantly from just short of a length. Essentially a player who thrived on the big occasion and the large crowd, he would probably have taken many more wickets for Sussex, if his county had been pushing for honours. As it was, his finest performances were usually reserved for Tests.

The other genuine international class bowler to come forward in this period was entirely dissimilar to Snow in both temperament and technique, Derek Underwood. Derek started life as a medium-paced left-arm seamer from over the wicket, who cut the ball a little. From the moment he entered on his First Class career, as a teenager, he picked up wickets and was difficult to score against because his style was unusual and his accuracy and control exceptional.

These virtues remained when he became an orthodox left-arm spinner of just under medium pace. His basic action makes the ball dip in late to the right-hand batsman and means that he is very hard to cut, except for left-handers, against whom he has never been quite so effective. Pleasant, naturally rather shy, unselfish and always keen to improve, Derek was the type every captain wants in his side. He caused no trouble and could always be relied upon to give his best. His best was to become a very good best, as he eventually developed into a great international bowler, a match-winner on a pitch giving him any assistance and the ideal person to act as an effective brake on plumb pitches. His pace through the air combined with his absolute mastery of line and length have meant that batsmen find him very hard to collar, and of course he proved a natural for limited overs cricket.

In his early days, critics would say that he would be a more successful operator on good wickets if he cut down his pace and gave the ball more air and time to turn. In theory this was excellent advice, but it did not work in practice, as I discovered when Derek was in a side I captained for the Cricketers' Club on a somewhat improbable tour to Cyprus.

The matches were played on the mat and I suggested to Derek that if he tried throwing the ball a shade higher, it should break more. Derek has always been keen to improve, but the experiment did not work, because he derived his spin more from his action and wrist and less from his fingers than most bowlers of his type. His method is really a cross between those of a spinner and a cutter.

Much of the county cricket was mundane and undistinguished. This was not surprising, because there was a shortage of outstanding players, as was evident in the English teams of this era, while the massive influx of overseas cricketers, which was to raise the overall domestic standards, was only just starting.

The outstanding county of the period was Yorkshire, who carried off the Championship in 1960, 1962, 1963, 1966, 1967 and 1968. There was nothing new about the Tykes being so successful, as they had frequently dominated the competition in the past. The surprising feature was that it was achieved by Yorkshire teams which contained players who would never have made any of their vintage sides. In the same way, some good Yorkshire players of the period, like Ken Taylor, Don Wilson and Phil Sharpe, were capped for England, although short of the class normally associated with true internationals.

Why did the White Rose manage to do so well? The main reason was that though they were not a great county XI, they were not only stronger than most of the opposing teams, but they also had a tradition of success behind them and the confidence, plus a belief in themselves, which went with it.

In addition, they possessed four very talented players: Fred Trueman; the new run-machine, Geoff Boycott; the all-round skill of Ray Illingworth, and that big enigma, Brian Close.

Brian had the basic talent to have become a great international, but for one reason and another has never established himself in Test cricket. However, when he was appointed captain of Yorkshire in 1963 he showed a new skill. His leadership was inspiring, both by personal example and in the tactical sense. He

was willing to stand in the suicidal position and to make runs when the going was at its most difficult, so that he welded the Yorkshire team into a compact fighting unit. In addition to his batting, fielding and captaincy, he also had the happy knack of picking up valuable wickets, not infrequently with very improbable balls. Ever blunt, uncompromising and ruthless in battle, a row over the delaying tactics he used in a match against Warwickshire ended what could have been a long and successful spell as captain of England, while Yorkshire eventually sacked him after a disappointing season because typically, though undiplomatically, he had expressed his disenchantment with Sunday cricket. The manner in which this was handled showed cricket administration in its worse light. He then joined Somerset and did much to assist them both as a player, and later as skipper.

The most romantic moment of the decade was when Hampshire won their first ever Championship in 1961 under Colin Ingleby-Mackenzie, with a mixture of luck and audacity, the batting of Roy Marshall, and outstanding seam bowling from Derek Shackleton, about whom it was said that they wound him up in May and he continued to send down over after immaculate over until the end of the season.

The best team in the middle period was Worcestershire, who won their first title in 1964, although they had only lost it by a whisker in 1962. In 1965, with the arrival of Basil d'Oliveira from South Africa, who went on to become an outstanding batsman for England as well as being a more than useful fourth seamer, they were even more impressive. They celebrated their centenary in the grand manner by winning ten out of their last eleven matches.

Their strength lay in well above average batting, two fine opening and contrasting bowlers, and adequate spin support, which was quietly and efficiently directed by Don Kenyon.

Tom Graveney, who had become more disciplined and run-hungry since his departure from Gloucestershire, was the main batsman, but he received splendid support from d'Oliveira, Horton, Headley, Dick Richardson and Kenyon himself. John Flavell, orig-

The perfect follow-through by John Snow, the Sussex and England fast bowler: his right arm chases his left across his body until stopped by his left thigh, while his left arm finishes almost as straight and as high as it was before he delivered the ball

inally a fast tear-away, had cut down his run, bowled close to the stumps and moved the ball sharply away in the air, with the nip-backer for variation. He became a very fine opening bowler who was well complemented by Len Coldwell, a natural in-swinger with a high action. In addition there was seam from d'Oliveira and Carter, and spin from Gifford, Horton and Slade.

The last Champions of the decade were something of a surprise, because even the keenest Welshmen did not expect it, and their very able captain, Tony Lewis, would have cheerfully settled for a place in the first six at the start of what proved to be a very memorable season for Glamorgan cricket.

Their previous Championship success had owed much to close catching, and fielding again played a vital part, but on this occasion their batting and, in particular, the speed with which they acquired their runs was the deciding factor. It not only enabled them to pick up a valuable number of bonus points, but also gave a slightly limited attack sufficient time to bowl out the opposition. The main run-getters were Alan Jones, a left-hand opener, who during a long career has had every reason to consider himself unlucky never to have been given an overseas tour, the brilliant Majid Khan and Tony Lewis. The main wicket-takers were three typical county seamers, Nash, Cordle and Williams, and that ageless purveyor of quick off-spin, Don Shepherd, who had started his career as an opening pace bowler.

THE SUNNY SEVENTIES

David Steele playing a push drive off his legs against the West Indies in the final Test in 1976. A sound, experienced front foot player, with plenty of courage and determination, David was originally brought into the England side the previous summer against the Australians. He immediately provided the team, still shell-shocked from their experiences in Australia, with the backbone required, which makes one wonder why the Selectors ignored him for so long. For several seasons he had scored with consistency for Northants and they may also have discarded David rather too quickly, because he certainly withstood fast bowling far better than most of his contemporaries

In 1968 when John Player first talked with the Test and County Cricket Board about sponsoring an entirely new competition, the Sunday League, which finally began in 1969, the game's finances in England were in a horrid state with the clubs sinking deeper and deeper into the red.

The obvious solution was increased sponsorship, but cricket's administrators, despite the success of the Gillette Cup, have never been noted for their forward thinking, and it took them a long time to realize the fact. In this connection it should be noted that it was not until 1977 that the County Championship was sponsored by Schweppes, and it was only after the threat posed by Kerry Packer in the same year that the Cornhill Insurance Company decided to sponsor the Tests, though there had been a substantial offer many years earlier.

Without the enormous increase of financial investment, which later included the Benson & Hedges and the Prudential Insurance Company Competitions, the Sunny Seventies would never have occurred, because membership—the life blood of every county—gate and television receipts on their own would never have been sufficient to maintain professional cricket on its present scale in times of galloping inflation and ever increasing costs.

Although it could well be that four competitions is one too many for what in effect are seventeen competitors, it has certainly increased the interest in cricket. Success usually leads to bigger gates and with four honours available each year the chances for every team to do well in one of them are far higher, which has appealed to the supporters.

Although there was more money available at the start of the 1970s, the standard of English cricket as distinct from domestic cricket was at a low ebb.

The two main causes were the big influx of overseas players and the reduction in staffs in the previous decade. The result could be seen in the small number of English cricketers of international class.

There had always been a number of players from abroad in the counties, like Jack Walsh and Vic Jackson for Leicestershire. Bruce Dooland, possibly the most successful of all, for Nottinghamshire, Roy Marshall for Hampshire, Bill Alley for Somerset, George Tribe for Northamptonshire, and Basil d'Oliveira for Worcestershire, but in the 1960s and 1970s there was a real invasion, not just of promising youngsters like Keith Boyce and John Shepherd, who became West Indian Test players after they had served their apprenticeship with Essex and Kent respectively, but also established stars, of whom Gary Sobers was the greatest.

Gary joined Nottinghamshire in 1968, but for varying reasons, including injury and absence on international duty, was never as successful as he had been with South Australia earlier in his career.

At the time he was the highest paid cricketer in the country, but his presence in the side never drew the crowds that had been expected, though it probably would have been a different story if his adopted club had won some tangible honour while he was there. The influx of overseas stars, who were able to play immediately without residential qualifications, inevitably raised the standard of county cricket, but at the cost of reducing the number of home-grown players coming into the game.

Although this was obvious, once again the cricket administrators took too long to realize the fact and did not tighten up on the registration rules until the mid-1970s. By this time the situation had reached the ridiculous state where it was possible to watch a county game in which over a third of the contestants had learned their cricket abroad.

It is impossible to judge to what extent the presence of mercenaries added to gate receipts. Unless success followed in the form of a title, it probably had no great effect. However, without them the chances of winning one of the four titles was small so that more and more counties tried to buy success. Yorkshire remained true to their code and suffered in terms of results, while the stars of the other clubs tended to cancel each other out.

The start to the era was anything but sunny, because the South African tour of England in 1970, by what promised to be their strongest and most exciting team, was eventually cancelled for reasons which had nothing to do with the game. The vast majority of cricket

Left In the early stages, most coaches will tell a boy to keep out the good ball and hit the bad. This is sensible advice, because there are normally quite enough of the latter. Batting becomes more difficult when the bowlers provide too few bad balls, and it becomes necessary to score off good length deliveries. This point was perfectly illustrated when Essex included a free-scoring club batsman in their side on a 'green wicket' at Derby, with Jackson and Gladwin doing the damage. He was fortunate enough to exist for more than an hour, and just managed to reach double figures, with the aid of a couple of snicks through the slips. He returned to the pavilion complaining bitterly that he had not received one ball to hit. Although it is possible to score runs in First Class cricket by relying on straight bat shots off the front foot, cross bat strokes and the nudge and deflection, the sure sign of the class performer is the ability to drive off the back foot to the boundary, a delivery which is only just short of a length. Here, that master of batsmanship Colin Cowdrey plays just such a stroke, scoring with a drive along the ground off his back foot

An unusual view of the Worcestershire CC grounds, taken from the cathedral. In addition to being one of the most beautiful grounds in the country, it is also one of the best on which to play cricket, thanks to the hard work of a succession of good groundsmen. In a fine summer the pitch is fast enough to give encouragement both to the strokemaker and to the bowler— an ideal state of affairs. The nets are always well above average standard, and if a team cannot field well on that outfield it never will

supporters wanted the Springboks to come, but there were other sections in the country who not only disapproved of the visit, but were also prepared to dig up pitches, interrupt the play and demonstrate in order to emphasize their dislike of South African internal policies.

Cricket, which ironically has shown greater tolerance than most sports, and about which it has been said that the French Revolution could have been avoided if the French nobles had played cricket with the peasants, suddenly found itself sucked into a bitter conflict. The issues, moral, political, ideological and racial were inflammatory in the extreme. These ingredients were exploited to the full by individuals and groups to suit their own ends and aspirations.

In an era when sectional demonstrations, both peaceful and violent, and legalized blackmail have become an accepted, if unacceptable part of life, cricket, which by its very nature is especially vulnerable, never had a chance, though the administrators fought a long hard battle for the fundamental right to ask any team they wanted to visit England.

The eventual outcome, after considerable pressure, innumerable meetings and finally an official request from the Labour Government was that the Test and County Cricket Board reluctantly called off the tour.

In a lengthy debate in the House of Commons, Denis Howell, the Minister for Sport and Chairman of the Sports Council, had said that the South African visit raised four emotive points. First, there was the effect on racial harmony in the country. Second, there was the question of law and order: the recent South African Rugby tour had led to clashes between its supporters and demonstrators, with the police inevitably in the middle and on the receiving end. Third, there was its effect on the Commonwealth Games, which brought the slightly cynical query in some quarters— what Commonwealth? Finally, there was the long-term interest of all sports.

Mr Howell 'strongly urged' the Cricket Council to withdraw its invitation to South Africa, because of the harm it would do to sport, especially multi-racial sport. Others argued with equal fervour that cricket lovers had the right to watch the South Africans in their own country and in peace. All in all it was a sorry start to the modern era.

With the South African Tour cancelled the TCCB decided to arrange five unofficial Tests, for which full England caps were awarded, against a Rest-of-the-World team under Gary Sobers. The series was sponsored by Guinness for £20,000 of which £13,000 went to the players and £7,000 to the counties.

The Rest-of-the-World XI was powerful, far stronger than most touring teams, and not surprisingly defeated England by 4 matches to 1. It included five South Africans, Barlow, Richards, Procter and the two Pollock brothers, Graeme and Peter; five West Indians, Sobers, Lloyd, Kanhai, Gibbs and Murray; two Pakistanis, Intikhab and Mushtaq; McKenzie from Australia, and Engineer from India, while there were other outstanding players from overseas available.

Although it would have been possible to pick an even better Rest-of-the-World team, there was no doubt as to the ability and the attractiveness of this group, all of whom, apart from three of the South Africans, were already resident in England. They played some marvellous cricket, but in the main the matches were poorly attended which showed that the cricket public are more interested in genuine confrontations between nations than England taking on a group of stars, however brightly they twinkle, and although in this case they included the rare treat of Sobers and Pollock in a long partnership.

From England's angle the most satisfactory feature of the series was that Ray Illingworth confirmed his ability as an international player and as a very astute captain, a post which he had gained by fate in the previous summer.

When Ray joined Leicestershire because his native Yorkshire would not grant him the length of contract he desired, nobody thought that this move would spark off a triumphant return to international cricket. Colin Cowdrey, who had been leading England spasmodically over the years, would have been in charge against the West Indies and New Zealand in 1969, but then he was injured and the Selectors, who have always tended to look to county captains, turned to Ray.

Although he had had only a handful of

Above Mike Denness is a classical batsman with a pleasing upright stance. He has always been an especially good player of spin, because he is not afraid to use his feet and drives very sweetly with the full swing of the bat. Here he is playing a drive during his fine 118 against India in the Lord's Test in 1974

Left One of the things that makes Ray Illingworth such a splendid off-spinner is that he bowls so close to the stumps from over the wicket. His left foot in this photograph is in front of the stumps, which means that he is able to drift the ball away from the bat This is a deadly delivery, as the batsman is looking for the break-back and frequently provides a catch for slip or keeper

Right As is so often the case with very tall men, Tony Greig is a good and powerful driver off his front foot, but inevitably suspect against a yorker in the early stages of an innings. Unlike most of the English team, he found that he could sometimes drive the Australian pace bowlers. In the second innings of the Sydney Test of 1975, where he led a brave but unsuccessful counter-attack, his fifty was the highest score

Overleaf The fate of so many England batsmen fishing outside the off stump—caught Marsh, bowled Lillee. On this occasion the victim is Alan Knott at Old Trafford in 1972. The jubilation of the Australian fieldsmen is easy to understand and to justify, because over the years Alan has often engineered a recovery just when the Australians felt that they were ready to move in for the kill

games as skipper of his new county, he possessed the invaluable background of years with Yorkshire and knew the game backwards. It turned out to be an inspired choice, but it almost certainly would never have occurred if he had not gone to Leicestershire. This emphasizes the point that the captaincy of a county should not be a necessary requirement for leading England, though it naturally has obvious advantages.

In the winter of 1970–1 Ray Illingworth was chosen to captain the MCC in Australia and New Zealand. In terms of results already achieved under his command, it was an entirely logical choice, but it was not helped by a vociferous campaign to give the job to Colin Cowdrey, who possessed greater personal charm and had established himself as a world class batsman.

After a long hesitation Colin, because he was such a nice person, decided to accept the appointment as vice-captain, though his life-long ambition had been to take the side to Australia. It turned out to be the wrong decision, because he never really came to terms with the position and lost confidence with the bat and in the slips, which reduced both the harmony and the effectiveness of the team.

To make matters worse the manager, David Clark, who had done such a fine job in India, where he had blended so easily with Mike Smith, was unable to establish any real rapport with Illingworth.

The situation which was obvious to anybody who knew the two, apart from the Selectors, was not helped when the manager, supported by two visiting MCC officials, Sir Cyril Hawker, President, and Gubby Allen, agreed to change the tour programme when the rain ruined the third Test and play another Test without consulting the captain or players. Not unnaturally, this was resented and provided yet another example of the lack of communication which has always existed between the establishment and the players.

These difficulties made Ray more determined and obdurate and he had the considerable satisfaction of returning with the Ashes by winning two Tests and drawing the rest.

The seventh Test saw the Australian Selec-

Left Derek Underwood, known as 'Deadly' because of his penetration on any pitch giving him just a modicum of assistance, bowls against Australia at the Oval in 1977. His pace is closer to medium than slow, and he is very difficult to collar, hence his effectiveness in limited overs matches, when he had so frequently provided the break that Kent required. He has been an invaluable member of the England team for many years, both as a shock and a stock bowler

Right The difficulties of a small man playing a short lifting ball: Alan Knott is airborne as he manages to keep down a delivery from Thomson

Right As well as ability, technique
and application, John Edrich
has plenty of physical courage;
which is why the England
Selectors turned to him again in
1976, when the West Indies fast
bowlers were consistently
knocking over wickets and
batsmen. Here he is playing a
typical Edrich square cut and
rolling his wrists to make sure
that the ball travels along the
ground. In 1977, John reached his
hundred hundreds, an achievement
which never received the
acclamation it deserved, but
which underlined the tremendous
service he has given to both
England and Surrey over the years

Far right Geoff Boycott
acknowledges the applause
of the crowd after reaching
a hundred hundreds in the
Headingley Test against the
Australians in 1977. This feat is
the hallmark of an outstanding
batsman. It shows the ability to
make runs consistently and in
profusion over the years. There
could be no more appropriate
setting for a Yorkshireman to
achieve it than a Leeds Test. This
was Geoff's year—not only did he
make a highly successful return to
international cricket, but he
became captain of England in
India after Mike Brearley broke
his arm. With the decrease in the
number of First Class matches in
England, it has become far more
difficult to score a hundred
hundreds, and Geoff could well
be the last Englishman to achieve
this for a very long time

tors panicked into picking one of the weakest teams in their history, while England were without their best batsman, Boycott, who had been injured earlier. The outcome was an absorbing game made so by the continually fluctuating fortunes, enlivened by a walk-off by the England XI after an incident between the every controversial Snow and a spectator, and eventually won by England by 62 runs.

The following summer saw Ray Illingworth lead his team to victory with a certain amount of luck over Pakistan and lose rather unluckily to India, and he was naturally still in charge when the Australians, under the dynamic if often undiplomatic Ian Chappell, arrived to see if they could regain the Ashes.

Although the Australians were unsuccessful in their quest as the series was drawn with two wins apiece and a draw, they did far better than had been expected and exposed several cracks in the England team. The batting looked insecure against the extra pace of Lillee and the prodigious late swing of Massie, and they had to do without the services of Boycott for the last three meetings. Although the batting line up had plenty of experience, it was on the elderly side, which showed in the field, and no England player hit a century in the series.

In contrast the Australians were young and improving. They had yet to reach their peak, while their opponents were already on the decline, though the bowling was still good in English conditions and Tony Greig again showed his potential as an all-rounder and the keenest of competitors.

With Ray Illingworth unavailable for the exhausting, and ultimately disappointing tour to India, Pakistan and Sri Lanka, Tony Lewis was entrusted with the captaincy and did a most praiseworthy job in difficult circumstances, both on and off the field. England took a surprise lead in the first Test, but eventually went down by two games to one in a five-match series. It would have been a different matter if they had included one class bat to supplement the efforts of Greig and Fletcher and to a lesser degree, Lewis and Denness. The last two had had good careers in county cricket over a considerable period and both were far happier against spin than extreme pace. In Pakistan all three Tests were

drawn on dead, unhelpful tracks and Amiss recovered the form which had deserted him in India.

Awaiting England at home in the summer of 1973 were an improved New Zealand, who came close to securing that elusive victory, and a West Indian team, who celebrated the end of a disastrous seven years in which they had failed to win a Test against England with two victories under Rohan Kanhai, and a particularly unpleasant drawn game at Edgbaston which merely served to tarnish the image of the game.

Their final victory at Lords, which became known as the 'Bomb Scare' Test, was by an innings and 226 runs and, apart from two fighting innings by Fletcher, showed up the many limitations of the English team, who were outbatted, outbowled and outfielded. Something had to be done and the axe fell on Ray Illingworth, who was not only the losing captain, but had had his least successful series as a player since he had taken over the captaincy.

With Tony Lewis a non-runner because of injury, the Selectors turned to Mike Denness to take the party to the West Indies, despite some obvious limitations in his batting and tactical knowledge. This decision did not appeal to Boycott, who as well as being in a different class to Denness as a batsman, was vastly more experienced in international cricket and was also captain of Yorkshire.

Although England appeared to be heading for certain defeat, they managed to tie the series, more through West Indian mistakes than their own ability. Greig, mainly in an off-cutting role, enjoyed easily his best all-round tour, Amiss scored prolifically and Boycott provided two big innings in the final Test, which England just managed to win by 26 runs. If that match had been lost the Selectors might well have turned to somebody else, but they decided instead to stick with Denness against India and Pakistan. The former provided little opposition and all three Test were drawn against Pakistan, so that the man in charge was given the daunting task of taking the MCC to Australia in the winter of 1976, where Ian Chappell and company were waiting for revenge and to regain the Ashes.

They achieved both without over much

trouble, because the combined pace and bounce proved too much for the English batsmen, who simply failed to score sufficient runs. By and large they lacked the skill needed to cope with a very fast lifting ball. To some extent they were bounced into submission. In a desperate attempt to shore up the fragile English batting, Colin Cowdrey was summoned out to join the main party and make a record sixth visit to Australia. Although he did not score many runs, his technique allowed him to appear more confident in coping with the speed bowling than most other members of that shell-shocked group.

The Australians scored more runs than their opponents, because the England bowling, though accurate, did not possess nearly as much venom, while the Aussies' close catching was far more deadly.

It was not a happy tour and the number of short-pitched balls by both teams was excessive, so that one was inclined to wonder whether the home umpires had bothered to read Law 46, as their interpretation of the word persistent was unusual.

However, it must be admitted that many of the nastiest of Thomson's deliveries were not bumpers, but simply rose sharply from just short of a length. The swearing and abuse by the players at each other and at the umpires could hardly have been in the best interests of the game; certainly manners and sportsmanship, once so closely associated with cricket, seemed to be very, very far away.

After a memorable World Cup of 1975, which was predictably won by the West Indies, the Australians undertook a shortened tour which included four Tests. The first they won by an innings, after Mike Denness had called correctly and invited them to take strike, possibly because he feared what the opposing attack would do under conditions which might have been expected to give them some encouragement. The gamble did not pay off, as the tourists scored a solid 359 and then proceeded to shoot out England for 101 and 173. Gooch, a newcomer to Test cricket, suffered the indignity of a pair and Fletcher, though never looking remotely confident, was the only person to reach 50. The English batting was a nightmare and the Selectors decided to appoint a new captain, Tony Greig,

one of only three current players who could at the time claim to be of true Test calibre, the others being Knott and Underwood. Amiss would have been put in the same category, but not against extreme pace, while Boycott was a voluntary Test exile, but scored over 2,000 runs in First Class cricket for Yorkshire.

Understandably, but rather unfairly, like so many England captains before him Mike Denness paid the penalty for one shattering defeat by losing the captaincy to Tony Greig, the new white hope. What was even more shattering was that within a year Mike had not only been sacked from the number one job in cricket, but had also lost the captaincy of Kent, which illustrates the uncertainty of the game and the game's administrators.

The England skippers of the 1970s make intriguing subjects for comparison. Ray Illingworth would probably have not played for England again if a stop-gap captain had not been required to take over when Cowdrey was injured, but he immediately made the most of the opportunity, both as a leader and as a player. His critics may say that he did not bowl enough himself and that he was a shade too cautious, but there can be no doubt that he was shrewd, dedicated and successful.

Tony Lewis led with distinction in India and Pakistan, but never established himself as an international class batsman.

Mike Denness was clearly a better captain in limited overs cricket. The tactical demands are more straightforward than in Test matches, where he sometimes displayed a certain naivety.

Tony Greig was a natural leader and a fine competitor, who was to lose his job when he became an agent for Kerry Packer. His captaincy, rather like his batting, was inclined to be erratic. A typical example occurred in the final Test against the West Indies at the Oval, when Tony took off Willis, who had just dismissed Greenidge for nought, after only two overs with the new ball on the first day, and brought on Underwood in his place. Presumably the thinking behind this move was that the pitch would take spin, but the 687 which the West Indians rattled up proved this to be incorrect. In India Tony did very well both on and off the field. His strong and pleasant personality and considerable pre-

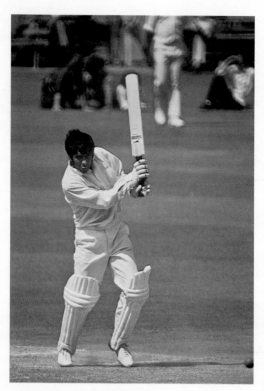

Above There have been few if any better batsmen at Cambridge since the war than Majid Khan. He was already an international class player, and at least two grades higher than any of his contemporaries. Subsequently, he has produced some very fine innings for Pakistan and Glamorgan, without ever shining quite as brightly as he had promised. Suffice it to say that if he had possessed the same total involvement in the job of run-getting as Geoff Boycott, he would unquestionably have made many more runs and broken more records than he has done, because he has exceptional ability. Possibly his refreshing outlook— that cricket is a game to be enjoyed rather than a business— has sometimes proved to be a handicap. This drive shows Majid in form, and there are not many better sights

Left Vivian Richards drives Underwood to the boundary at the Oval in 1976, a rare occurrence for the Kent bowler. This has been a good length delivery, but Vivian has hit through the line of the ball and kept it on the ground, although it was rising at the moment of impact. The picture shows completion of the powerful follow-through. A six by Richards tends to land high in the stand or out of the ground. He holds the record for the number of boundaries hit in a season of John Player League games

Right Bishen Bedi is a slow left-armer in the classic mould, who floats in from four paces and combines the subtleties of flight and spin, so that he is able to deceive the batsman both in the air and off the pitch. His gaily coloured patkas proclaim him to be a Sikh and make him instantly recognizable on pitches all over the world. Bishen is an artist who has to live in a world of cricket which is often rough and tough. His beautifully grooved action helps him to maintain immaculate length and direction for hour after hour, and assists him to disguise his pace. From time to time Bishen has been forced to bowl for too long: it is frequently forgotten that the fingers of a spinner eventually become tired

Far right Mike Procter has become a world class fast bowler with an open-chested hopping action, which might make some purists shudder. But though he hops immediately before his delivery stride, fails to utilize his left arm to the full, and never adopts the classical side-on position, his action obviously suits him, since his speed—he was a really fast bowler before his injury—comes primarily from his right arm and back. Small boys have often been discouraged from bowling in the Procter style, which has been termed 'off the wrong foot' (though this is strictly speaking incorrect, because everyone delivers the ball off his front leg). This illustrates the dangers of coaching bowlers. I once

manufactured a beautiful action
for a young boy with a bad one:
it looked very good, but he
stopped taking wickets. Because
of his open-chested action, Mike
is essentially an in-swing bowler,
who moves the ball a good
great deal in the air, enough to
get l.b.w. decisions from round
the wicket

sence proved an enormous asset. Very articulate, he conducted his press conferences in masterly fashion. Occasionally his choice of words was ill-advised, as instanced by his declared intention of making the West Indians 'grovel', but he looked as if he would be England's skipper for many years to come when the well kept secret that he had signed up for the Kerry Packer television series broke.

His activities as an undercover agent for the Packer organization were hardly suitable for the elected captain of England. As a signed up member of the Packer organization, moreover, he had committed himself to play in Australia, which automatically meant that he would be unavailable to take the MCC party to Pakistan and New Zealand and, in the following winter, to Australia. The inevitable outcome was that he lost his job and was replaced by Mike Brearley for the series against Australia in the summer of 1977.

A year earlier the betting would have been against Mike being picked for England, let alone as captain, but with so many of the counties being led by overseas cricketers, and others out of the reckoning because of age, the choice was severely limited. Middlesex had also won the Championship under his command and he had shown himself to be a sound tactician with a well above average intellect. He proceeded to lead England quietly and efficiently to a comfortable victory over what must surely have been just about the weakest Australian party to have ever visited this country. As a batsman he has his limitations, but he has always possessed plenty of courage when facing quick bowling and he successfully applied himself to the job without ever quite suggesting that he was a true international opener.

Tony Greig's short reign as captain of England began with three drawn games against the Australians, which represented a considerable improvement after the severe thrashing that had been administered at Edgbaston. In David Steele, the Selectors found a dependable barricade who stood up to the pace bowling with the straightest of bats and a pronounced forward movement.

However, hopes that these three draws under the new skipper marked a genuine revival were to be ruthlessly shattered by the West Indian touring party of 1976, who merely exposed the many weaknesses in England cricket. Rather strangely, the West Indians themselves had been more severely beaten by the Australians in Australia than the MCC party of Mike Denness, while their performance against India in the Caribbean had been undistinguished.

The tourists, who were led by Clive Lloyd, won the Test series 3–0, with 2 draws, took without difficulty the Prudential Trophy 3–0, and their complete playing record of played 26, won 18, lost 2 was most impressive. They delighted the big crowds who came to see them with the splendour of their batting, the speed of their bowling and their spectacular fielding.

The difference between the two teams was considerable. If one had had to choose the best XI from the players in the series, only three England players would have warranted serious consideration. Alan Knott was much the better wicketkeeper and also a far more effective batsman than Derek Murray. Derek Underwood was the only class spinner and Tony Greig might just have gained the all-rounder spot, though more on past potential than for what he actually achieved in the summer.

The West Indian batting was not only exceptionally strong, but was almost invariably entertaining, with Vivian Richards the brightest star in a galaxy. Their bowling was built round three genuine quick bowlers, Roberts, Holding and Daniel, with support from the lively Holder and the medium-paced King. They lacked a good spinner, but in the fine summer of 1976 and with England's vulnerability against pace, this did not prove to be the handicap it would have been in different circumstances and on different wickets.

At the start of the trip their manager, Clyde Walcott, had said that the time was fast approaching when the West Indies manager would fly to England to pick up his team there, and on this occasion a high percentage of the party were regular county cricketers. In these circumstances it was rather strange that they were not as popular as earlier sides, perhaps because they had become too professional and had lost some of their fun. It was also, of

Greig is yorked comprehensively by the pace of Holding in the Old Trafford Test against the West Indies in 1976

Above Craig Sarjeant is caught
behind the wicket off the bowling
of Old in the Jubilee Test at
Lord's in 1977, much to the
delight of the two slips, Greig
and Brearley

Left Brian Close: the man who
did not know the meaning of
fear. Brought back as a veteran
to combat the West Indian pace
quartet, he never flinched. On
this occasion, he has been struck
by a bouncer from Daniel. He did
not even bother to rub the spot:
bruises were just part of the
game to Brian. During his long
career he collected more than his
share, both when batting and
when fielding in a suicidal
position, literally inches from
the bat

course, true that it was far less of a novelty watching Lloyd, Roberts, Richards and Greenidge as they could be seen regularly in domestic cricket.

The following winter the MCC went to India and Sri Lanka and concluded their tour with the Centenary Test in Melbourne, which more than lived up to the hopes of the organizers, who not only laid on an enthralling match but assembled the greatest gathering of past and present players the world has ever seen.

Everything went according to plan; the cricket was exciting, the weather ideal and the crowds enormous. Even more strange, the game ended in a win by Australia by exactly the same margin as had occurred in Melbourne one hundred years before.

On the evidence of the match, it was obvious that England had started to improve and that Australia, who had lost many of their finest players, were on the decline, so that there was a strong chance that Tony Greig would regain the Ashes the following summer. But this failed to take into account the Packer Revolution which was to shake the entire cricketing world.

The most intriguing feature of domestic cricket in the 1970s has been the even standard of the First Class sides. This has meant that one outstanding player, usually from overseas, can when enjoying a good season take his team from near the bottom to the top of the table, or to success in one of the knockout competitions. In this connection, it has been significant that Yorkshire, who rely entirely on home-grown talent from the county, have never been at the top, or won any honour in this period.

On paper, the strongest team have been Kent, despite the handicap of frequent Test calls. On a good wicket their attack has been lacking in penetration, but their depth in batting has been exceptional, while Underwood has been deadly in certain conditions, and their seamers more than adequate on 'green tops'. They have always been up near the leaders and have carried off the title twice.

Middlesex won the Championship in 1976 and shared it in 1977, a fine all-round performance that owed much to a well balanced attack of both spin and seam with reasonable,

Mike Brearley suddenly found himself captain of England because Greig had acted as an under-cover agent for Packer. He led his team to victory against Australia in 1977 and batted with commendable determination, wearing defensive protectors inside his cap and over his ears as a counter to the bouncers. Here, he is forcing the ball through the off-side off his back foot

if not excessive batting support, and first class fielding.

Leicestershire, under Ray Illingworth, were successful in 1975. They owed much to his captaincy, an unusually varied bowling line up, the early thrust posed by McKenzie with the new ball, the positive batting of Davison and Tolchard complementing a sound first three, and a most resilient tail.

The surprising thing about Hampshire becoming Champions in 1973 was that they achieved this before the arrival of Roberts, who brought that added bite to an attack which was somewhat limited; and but for injuries, weather and the West Indian tour, which deprived them of the services of both Roberts and Greenidge, they must have reached the top again. In Richards and Greenidge they possessed what was probably the most devastating pair of opening batsmen in the world.

In the early 1970s Warwickshire were a very formidable team, which included no fewer than four West Indian Test cricketers— Kanhai, Kallicharran, Murray, and Gibbs, who had by now completely adapted himself to the requirements of bowling offbreaks on English pitches. To these were added the run-hungry Amiss, the still prolific M. J. K. Smith, the power of Jameson, and the added pace of Willis, whom they had just acquired from Surrey. They took the title comfortably in 1972 and were only beaten on a technicality by Surrey in the previous year.

Surrey had eventually won the Championship in 1971, when they secured their second bonus bowling point against Hampshire in September. This made them level on points with Warwickshire, but they had secured the greater number of wins. Although they were a good all-round side, there was still a lack of harmony in their dressing room, which to some extent is why they have failed to repeat the performance. Over the years they have never consistently played up to their considerable potential.

Like their near neighbours Warwickshire, Worcestershire contained rather too many players who were not eligible for England to be in the best interests of the game. When they snatched the title from desperately unlucky Hampshire who had to contend with five days'

continual rain in their last three matches and watched the title drift away from them by only two points, their leading run-scorer was the New Zealand Test player, Turner; the West Indian Holder was their most effective bowler; valuable runs were also forthcoming from Headley and Parker, of the West Indies and New Zealand respectively, while of course Basil d'Oliveira, who had a great season with bat and ball, had learned his cricket elsewhere.

Once considered the chopping block for more powerful opponents Northamptonshire, thanks very largely to imported players, firmly established themselves as one of the stronger teams, while the sides most regularly found near the bottom of the table were Nottinghamshire, Derbyshire, and a perpetually disappointing Sussex.

What must have made life all the more galling for Sussex was the way that Kent, who have such a similar background, were not only doing well but also constantly finding good young cricketers as a result of probably the most thorough coaching system in the land.

A lack of belief in themselves prevented Essex from winning a major honour, especially in limited overs cricket which has always eluded them, and the same might be said for Somerset, who have also brought on some good young players.

Lancashire, apart from a period under Bond in the one-day game, are a county who have consistently failed to fulfil their promise during the 1970s. They have had some fine players, but their results in Championship cricket show that a vital spark is missing. Glamorgan have never looked capable of repeating their totally unexpected triumph of 1969; their imports from abroad have, by and large, failed to live up to expectations, while their youngsters have tended to take longer to establish themselves than had been hoped.

LIMITED OVERS CRICKET

Top Leicestershire celebrate winning the John Player League in 1977, after they had beaten Glamorgan in the last game of the season at Grace Road

Bottom left Ray Illingworth holds aloft the Benson and Hedges Trophy, which Leicestershire carried off for the second time under his command when they beat Middlesex at Lord's in 1975

Bottom right Mike Denness and the rest of the Kent team with the Gillette Cup, which they had just won at Lord's by beating Lancashire. The Gillette Cup is the oldest and most important of the limited overs competitions. The final is always played on the first Saturday in September, and there has been a wonderful record of good weather for this major cricketing occasion, which always draws a large and enthusiastic capacity crowd. However, this 1974 final was unusual as heavy pre-match rain, combined with more showers on the morning of the match, prevented any cricket on the Saturday, and the contest was held on the Monday

Professional cricket has never been a financially rewarding game and the First Class counties have always had to struggle to survive. In the early days, apart from membership, which was and still is the lifeblood of any club, they received considerable assistance from wealthy patrons who have long since been taxed out of existence or are living abroad. The inclusion of numerous amateurs of independent means, another extinct species, also helped to reduce costs.

After the last war, the counties were able to use the proceeds obtained from football pools to help meet the ever-increasing expenditure, with Warwickshire the most successful exponents of this particular form of fund raising. Supporters' clubs and their attendant pools played an important part in keeping the clubs solvent, especially when the gates for First Class matches began to slump alarmingly.

The substantial decline in attendances for county games was due to a number of factors, many of which had nothing to do with the way the game was played. Families who would once have gone to a county cricket game were seeking other forms of amusement. The spin in the car, fishing, an upsurge in golf and squash, continental package holidays and television all took their toll. First Class cricket was not the only spectator entertainment to feel the pinch. Cinemas were closing in ever increasing numbers and although football still draws big crowds for certain key matches, the present position with the League Clubs approximately £13,000,000 in the red is very unhealthy, while crowds for Third and Fourth Division and senior amateur games have dropped far more than they have for cricket.

The fact that England is the only country in the world where cricket provides a livelihood for players, and not just for star performers, underlines its economic problems. It is also significant that overseas cricketers, unable to make a living in their own countries, have flocked in ever-increasing numbers to make money in our domestic cricket.

The financial weaknesses of the game, when it has to make a profit, are many. It takes up too much time—six hours per day for six days, often seven, in a week. It is over-dependent upon the weather. It is costly to stage, as (quite apart from the wages of the twenty-four players) two paid umpires, scorers, groundstaff, gatekeepers, scoreboard attendants, scorecard sellers, catering staff and administrative staff are all required, even when the total receipts for the day are below three figures.

The cricket follower, like his football and boxing counterpart, has become far more choosy. He can see the best performers in the world by simply switching on his television, and is therefore less keen to attend when the second best are in action.

In the 1940s and 1950s the crowds for county games, particularly those of special interest like the Roses Match or Middlesex *v.* Surrey, were sufficiently large, when backed up by Test match receipts and membership, to keep the clubs going, but from then on, despite some outstanding supporters' associations, the clubs began to sink further and further into the red. The worsening situation was not helped by an increase in seam bowling and a more defensive approach.

It could be said that membership of a county club, often a mere £3 per season, was too low as costs continued to increase, but it was also true that many of the members regarded their subscriptions almost as a donation because they seldom used the available facilities.

The MCC tried several ways of artificially livening up the game—shorter boundaries, new bonus points, the limitation of leg-side fielders and a first innings limited to a hundred overs—but still the crowds did not return, so something had to be done.

The answer eventually turned out to be limited overs cricket allied to sponsorship. The first experiment was with the Gillette Cup, which started in 1963. From its inception, this competition has not only proved to be a tremendous success both from the playing and from the financial angles, but is clearly the most satisfying of all the one-day competitions.

I had the pleasure of sitting on the small committee which drew up the original rules for this competition. It was unquestionably the best, and most incisive, of the cricket committees on which I have served. The greatest source of satisfaction was that all our recommendations were accepted by the counties, and there has been no need for any major changes. It is not often that one finds the right formula first time.

There were two points about which I felt very strongly at the time; in retrospect I was wrong about the first and right about the second. I did not approve of the artificial limitation of the number of overs allowed to the bowlers. I felt that if Fred Trueman had taken two wickets with successive balls, he should be allowed to carry on, and not have to come off because he had used up his allotted span. After all, there was no such limitation on the batsmen: they could bat for the entire innings, as was perfectly demonstrated by Richards and Greenidge for Hampshire against Nottinghamshire in the Gillette match in 1977. However, in retrospect I feel that being forced to use a minimum of five bowlers has added to, not detracted from, the Gillette Cup, and indeed it has become an accepted feature of all the major limited overs competitions.

The second point was what to do if bad weather did not permit the agreed number of overs to be bowled. Although, with three days available for every match, this was unlikely to occur, it was in my opinion vital to avoid a situation where the result of a game might be decided by the spin of a coin. As an insurance against this, it was agreed that in the unlikely event of no decision being reached, the two contestants would play a ten overs match, if necessary in conditions which would not normally be tolerated. This might not be pleasant, but it would be the same for both teams and was clearly preferable to tossing a coin. This avoided the charge that a county could reach the final simply through the ability of the captain to call correctly. Fortunately, the number of really foreshortened games has been negligible.

The original Gillette Committee appreciated that the new competition had three great advantages over other forms of cricket. First, it had the basic appeal of instant death. Second, it guaranteed a definite result, which automatically eliminated one of the game's less attractive features, the dull draw. Not, let it be added, that a draw is of necessity dull as it can, and often does, provide entertainment,

One of the outstanding features of limited overs cricket has been the brilliance of the fielding. Here, Viv Richards is running out Alan Turner in the Prudential World Cup final at Lord's with an electrifying piece of ground fielding

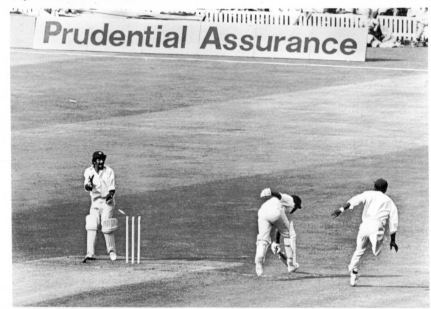

Ron Headley, Worcestershire, hooks the Northants fast bowler Dye for a big six in a Benson and Hedges match. Ron, the son of the great West Indian batsman George Headley, learned most of his cricket in England and became a fine county player. He was also capped for the West Indies

One of the many strokes used by Gordon Greenidge in his record breaking limited overs innings of 177 for Hampshire against Glamorgan in a Gillette Cup match at Southampton in 1975

but in a knock-out cup, when time would not allow replays, it had to be eradicated. Third, the spectator was, weather permitting, able to see the entire game within a day.

We all implicitly believed that not only would the new competition provide excitement, but that it would help the counties in their fight for survival. It would also give the Minor Counties a fresh incentive, even though they have in the main been chopping blocks for the First Class clubs.

Looking back to the early days, when we were uncertain as to how well this new form of the game would be received by the supporters, we even cut down on expenses by arranging for the home county to put up the visiting county privately.

The first ever Gillette game played by Essex was at Old Trafford. It was a long drive in those days without the motorways. We were met by Geoffrey Howard, the Secretary of Lancashire, and some of their side at the Altrincham police station shortly after midnight. From there we were ferried to various homes for the night. It may not have been the ideal preparation for a vital knock-out game but it saved money, which after all was the main object of the exercise at that time.

With the FA Cup Final as the model, the Gillette Committee naturally recommended that the Gillette Final should be staged at Lord's on the first Saturday in September. The success of the Lord's final in terms of both the cash taken and the interest aroused ensured the success of the competition. It is also true that the weather over the years has proved incredibly kind.

However, it is doubtful whether the counties would have taken the gamble of starting something entirely new without the guaranteed sponsorship of Gillette, who in turn were to be followed by many more sponsors, helping to save the First Class counties from extinction in their present form.

The game's administrators have always been inclined towards caution and conservatism, and it was Bagenal Harvey, a shrewd businessman, who first appreciated the possibilities of instant cricket, played on Sunday afternoons and televised. Bagenal was agent for many of the leading cricketers. His first client was Denis Compton, and he was subsequently to have most of the England team on his books because he was able to make money for them by exploiting their considerable value in the commercial world.

Bagenal founded the International Cavaliers, who were sponsored by Rothmans, and for four happy summers they played Sunday matches against county clubs, often in aid of the current beneficiary. The Cavaliers' team was filled with famous players from all over the world, like Gary Sobers, Clive Lloyd, Barry Richards, Graeme Pollock, Fred Trueman, Ted Dexter, Jim Laker, Bobby Simpson etc., and they drew large crowds. The BBC quickly realized that these games, with money at stake and tailor-made to fit the requirements of television, made excellent and comparatively cheap viewing.

After four years of fun which produced a profit for cricket, the players and Bagenal himself (though the amount was not nearly so large as was assumed), the MCC at last realized that this form of the game could be used to bolster the tottering finances of the county clubs. The outcome was that the MCC, after some rather unpleasant infighting, pinched both the idea and the television rights, and so the John Player League was born. Not surprisingly, a bitter and disillusioned Rothmans withdrew entirely from cricket sponsorship. Quite apart from the Sunday League, they had generously sponsored several tours which had benefited English cricket. The John Player League, because of its limited run-ups and short duration, is the least satisfactory, from a player's angle, of the one-day competitions, yet it has several attractive features: the matches take place on the day, Sunday, with the largest crowd potential, and the competition continues throughout the summer; on the main it provides excellent television, and as it is usually exciting it attracts many spectators who are unable to appreciate the subtler nuances of the First Class game.

The John Player league has done much to stabilize the finances of the counties, as a result of the sponsorship, the television rights and the gate receipts, but it could still be improved. One would like to see more occasions when the two opponents for the Sunday League game are the same as for the

Two moments from the first ever cricket World Cup, held in 1975. **Left** Clive Lloyd holds aloft the Prudential World Cup, which has just been presented to the captain of the West Indies by Prince Philip after a magnificent final
Right The final itself, between Australia and the West Indies: Kallicharran hooking Lillee. The contest proved a great success and really caught the imagination of the general public. It will certainly be held again

First Class match on the Saturday. This would automatically reduce travelling and expenses.

In 1972 came a third inter-county limited overs competition, the Benson & Hedges Cup. In terms of cricket it was not needed, but it has provided a welcome financial adjunct for both the players and the clubs. With its limitation of fifty-five overs, it is part league and part knock-out. The early rounds are fought among the First Class counties, plus two teams representing the Minor Counties and a combined Oxford and Cambridge XI added to balance the numbers taking part. The opening zonal matches, which are staged in the early part of the summer, attract only limited interest and support. It could be said that the competition does not really come alive until the knock-out stages. A serious weakness is that counties who have been eliminated find themselves without matches in the best part of the season, while there is something vaguely farcical about teams going for the quadruple.

If it was felt necessary to increase the amount of limited overs cricket, apart from financial considerations, a more logical solution would have been to extend the Sunday League to include the Saturday, although this would reduce the opportunities for the minority who prefer First Class cricket to see it at the weekend.

The success of one-day matches was so obvious that it was only a matter of time before it was introduced into international cricket. This occurred first during the Australian tour of 1972, when three one-day Internationals, sponsored by the Prudential Insurance Company, were played between England and Australia after the Test series. From the purely commercial angle, these games were satisfactory, as they were watched by 55,000 spectators and apart from the £30,000 paid for the sponsorship produced £46,000. However, the cricket was less convincing, almost as if the two opponents had agreed to split the prize money, and clearly the Prudential One-Day Internationals would have greater appeal if they took part earlier in a tour, before the Tests. This did occur in 1977, but even then some of the bite was missing, as the Australians used them primarily as preparation for the coming fight for the Ashes.

The Prudential Cup, which really caught the imagination of the cricketing public, took place in 1975. It was run on soccer World Cup lines and was eventually won by the West Indies, who beat the Australians at Lord's in an epic final. The sponsorship, which was in the region of £100,000, the large gate receipts and the wonderful weather throughout the competition made the venture viable, and everyone is looking forward to the next time a Cricket World Cup is staged in England.

The benefits that one-day limited overs cricket have brought have been considerable. It has increased the revenue and the interest in the game at a time when both were on the wane. It has improved the athleticism of the fielding and throwing, though not of the close catching, and it has placed an even greater value on batsmen who are able to hit the ball hard and on quick running between the wickets, but it also has its disadvantages. These all stem directly from one fundamental difference between this and First Class cricket. In limited overs cricket it is not necessary to bowl out the opposition, or rely on a declaration in order to win a match. Because the winning team simply has to score more runs in a certain number of overs, the draw has been eliminated.

This has automatically changed the thinking of bowlers. Their first consideration is to stop the batsmen scoring rather than to bowl them out, and at the same time their allies, the fieldsmen, are more concerned with preventing runs than anything else. Conversely, the batsman has to take more chances. In a five-day Test match a score of 100 for 0 in 60 overs represents the foundations on which to build a victory, but in the Gillette Cup this would be the recipe for disaster.

The one-day game has produced a race of medium to fast-medium seamers, who bowl a line and a length. They tend to attack the leg stump which restricts the scoring arc more than if they bowled at the off stump. They are difficult to score off, but many of them would bowl a batsman in, rather than bowl him out, if he could afford to take his time.

The success of the medium-paced 'dobbers' has been largely attained at the expense of the

A prize wicket: Hampshire's great South African, Barry Richards, is clean bowled by Leicestershire's fine Australian fast bowler, Graham McKenzie

slow bowlers, who are so much more interesting to watch in action. It is not that the slow bowler, providing he has mastered his difficult craft, cannot be successful in limited overs cricket, but he tends to abandon such vital arts as spin and flight, and to bowl flat. In a Test match the good slow bowler will invite a batsman to try to hit him in the hope that he will deceive him with the break, or in the flight, but in the one-day game a maiden represents a positive attainment.

In a different way, the fast bowlers have also been affected. Without the conclave of close fielders they are less likely to take wickets, but if they can put a brake on the scoring they have done their job. Their role in a Test is that of a shock bowler, but in limited overs matches they are frequently reduced to being stock bowlers.

One of the less acceptable sights in the one-day game is Roberts or Procter bowling to some indifferent tail-enders with nobody near the bat, 60 runs still required, and four overs remaining. They do not have to worry about bowling them out, as four maidens will be just as effective.

From the batting angle, the ideal position in one-day cricket is number one, because this provides the opportunity to have a reasonable look at the bowling and to some extent build an innings, whereas the role of someone in the middle order is often either to throw the bat or to improvise, neither easy for a youngster trying to establish himself in a county XI. It has certainly handicapped many promising English players, and is made worse by the fact that most of the counties naturally employ their star imports from overseas in the key batting spots.

However, although limited overs cricket is not invariably exciting and it is often easy to predict the result long before the end, it has provided much outstanding entertainment, which over the years has more than compensated for its deficiencies.

Some of the innings produced by Barry Richards have been as close to perfection as makes no difference. They have included such moments as when he has moved outside his leg stump and played a lofted off drive for six. Clive Lloyd has frequently taken an attack by the scruff of its neck, made defensive field placing appear superfluous, and won the game by brutal power of his stroke play. Keith Boyce with his bowling, brilliant fielding and uninhibited hitting epitomized the joy it so often provides.

However, it has by no means only been the great strokemakers who have scored the runs. Brian Luckhurst showed for Kent just how to pace an innings and achieve the right result.

Close finishes have always been one of the best features of limited overs cricket, and by the very nature of things these are more prevalent here than in any other form of the game, while the spectator has the satisfaction of knowing that, weather permitting, he will have the opportunity of witnessing an entire game with a definite conclusion, which does much to compensate for the monotony of an almost non-stop diet of seam bowlers, the keeper standing back, and the stereotyped defensive fields.

Although there is an increasing amount of sponsored one-day cricket in other parts of the world, it has so far not proved as popular or as important as in England, because elsewhere the economics of supporting a professional as distinct from a partially professional sport do not apply.

HARD MEN IN BIG GREEN CAPS

Above Two Australian 'Demons': Spofforth (top) and Lillee (above). Both had the same determined chin, strong aggressive features, fierce dislike of opposing batsmen, mastery of their chosen profession (neither relied on pace alone), determination and fine physique

Left Doug Walters is a much feared and respected strokemaker, except in England, where he has failed to adapt his technique sufficiently to reach his potential. He is also a useful medium-paced bowler and a first rate outfield. Here, he is playing a somewhat unorthodox instinctive hook against England on a lively Perth wicket, during the Second Test in 1974

Sweeping generalizations, like 'Italians invariably make good lovers', or 'the Irish are stupid', or 'the Scots are mean', are usually wide of the mark. This is certainly true of the fallacy that all Australians are cricket enthusiasts, because there are very many, and not only the 'new' Australians from Europe, who are not interested.

On the other hand, the Australians must have a higher proportion of first class sportsmen than any other nation in the world, which is why over the years their cricketers have been so successful. The same applies to all their sportsmen and sportswomen in a very wide range of activities, including lawn tennis, golf, athletics, rugby, swimming, speedway, cycling and squash; while it should not be forgotten that they once reached the last sixteen of the World Soccer Cup.

There are two main reasons. First, they have the finest of all coaches—climate and space. Second, the Australian is a natural, aggressive competitor with a built-in hatred of losing. It is interesting to note that they have achieved their remarkable successes in the sporting world without the intense drilling, screening and coaching at public expense as happens to the young of East Germany, for example.

Attendances at cricket matches, outside the Anglo-Australian and, latterly, the West Indian Tests, are not large. Their inter-state games do not draw big crowds, which is why the game has never been considered a profession out there, though in recent times some of their best players have earned considerably more than their professional counterparts in England.

Most Australian cricketers have a full-time job and spend their holidays playing for their state. If they should be chosen for the International XI, many firms are prepared to give them time off. The financial rewards are also becoming increasingly attractive.

With usually small crowds, why are many Australian Test match grounds larger than those in England? The reason, quite simply, is that all Australian towns, let alone the big cities, have a playing oval. On this they play cricket in the summer and football in the winter, comprising a certain amount of Rugby Union and Rugby League, an increasing

amount of soccer and their own speciality, Australian rules football, a high-scoring, spectacular game, especially popular in Victoria, which, with eighteen-a-side, takes up the whole of a full-size cricket ground. For the grand final at the Melbourne Oval, where the Olympic Games were staged, as well as Test and state cricket matches, there is usually a crowd of 100,000.

This multiplicity of purpose on the ovals is made possible by the fact that one is able to play right across the square in the winter and still produce a beautiful batting pitch in the summer, something which, unfortunately, is not possible in England where cricket grounds, apart from occasional games of hockey on the outfield, remain bare and empty most of the year. Had it been feasible in our climate to stage football matches on English Test grounds throughout the winter, they would assuredly have been developed into vast stadiums long since.

A high percentage of those who come to watch a Test will not see any other First Class cricket that season, they are inclined to be less knowledgeable, and certainly noisier, than English Test crowds, although these have become less sedate in recent years due to the exciting influence of limited overs games and the enthusiasm of the volatile West Indian immigrant population.

The Australian spectator has always liked to barrack, and the barracking becomes increasingly more pronounced later in the day, as the considerable quantity of 'grog' he has brought with him in his icebox is drained away. The shouting is in the main humorous and somewhat monotonous, with an occasional shaft of wit to punctuate cries of 'Have a go, yer mug!', or 'Get a bag, yer mug!', when someone drops a catch.

One of my favourites occurred at Adelaide. As I made my way down to fine leg after each unsuccessful eight-ball over with the temperature in the high nineties, I was greeted with 'You'll never get 'em out, Bailey!', which was sadly all too true. After my seventh over, one lone but penetrating voice came out with: 'Bailey, your bowling is just like a lavatory seat—straight up and down.' I have always treasured this, along with a suggestion from a frustrated Brisbanite, as I raced into the high 'teens after some two or three hours of crease occupation, that I should 'Climb out of that iron lung!'. A less welcome form of barracking is provided by the banging together of countless numbers of empty beer cans, while a chant of 'Kill!' as Lillee runs in to bowl could be said to be more apposite to a gladiatorial meeting in ancient Rome than an Australian cricket ground.

To many Australians the Tests represent not just a cricket match, but something of an occasion, a break from the beach and the delights of surfing and horse racing.

The Sheffield Shield is the principle domestic competition, fought between five states—Victoria, New South Wales, South Australia, Queensland and Western Australia. To this established quintet is now added Tasmania, who for the time being will meet the other states only once a season, instead of on the home-and-away basis which applies to the rest.

Melbourne and Sydney are the largest cities in Australia, and there has always been great rivalry between them. Thus, in order not to cause offence, the MCC play two Tests in Melbourne on one tour and two in Sydney on the next, even though the capacity of the former is much greater.

The home ground of the Victorian Cricket Association in Melbourne is the biggest in the country, with excellent facilities, but it is a stadium first and a cricket ground second. Functional and rather ugly, with an enormous playing area not unreminiscent of an outsize bull ring, it could be said that the outfield is too large, and certainly sixes are something of a rarity. The massive stands are inclined to make the play look rather remote and impersonal. Unless there is a big crowd, which engenders its own excitement, the ground is rather lacking in atmosphere. It is the cricket equivalent of Wembley stadium, although the surroundings are infinitely superior, with a number of good hotels within walking distance.

It has often been said about New South Wales, rather in the same way as it was true of Yorkshire and England, that a powerful New South Wales team means a good national XI. Their supporters, though they will strenuously deny it, were for many years inclined to regard the Sheffield Shield as their own property. They certainly won it enough times.

The Western Australia CA is, apart from just elected Tasmania, the baby of the cricketing states. Their development was originally held back by their isolation, which is best illustrated by the probably apocryphal tale of the WA batsman who was picked to play for an Australian XI in Brisbane. He had to be granted a long leave of absence from his firm, for the involved train journey, including three days and nights across the Malibu plain, the game itself, and a little pre-match practice took up the best part of a month. As the unfortunate managed to 'bag a pair', some doubted whether his journey was really necessary.

In the early days, Western Australia played the opposing states only once a season, and there is no doubt the advent of easy air travel has played a very big part in their advance from the weakest side in the Sheffield Shield to the strongest. For the past decade they have been the leading state, which stems directly from having the most thorough and productive coaching system in the whole of the country. Their administrators still possess some of the pioneering enthusiasm which was needed in the immediate post-war years, when their captain, Keith Carmody, achieved so much with strictly limited material. They have remained forward-thinking and have avoided the complacency which can still at times be found in New South Wales.

The Perth pitch has retained its reputation for being the fastest, and the stadium has more than justified its inclusion as a regular Test match venue.

The Adelaide Oval, which is the home of the South Australia CA, is easily the most attractive of the major grounds, because like the city it has retained the grace and charm of an earlier age. The pitch has proved a paradise for batsmen and there have been numerous occasions when it has typified that cricketing contradiction, a wicket that is too good. It has reduced great bowlers to near impotence with its utter docility, and the short boundaries on either side of the pitch, as distinct from the very long straight ones, make the cut and the hook especially rewarding strokes.

Brisbane is a friendly, essentially Australian city, less Americanized than Sydney, less sophisticated than Melbourne, less cultured than Adelaide and less ambitious than Perth, but a very good place to live. The Queensland CA's ground, the Gabba, takes after the city. Where else in the world would you find the leading citizen taking over the preparation of a Test match wicket.

It was also the last Australian ground to provide a 'sticky' for a Test against England. Since that tour in 1950–1, all Australian wickets have been covered, unlike the situation in England where they remain open to the weather during the hours of play. The reason is that while it is possible to make runs on English pitches after heavy rain, even if hot sunshine and a high class spinner make life difficult, heavy rain on an Australian wicket produces nearly unplayable conditions because the quicker bowlers are able to make the ball rear head-high off a full length.

The overall standard of umpiring in Australia is not, understandably, as high as in England, because they do not have the same amount of both playing and practical experience for what is an extremely difficult job. However, from personal experience both as a player and a spectator, I would rate Australian Test umpires very highly, and indeed they are often better than their English counterparts.

To walk, or not to walk, is a vexed question. If *every* batsman invariably walked when he gave a catch to a fielder, and every fieldsman were honest, then 'walking' would certainly help the umpire and probably be in the best interests of the game. Most players will not wait for the umpire's decision in county cricket, and some acquire a reputation for being 'good walkers'. They are off to the pavilion before the umpire has had time to raise a finger, until they meet that really difficult one, when a ball has flicked a glove in a vital situation, and they stay.

The Australian inclination is to leave everything to the umpire. If the batsman is given not out, even though he has hit the ball, there will be times when this will work the other way round. Providing both teams adopt that attitude, it should mean that there is no bitterness. After all, bowlers and fielders frequently appeal when they know the batsman is not out, and it is a common sight for most of an Australian side, wherever stationed, to leap and call in unison for an l.b.w., let alone a catch behind the stumps.

Not unnaturally, this has been copied by their opponenents and has eventually developed into what is known in Australia as 'sledging'. This works on the theory that if the fielding side shout often enough and hard enough there is a good chance the unfortunate umpire will make a mistake. A less attractive feature of 'sledging' is that it now embraces verbal abuse of the opposition and the officials.

Although Australian cricket is temporarily at a low ebb, for much of the time since the war they have been the unofficial world champions, apart from a period in the 1950s, when England and later the West Indies took over. At the time when South Africa were cast into the wilderness, they were also challenging strongly for the title.

Australia's success has stemmed not only from an abundance of high quality players, but also from a fierce competitive streak and a positive hatred of losing, which has enabled them more than once to beat potentially superior opposition, especially from the West Indies. An Australian team is never more dangerous than when it appears to be well beaten. This is when their batsmen have the knack of launching a positive counterattack, or their bowlers will suddenly produce that little extra, for until their disastrous tour of England in 1977 there had always been a hard core of top quality players who were also first class competitors, and some excellent captains with material to match.

They began the post-war era under the leadership of Sir Donald Bradman, still a superb batsman; in fact so good that he was to some extent rather a liability to succeeding generations of Australian players when labelled with the impossible tag of 'another Bradman'. Three of his team who had pre-war experiences were Lindsay Hassett, Don Tallon and Sidney Barnes.

Hassett was one of the most complete of all their batsmen. His near perfect technique meant he could bat very well in all conditions and against all types of bowling. He was neat, dapper, quick on his feet, with a delicious impish sense of humour that later made him a very popular skipper. Tallon was not only brilliant in a long line of outstanding wicket-keepers, but was also elegant and brought grace as well as agility to his craft.

Barnes was a great batsman, who would have made even more runs had he not, either consciously or subconsciously, rather resented the overpowering presence of the 'Master', and had he been less interested in commercial opportunities, as well as fighting a continual battle with a distinctly conservative establishment. How he would have loved the rich contracts that increased sponsorship has brought to the game in the 1970s! A natural loner with a shrewd business brain, who could be and often was extremely difficult, I liked him and can think of few, if any batsmen, apart from the Don, I disliked bowling against more.

The first requisite of any captain wanting to win an international series is a great pair of fast bowlers. These are able to open up the opposition with the new ball, undermine the confidence of the timid, and blast out the tail. Australia have produced two pairs in the post-war period; Ray Lindwall and Keith Miller, and Denis Lillee and Jeff Thomson, all very different in style, but all genuinely fast.

Lindwall had a beautiful rhythmic approach to the wicket, a powerful body action, in which he dragged his right foot, and a not very high right arm, which meant he had to drop his bouncer a shade shorter than Miller, who released the ball from a greater height. Ray was essentially a swing bowler, moving the ball more in the air than any other of the really quick post-war bowlers, as distinct from the fast-mediums.

His natural delivery was the away swinger, which he could start on or outside the leg stump. A perfect example of this occurred in an MCC game at Lord's when Reg Simpson was attempting to play a ball of full length from outside his leg stump to the on-side only to be caught in the gully off the inside edge. Later, Lindwall introduced the in-swinger into his considerable repertoire, which included a superb yorker and a well-disguised slower ball. He was the complete fast bowler with exceptional control and enormous stam-

ina.

Miller was entirely unpredictable, a bowler of moods, who could drop a ball on his short run up, pick it up and carry on without any noticeable difference in pace. Although naturally formidable with the new ball, his greatest asset was probably the knack he had, midway through a hot afternoon on a perfect pitch with no shine remaining, of suddenly producing a near unplayable delivery, pitching leg and hitting the top of the middle-and-off.

Although Ray was a dangerous lower middle order batsman with a love for the cut, Keith was top class, and this, when taken in conjunction with his fielding, made him one of the greatest, possibly the greatest, of all Australian all-rounders. An exciting stroke-maker with a high backlift, he drove with immense power, especially off his front foot. With a less volatile temperament, he would certainly have made even more runs, but then he would have lost some of that charisma which made him so attractive to watch.

Comparing Lindwall with Lillee is rather like comparing Joe Louis with Rocky Marciano, both unquestionably world class boxers, but from different eras. In the matter of sheer pace there could have been little between the Lindwall of the 1940s and Lillee of the early 1970s. They were both unpleasantly fast.

Lillee does not move the ball as much in the air, but he does more off the seam and his bounce is steeper. Although his action is excellent, it puts far more strain on his back, so that his life span as a fast bowler must inevitably be shorter. One advantage Lillee does enjoy is that Australian outfields and pitches are far grassier than they used to be, which means the shine lasts far longer and, in addition, the inital gloss appears to be impregnated more. After a full day's play in most Tests nowadays, the ball is still smooth, whereas it used to be rough and ragged, which is one reason for the increase in the number of successful pace and seam bowlers and a corresponding decrease in the number of effective spinners.

Like most of his kind, Lillee on the field is fiery and detests batsmen. He posses great determination, as he showed by continuing

Top A view from the famous Hill at Sydney during a Test between England and Australia. The Hill has always been the natural habitat of the Australian barracker, who tends to become noisier as the day wears on and the beers go down. An elderly member of the party I took to Australia in 1970–1, when Ray Illingworth won the Ashes, insisted that he intended to sit on the Hill, and somewhat injudiciously planted a Union Jack. He came back with a cut on the head, the result of a flying beer can, but his only comment, accompanied by a broad smile, was 'Scars of war, my son!'

Bottom The Adelaide Oval is the most beautiful of the Australian Test grounds, with a very long, straight carry; but it has comparatively short boundaries, square to what over the years has been the most placid of Australian pitches—great for batsmen, but often a graveyard for bowlers

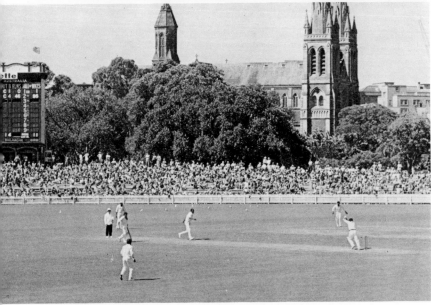

after a back injury in the Caribbean threatened to end his First Class career. Not only did he come back, but he improved as a bowler. He added to his armoury and, like Lindwall, now varies his pace and can therefore keep going for much longer spells when required. He is a world class fast bowler that any captain would like to include in his side and hate to have in the opposing ranks.

Thomson is something of a rarity, a fast bowler who derives his speed from something closely akin to a slinger's action. Although he employs a very long amble up to the stumps, one gains the impression he could be just as quick off half that distance, because his pace is derived essentially from body and arm. He lacks the subtlety of Lillee and seldom moves the ball much in the air unless he starts it outside the off stump, but he does cut the ball back sharply off the seam. His greatest asset is the amount of lift he can get from only just short of a length. Batsmen are frequently in trouble against the bouncer, but the really unpleasant delivery is the ball which is not especially short so that it has to be played around the chest.

As would be expected from anyone who depends so much on sheer speed for his effectiveness, Jeff is relatively far more potent in Australia than in England, because the pitches tend to be quicker and the ball travels through the air a fraction faster. At the moment he is inclined to bowl everything from the extreme edge of the crease. In fact, he frequently breaks the return crease with his right foot and only the fact that the umpire is concentrating on where he is putting down his left foot saves him from being no-balled. If he can bowl from closer to the stumps he might well become an even better bowler—and he is already a very good one indeed.

Unlike the 1930s, when spin was their main weapon, the modern Australian attack, particularly in England and increasingly at home, comprises fast or fast-medium bowlers, and there has been no shortage of these.

The most distinguished was probably Alan Davidson, for a time probably the most feared new-ball bowler in the world. He was originally a good, typical Australian all-rounder; a brilliant all-purpose fieldsman, a fine, very hard hitting bat and a useful third or fourth

Left It is impossible to overrate the importance of having a top class wicketkeeper. Not only is he the hub around which the fielding revolves, but he also has more chances than anyone else of effecting a dismissal. The Australians have long appreciated this point and have turned out a whole succession of fine keepers, including the elegant, neat and dapper Oldfield, pictured here, the graceful Tallon, the ultra-dependable Grout and the indestructible Marsh

Right Ray Lindwall was the best fast bowler with a new ball that I have ever seen, because he moved it so much and so late. He possessed a rhythmic approach, a beautiful body action, a well disguised slow ball, a devastating yorker, which he could produce at will, and superb control. He was poetry in motion

seamer, a little faster than his short run-up suggested and giving little away. All this changed in the mid-1950s when Davidson suddenly found the ability to dip the ball in late to a right-hander from on or outside his off stump. Because he bowled left-hand over the wicket, he automatically made the ball leave the bat by his line, irrespective of any additional movement in the air or off the pitch. This nearly doubled his menace and forced batsmen to play at deliveries which formerly they could have afforded to leave alone.

Bill Johnston and Garth McKenzie were entirely dissimilar in style—a fast-medium left-arm, who occasionally reverted to spin with a fine, almost languid action, and a quick right-hand rhythm bowler who, when everything clicked, was distinctly sharp and certainly hit both the deck and the bat. Each also had an unusual characteristic for quick bowlers, let alone the Australian variety: in entirely different ways they could be described as lovable, lacking the fierceness, and the frequent malice, of most of their breed. Bill bubbled with good humour; Garth was quieter, easy-going and placid. Two of the game's 'nice guys'.

Of Australia's best fast-medium bowlers post-war, Neil Hawke and big Max Walker stand out because although they had ugly actions both swung the ball a great deal and never stopped trying. Neil was a genuine swing bowler. He could move the ball either way, had excellent control and considerable variety. He worked at his bowling and took the trouble to appraise the weaknesses of opposing batsmen. Max has a very open-chested action, so it is hardly surprising his stock ball is the big in-swinger. Although he does cut the ball back off the wicket and away from the bat from time to time, this seems to happen only when it is pitched outside the off stump. His away-swinger tends to go earlier and not as much as his in-swinger and he possesses a formidable 'nip-backer'. He has achieved more bounce on the harder, faster wickets of Australia and the West Indies than in England, where one feels he has not fully exploited the conditions, which should have suited his style, quite as much as his ability warrants. This is largely due to the fact that he is inclined to bowl a shade too short and too wide of the off stump to the accompaniment of a host of slips and gullies. If he attacked the stumps and employed more close catchers on the leg-side he would probably meet with greater success.

Alan Connolly began as a tall, rather ungainly fast bowler, who later reduced both his pace and run to become a very good fast-medium seamer, who moved the ball around and had a well disguised slower ball, and the odd quick one.

Best of the Australian spinners was Richie Benaud, who went on to capture more Test wickets than any other Aussie bowler. A very accurate wrist-spinner, like many of his kind he did not have too much joy in England where the pitches were unsuited to his style, and he was infinitely more effective in Australia and other countries where he was able to get more bounce and yet still turn the ball sufficiently to find the edge, even though he was never a big spinner. He had a deceiving loop to his flight, a 'flipper', which was difficult to pick and hurried off the wicket, and outstanding control, which meant a batsman could not afford to wait for the bad ball, because these were few and far between.

Richie was also a fine attacking, often spectacular batsman, who liked the ball to come on to the bat, and a great fieldsman, especially in the gully. But he will probably be best remembered for his captaincy; shrewd, imaginative, diplomatic and articulate. His press conferences were masterly. The only criticism was that some of the correspondents felt he would have liked to have written the copy for them as well.

John Gleeson was also a wrist-spinner, but with a flatter delivery than Benaud. He had a deceptive googly, which owed more to the fingers than to the wrist.

Although Ian Johnson and Ashley Mallett were both off-spinners, their techniques were very different. Ian was essentially a flight expert who could beat batsmen in the air and invited them to come down the pitch at him. The traditional spinner of this type can be safely negotiated from the confines of the crease, but he was so slow that he could prove dangerous on a fast pitch because of the bounce, rather than the turn he achieved, and the way he drifted the odd delivery away from the batsman. Ian could not adapt his style to suit English conditions, even when these favoured more orthodox finger-spinners and Jim Laker and Tony Lock were having a ball. He was simply too slow through the air. His right arm was reminiscent of a corkscrew, and in another era he would have been no-balled for throwing, as, indeed, would Lock.

Ashley Mallett, a standard off-break bowler, was frequently used in the role of a defensive stock bowler to keep down the runs and rest the main strike force. Here his accuracy from either over or round the wicket was a great attribute. Never less than tidy, and always difficult to get after, Ashley played in exactly the same number of Tests as Gleeson, bowled a comparable number of overs and took roughly the same number of wickets, but these cost at least 10 runs a wicket less—a tribute to his unfailing 'tightness', which is also probably why he did not achieve as much turn as expected on the odd occasion when one of his kind should have been a match-winner.

Australia has always had an enviable record for producing high quality left-hand batsmen, though, strangely, not left-hand bowlers, and the post-war era was no exception, with Neil Harvey, Bill Lawry, Arthur Morris, Bob Cowper and Ken Mackay.

Harvey tops this list for both the quantity and quality of his runs. He found a style which suited him and included driving quick bowling off his back foot from over rather than from behind the batting crease, with both shoulders facing the bowler. It may not have been textbook, but it was certainly effective and, of course, he remembered the one vital rule of bringing his bat down perfectly straight, while his timing allowed him to keep the ball along the ground even though he had struck it on the up. His footwork, as might be expected from a small man, was quick and he was never happier than when dancing down the pitch to the spinners, or hooking the quickies. He frequently savaged a quality attack, but he also possessed an excellent defence. As a fielder, Neil ranks with the greatest of any era, very fast, very safe, a superb pair of hands and a deadly flat throw. Later he was to become an outstanding slip.

Although Greg Chappell will be remembered for his on-driving, he had a masterful technique, a wide range of strokes, and was one of the most correct batsmen Australia has ever produced, able to make runs with genuine style against all types of bowling and on all kinds of pitch. Here he is seen executing a square or back cut in the second Test against the West Indies in 1973

In complete contrast, there was nothing basically exciting about Bill Lawry. He was a watchful accumulator, imperturbable, immovable, the perfect sheet-anchor, nudging, pushing and occasionally putting away the bad ball. Bill was not the kind to create a stampede through the turnstiles, at least not into the ground. But he was an invaluable asset to his country because he provided the stability every team needs, while under the apparently dour exterior and hook-like beak lurked a delicious laconic wit. A sound tactical captain, he suffered from the disadvantage of leading a team that was on the decline.

Arthur Morris was not only a very sound opener, but could change gear in mid-innings and increase the tempo to suit the situation. He was exceptionally strong off his legs and used an angled bat to run the ball down through the gully without appearing to take any chances. Although a better player, Arthur's technique reminded me of Worcester and Kent's Peter Richardson. He was a quality workman with a fine temperament who acquired his runs methodically without the basic excitement of a Harvey, or a Woolley, or a Sobers.

Bob Cowper lacked the class of Harvey and Morris and the solidarity of Lawry, but he was a good stroke-maker who gave the best of bowlers little chance. Rather sadly, his fine business acumen lost him to the game after a career which was all too brief. He would probably have made an outstanding captain.

Ken 'Slasher' Mackay was the most efficient blunter of pace bowling in Australia. Few have possessed better judgement of what to play and what to leave alone. His watchful defence repeatedly held his side together from the middle of the order. Although he experienced problems on an English pitch, and was almost unbelievably bad against the Surrey twins, Laker and Lock, in England, his overall value to Australia was considerable and rather more than statistics suggest. Slasher also bowled a nagging medium pace which would have caused little trouble in the 1930s and 1940s, but made him a very useful support seamer on pitches and outfields that were becoming increasingly greener.

When Norman O'Neill first burst into prominence, he was hailed by the Australian press as the 'new Bradman' and indeed he was a most impressive player, with the gift of being able to hit good-length bowling to the boundary with powerful straight-bat strokes. He was, however, just another fine forceful strokemaker, not a genius. A notoriously bad starter, fast, short-length bowling gave him far more trouble than it should have done.

Bobbie Simpson was a very good model for any aspiring player. He had a sound defence, a wide range of strokes, and his technique was pure textbook. As a result, he was better able to cope with the many different English pitches than most of his compatriots, and was an exceptional, complete batsman. True, Fred Trueman fancied him round his off stump, but there have been few batsmen Fred did not think he could remove.

In addition, Bobbie was a superb first slip, a competent leg-spinner and a sound orthodox skipper. When the Selectors found they had lost most of their current Test team to Packer, they solved one of their major problems by calling Bobbie out of retirement and making him captain of Australia once again. Considering his long absence from top class cricket, he did splendidly.

The most baffling of all post-war Aussie batsmen is Doug Walters. His build, the way he wears his green cap, his neat footwork, wonderful eye and ability to conjure up brilliant, unconventional shots make him closer to the Bradman image than anyone else. There is a touch of genius about Doug's batting, but he lacks the Don's analytical mind and absolute dedication to the task of making runs, which is, of course, why in four tours to England he never made a Test century. He has not bothered to learn to adjust, otherwise he would not continue to give the two gullies, especially placed immediately he arrives at the crease, the catching practice he does.

In England Doug has been a disappointment, but elsewhere he has played a whole series of exciting and dramatic innings spiced with spectacular strokes. These include his 'come to attention shot', in which his two feet click together on the crease facing up the wicket and the ball is dispatched to the midwicket boundary off the middle-and-leg with a straight bat. He has always been

Richie Benaud was an outstanding captain and leg-break bowler, a flamboyant, swashbuckling batsman and an extremely athletic fieldsman with a very safe pair of hands. His bowling was noticeably more effective on hard pitches, and he found English wickets rather too slow. Not a prodigious spinner, he relied to a great extent on accuracy, a looping flight and the ability to make the ball bounce

Because most of the Australian players had joined the Packer brigade, their Selectors were not only short of players for the 1977–8 Tests against India, but desperately needed a captain. The choice of their former skipper, Bobby Simpson, whom they persuaded out of retirement, proved to be inspired. Bobby did a magnificent job with his young side in a wonderful series which was still in doubt on the last day of the final Test. He captained with his customary skill, batted with distinction and even managed to convince his players that extreme scruffiness is not an essential requisite of the Australian Test cricketer. In this photograph, from the 1965–6 series in Australia, Bobby is being congratulated by Bill Lawry on completing his century against England. Together they put on 244 runs for the first wicket and Bobby eventually reached 225. Like most Australian cricketers, he retired early from senior cricket; far to early, judging by the form he showed on his return

Ian Chappell—a typically aggressive shot from the World Cup Final in 1975

suspect against the bouncer, and has naturally received more than his quota. His great asset is that if he stays any length of time runs will flow rapidly, which is why he is so feared by opponents and so liked by spectators.

The Chappell brothers make a fascinating contrast, boxer and fighter, Greg's bat is a rapier, a deadly weapon to be used with elegance and panache, while he has the poise, the footwork and the timing to match. It is usually possible to tell when Greg is about to play a major innings. From the moment he arrives at the crease he will be middling the ball and finding the gaps with all the hauteur and certainty of a master duellist.

Ian's bat was a cutlass for hacking his way through a sweaty, swearing battle, when speed of eye, power of blow, and quickness of reaction counted for more than the niceties of stylized fencing. He often looked out of touch at the start of an innings, played and missed, edged it here, and snicked it there, but five and a half hours later he would still be there batting away and with a hundred to his name. His only concern was staying in and making runs; the manner in which these were obtained was of no real significance, although he was a spectacular hooker and an outstanding cutter.

Greg was the more naturally talented and polished performer, who could destroy an attack with his wide range of delightfully executed strokes, including a wonderful on-drive, but many bowlers prized Ian's wicket more, because he was a born fighter who made fewer mistakes. This, of course, was why Ian made such a fine captain—tough, knowledge-able, completely ruthless and prepared to bend the rules to suit his side. His object was to win matches and it did not worry him that in the process he should upset opponents and authorities; in fact, one gained the impression he went out of his way to do so. He certainly deliberately flouted conventions and must have been to some extent responsible for the 'ugly Australian' image which grew up during his reign.

The team Greg inherited from his brother was on the decline, so it is difficult to judge him as a captain. He was more withdrawn than Ian, but although he did not possess the same personal magnetism, he would probably have done well had it not been for the shadow

cast by Kerry Packer, and if he had had better players under him in 1977 when his team lost the Ashes and he announced his retirement from Test cricket.

Wally Grout, with his twinkling eyes, ready laugh and slightly rotund frame, looked more like a jolly inn-keeper than a wicketkeeper, let alone an outstanding international cricketer. Even on field his appearance was deceptive. His pads never seemed quite to fit, his gloves might have been borrowed and he was not graceful. It was not until he was in action that one realized why he was one of the most reliable of all Australian wicketkeepers, and effected most dismissals in Tests. He stopped nearly everything that passed the bat and held a remarkably high percentage of all possible, and some nearly impossible, catches that came his way. Like everything he did, his stumpings were fast and efficient rather than elegant and graceful.

When he started in First Class cricket, Rodney Marsh was essentially a good stop-per, rather than a keeper; an extremely dan-gerous left-handed striker of the ball, always capable of transforming the course of a match, a tough, uncompromising and most determined character. The last attribute en-abled him to improve his work behind the stumps until he became a very accomplished, often brilliant performer and an integral part of a highly successful Australian XI, in which the pace of Lillee and Thomson, combined with occasional uncertainties as to line and length by the latter, ensured that both bravery and agility were essential behind the stumps.

Rick McCosker batting in the Centenary Test at Melbourne, in spite of a broken jaw. This injury was the result of an indifferently executed hook at a bouncer from Bob Willis. It required considerable courage for Rick to bat again with his jaw wired and strapped, but his innings certainly helped Australia to victory. It takes time for a batsman to recover from a blow of this nature, and though Rick has plenty of determination it was bound to undermine his confidence. This was probably the main reason why his second tour to England was less successful than his first

Tony Greig dives to make a spectacular catch in the slips to dismiss Gilmour in the Centenary Test in Melbourne. Tony's all-purpose fielding in international matches was a continual source of inspiration to the team

CARIBBEAN CALYPSO

Sobers has another left-hand opening bowler, Alan Davidson, caught behind by Gerry Alexander in the fifth Test against Australia in 1961. Alexander not only kept extremely well in this series, but batted with great aplomb

Because West Indian cricket has always been so full of life, laughter and excitement; because their players tend to hit the ball harder and further than most; because so many of their cricketers have also been entertainers, and because of the excitement which they so often generate, a myth has been built up. They have been hailed as cricketing calypsos, noisy and boisterous, who play for fun; yet nothing could be further from the truth.

The West Indian takes and has always taken his cricket very seriously. He plays to win, not for fun. Anyone who has experienced club games, let alone First Class cricket, in the Caribbean will vouch for this fact. They have difficulty in coming to terms with the situation in a 'friendly', when the opposition are 70 for 7 on a good wicket and in England the fielding captain would allow the enemy some easy runs in order to prolong the contest.

This approach is entirely foreign to West Indian nature; friendly or no friendly, you move in for the kill, the bigger the better. The carefully manufactured finish is not their scene, and if one examines their cricket history it is easy to understand why.

The sport was introduced into the West Indies when they were part of the British Empire and, as in other parts of the world, soon became very popular with the local inhabitants, the majority of whom were the coloured descendants of slaves from Africa or indentured servants after the abolition of slavery. The islands at the time might be described as reasonably benevolent planto-cracies controlled by a small but powerful white, or nearly white, minority consisting of the colonial administrators and those who had decided to settle permanently, even though in the main they still considered England their real or at least their spiritual home.

It was inevitable that this white oligarchy would dominate cricket administration as they did everything else, but just as in England the wealthy landlord was prepared to play alongside his tenant, the whites encouraged the black population to participate.

On the cricket field as in law all men were equal, or nearly equal, although every island or combined West Indian team was automati-cally captained by a white man. At the time this was not considered an ethnic decision, but a natural social one. In exactly the same way, it was not until well after World War II that a professional was allowed to captain England, and even then it was accepted reluctantly, while the counties were almost invariably led by amateurs.

In the Caribbean the main cricket clubs were built up around the cities, and naturally the biggest were white dominated. But with the growth of competition, black and brown-skin clubs were formed.

It has been said with truth that it was once more difficult for a black man to be accepted in a brown-skin club than in a white-skin one. These subtle nuances of colour, position and wealth were not cricket, and at least on the field everyone was equal, which added extra bite to the contests. Here the black man could show he was the equal, and often the superior, of his master, in exactly the same way as the English professional was able to do in the Gentlemen v. Players matches of Victorian and Edwardian England.

With this background it was inevitable that West Indian cricket, although played with a fairness sometimes missing in England and Australia, was not to be taken lightly. It was for real, not for fun, yet it never lost that volatile exuberance which has always been such a feature of their game.

Another reason why the West Indians have always taken cricket so seriously was the close relationship that used to exist, and to a lesser degree still does, between senior club, inter-island, and Test cricket, and which was fur-ther intensified by the comparative smallness of each centre. It has meant their First Class cricketers were always playing alongside or against ordinary club players. This not only automatically raised the standard, but meant nobody could afford to cruise. The established top class player had to justify his reputation, while the club man was just as determined to cut him down to size. You have to be serious when batting against a Wes Hall or a Learie Constantine. Furthermore, bowlers of that calibre do not take kindly to having catches dropped and are prepared to express them-selves forcibly on the subject. Nobody enjoys having his bowling smashed all round the ground. Therefore the club bowler had

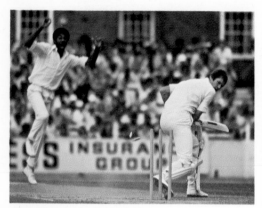

Above Balderstone was brought into the England XI in 1976, after showing consistency with Leicestershire, but found the extra pace of the West Indian attack too much for him. Here, he has been beaten by the excessive speed of Holding

Right In an international career which began in 1958 and ended in 1976, Lance Gibbs played in seventy-nine Tests, and took 309 wickets at 29.09 each, passing the score of the previous record holder, Fred Trueman, by two wickets. However, it should be pointed out that Fred secured his victims in only sixty-seven Tests at a cost of 21.57 apiece. With the ever growing number of international matches, it is inevitable that aggregates of both runs and wickets should increase. The legendary Sydney Barnes, for example, picked up his 189 wickets at 16.43 in a mere twenty-seven appearances! Lance was a superb off-spin bowler with a somewhat open action, a gloriously high right arm, a short bustling approach, long and powerful fingers and a deceptively fast arm action. He was remarkably accurate and could be used in an attacking role, or as a stock bowler on a perfect pitch. Unlike most slow bowlers, he had the temperament of a quickie and detested batsmen. This picture of Lance against Australia catches the loop in his flight which could be so disconcerting, because what appeared to be a half volley waiting to be hit so often turned out to be of perfect length

Absolute perfection: Sir Gary Sobers playing the straight drive at Edgbaston. This stroke had everything—correct footwork, elegance, grace, power and timing. It started with a high back lift; contact was made with the full face of the bat, and the stroke has been completed by a truly majestic follow-through

to concentrate even harder when bowling against a George Headley or an Everton Weekes, and there was always the chance of dismissing him, which would provide a memory for life. The outcome was that although club cricket in the Caribbean has always contained plenty of shots and fun, it has been played hard.

Having First Class cricketers performing regularly in local games not only automatically lifted the overall standard, but meant that the general public came to know the stars in their particular island more intimately than in England, where the County Championship tends to isolate them. As a result, the locals followed the progress of their hero in Tests and inter-island cricket with special interest, because he was one of them.

A perfect example occurred back in 1900 when a combined West Indies side went to England. Sir Learie Constantine's father, 'Cons' as he was affectionately known, was invited to make the trip, but had to decline because he could not afford to pay his own way and there was no professionalism in the West Indies. Although Cons was considerably better off than most black men—he was an overseer on an estate—he simply did not earn the type of money which would enable him to maintain a large family and spend the whole of the summer playing cricket in England. When it became known that much admired Cons was not going, a public subscription was quickly raised among the local community and he was put on a launch that just enabled him to join the rest of the party, who were already on board ship. Cons's subsequent feats, which included making the first West Indian century in England, must have given all those who subscribed, many of whom could ill afford it, enormous satisfaction, but especially the black community. At that time black cricketers were, rather like the English professionals, predominantly bowlers, with the white men, like the English amateurs, being considered the main run-scorers. This state of affairs continued into the 1930s and was not finally ended until the arrival of the three Ws in the 1940s.

Another important reason why the West Indian took his cricket seriously was that it provided a way, especially for a coloured player, to improve his lot, both socially and financially. The Caribbean is very beautiful, but the number of well paid jobs there is still limited, so a black lad from a large family, often with a limited education, had the utmost difficulty in bettering himself. However his chances could be dramatically improved if he excelled at cricket. Originally this took the form of patronage from a firm or employer prepared to allow a promising player time off to represent his island or the national XI. Sometimes he would be found a job which was something of a sinecure, but it did not produce big money or permanent security. There is still no real professional cricket in the West Indies. The players are better off, and in some cases well rewarded, but gate receipts are relatively small.

Inevitably, the best of their coloured players began to look towards England, where people were paid for doing the job they loved. The pick of them began in the 1930s to accept lucrative contracts in the Lancashire League, where they were generally both successful and popular. This trend has continued, although formerly none of them joined the county circuit.

Sir Learie Constantine began the movement because the jobs then available to him in his native Trinidad were not rewarding enough. He was to be followed by nearly all their finest players. At the start of the 1976 West Indian tour, Clyde Walcott said jokingly, although his words contained more than a hint of truth, that 'the time has nearly arrived when the West Indian manager could arrive in England to be met by his team.' Their players are the leading cricket mercenaries in the world. 'Have bat will travel' is their slogan.

This exodus provided problems for West Indian cricket. From the playing angle, it meant that their best performers were no longer regularly taking part in local club games. From the financial angle it meant that if they wanted to field their strongest team, either nationally or for their island, they had to bring the players back from England, and also make it financially attractive enough for them. This costs a considerable amount of money which previously would have been used for the general benefit of the game but

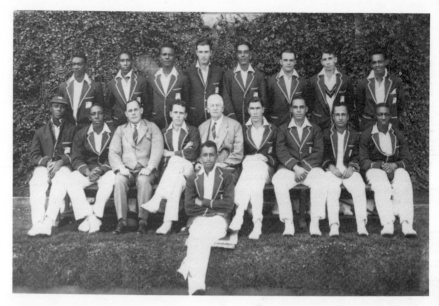

The West Indies team that toured Australia in 1930–1. It included a great batsman, George Headley, the irrepressible Sir Learie Constantine and some good fast bowling, but it lacked depth in batting. The players did not have complete faith in themselves as a team, and this did not change until after World War II

now goes to the big names.

Another outcome is that the West Indian Board are no longer able to pay the members of their touring party a near pittance, because they are dealing with professionals who realize their worth and also know what other tourists receive. A further intriguing development is that some West Indians, because of the length of time spent in England, have become better players under our conditions than at home. This is probably why Gordon Greenidge failed to score as many runs in Australia in 1976–7 as his ability warranted. He found that playing the ball as late as he does in England was not possible Down Under.

Because success can bring rewards far in excess of the undoubted satisfaction resulting from scoring heavily, or capturing wickets, the ambitious cricketer realizes at an early age that he cannot afford to play just for fun. If he makes the grade it can mean an escape to a materially richer life, though whether it is a happier one will depend upon the individual. All their most successful players have taken their cricket very seriously. In recent years they have tended to work at it harder and study it more than their English counterparts. While it is impossible to become a great cricketer without natural ability, it is equally impossible to reach the top without much hard work. However, the West Indian player

Below and right The three Ws— Clyde Walcott (below left), Frank Worrell (below right) and Everton Weekes. They all came from Barbados and were the most potent middle-order batting trio in history. All were world class players, with different styles: Everton was a short, neat killer, particularly devastating off his back foot; Frank was the classical artist, with a graceful, flowing style, while the massive Clyde was a 'power house' batsman. I have seen Clyde hit Jim Laker off his back foot for a straight six. Frank was also a more than useful left-hand

medium quickie, and sometimes a slow bowler. He became the first black player to captain the West Indies, a job which he carried out with all the charm and efficiency he displayed as a batsman. He was also the second West Indian cricketer to be knighted

has also retained his basic enthusiasm for the game itself, which is why he is so popular with crowds throughout the world. There are signs, though, that some of them are in danger of being contaminated by the cynical expediency to be found in England.

The West Indian Board of Control and West Indian Selectors have always had a more difficult job than their opposite numbers in other parts of the world, because the West Indies do not have a strong central government. They are a loosely knit group of islands, plus a small chunk of South America, who were once part of the British Empire and possess a passion for cricket. They have different backgrounds and histories, with different financial, political and ethnic problems which have tended to increase rather than decrease since independence. Large distances divide them—Barbados must be about as far from Jamaica as London is from Moscow. Inevitably, the loyalty of the inhabitant is to his island, not to the West Indies. To make matters worse, jealousy has always existed between the islands.

As a result, the West Indian Selectors have been unable to pick a team entirely on merit. They have to take into account geographical considerations, because it was inconceivable to stage a Test match in an island without including a representative from that area. In the same way, a major concern when choosing for an overseas tour is to make sure that every First Class centre, which now includes the Combined Islands, is represented.

The need to change the constitution of the West Indian XI from island to island was even more pronounced before their Selectors had a squad of cricketing professionals from England at their disposal.

However, inter-island rivalry still exists. Only recently a very insular Jamaican politician called on Jamaica to secede from the West Indian Board because there was no representative from his island in the West Indian team for a Test in England.

Back in 1954 the MCC were unhappy about the standard of umpiring in their match against Guyana, although, let it be emphasized, the tourists had won by the largest of margins, but they still decided that the two officials concerned were unsuitable to stand in

the Test there. The English captain (Sir Len Hutton) asked for an umpire from Jamaica and another from Barbados. Both had officiated in either the first or the second Tests which had been lost by England. His request was turned down, not because it was unreasonable, but because it would have offended the sensibilities of the local community. As a result the Guyana Test was umpired by the head groundsman and a Chinese gentleman, who had previously said that he would not stand again as he had been the subject of some abuse by another touring party a year earlier. In fact this oddly assorted pair did rather well, even though the first unofficial 'bottle party' held up play for some time, and one of the officials needed a police escort after giving his third decision in England's favour.

West Indian cricket has managed to survive for some seventy-five years despite numerous threats to its existence from social, economic, financial and political disagreements, as well as the inevitable dissatisfaction which occurred whenever one centre thought it had been badly treated. The game has been able to withstand the setbacks and the problems because most West Indians love it and cricket would surely suffer, from both playing and the economic angle, if there were no national XI and no Board of Control to manage the inter-island matches. The West Indies as a whole—Trinidad is very much the exception—is not a wealthy area, so that it would be fair to say that without the revenue from Tests, especially overseas tours, and commercial sponsorship, First Class cricket in its present form could not exist out there.

What makes the latest threat more serious than those in the past is that it has nothing whatsoever to do with the game, but is politically motivated. The West Indies have naturally resented the apartheid policies to be found in varying degrees in Rhodesia and South Africa, but in the past decade this resentment has taken on a more militant aspect. Because of the publicity that the sport enjoys politicians have exploited it in order to draw the attention of the media to events that are not remotely concerned with cricket.

The first indication of this occurred when Sir Gary Sobers, at that time captain-elect, returned to Barbados in 1970. That summer

Julien bowling to Illingworth in
the third Test at Lord's in 1973,
supported by an ultra-attacking
field. Note the deep backward
short leg stationed there
deliberately for the mis-hook

he had led the Rest-of-the-World XI, which had included several South Africans, to victory over England. After the English season he agreed, as a professional cricketer, to take part in a double wicket tournament in Rhodesia, believing that he was aiding the cause of multi-racial sport in Africa. He was bitterly attacked. The Prime Minister of Guyana, Burnham Forbes, demanded an apology from Sobers for his 'foolish and ill advised stand', or there would be no welcome for him in Guyana.

This affair very nearly split West Indies cricket and was ended by a compromise, in which Gary signed a carefully worded letter of regret, not an apology, to the Board of Control. But the danger remained. In 1975 Greenidge toured South Africa and Rhodesia with the International Cavaliers. When he was selected to represent Barbados in Guyana, the Guyanese government said they would not accept any cricketers who would play or had played in South Africa, and the game was called off. This attitude also led to the cancellation of the scheduled visit to Guyana of the English Youth team, as some of the players and the assistant-coach had previously been to South Africa.

Unless something changes dramatically, this must surely mean that no Test will be played in Guyana against England, Australia or New Zealand, who somewhat naturally have no intention of allowing Guyanese politicians to tell their players what to do as private individuals; while a cynic might be tempted to ask who wants to go to Guyana anyway?

Of course, it is still possible to tour the West Indies without Guyana, and the Board of Control are preparing an itinerary on that premise. But if Jamaica follows suit, it would be very difficult to find two extra venues.

The sad thing is that the many cricket-lovers in Guyana may be denied, for political considerations, the opportunity to watch the best players in action. It is also rather hard to understand how it is wrong for a Guyanese cricketer to play against Tony Greig, who was born in South Africa, in Guyana, and right to play against him in Trinidad or England. Could it possibly have something to do with the cash that would be lost by both the player and the association?

It is also tragic that cricket, which has done so much good for the cause of the black man throughout the world, should now be used as a political vehicle of doubtful value and less effect, apart from making West Indian cricket the poorer in all respects.

The West Indies did not become a world force in cricket until after World War II. Until then the game had been dominated by England and Australia, with South Africa a comfortable third. Although their record against Australia has been disappointing and they have never done battle with South Africa, who for a period in the latter part of the 1960s were probably the most powerful team, they have certainly produced more great players in this period than any other country.

It began with that remarkable triumvirate, Weekes, Worrell and Walcott, who scored their runs with a grace and regularity which were truly remarkable. Certainly, few if any teams have been able to boast a middle order of this calibre.

What was so fascinating about the three Ws, apart from the fact that they came from the same little island of Barbados, was that they were so different in style and temperament. Everton Weekes, small, neat, very quick on his feet, had more than a touch of Don Bradman about him. He became the best West Indian player on a slow turning wicket, with the possible exception of George Headley, and although he never had the chance to lead the West Indies, he showed for Barbados that he was a shrewd and thoughtful captain with considerable tactical knowledge. When a bad knee forced his retirement from Test cricket, he was still on one leg a far better batsman than most people on two. Like all the truly outstanding players he saw the ball early, always appeared to have plenty of time, and could hit the good ball to the boundary with a correct attacking stroke.

Frankie Worrell was the most graceful of the three Ws, less machine-like than Everton and less powerful than Clyde, with runs seeming to flow from his bat, so that his front-foot driving was something to savour and treasure. Once, at Lord's, Alec Bedser bowled one of his very few half-volleys just outside the off stump. It could have been driven for four, but Frankie caressed it to the boundary with the most delicate of late cuts. In addition to his batting, he was a useful left-arm seam bowler who swung the ball considerably and could also bowl left-arm orthodox, but his biggest contribution to West Indian cricket was undoubtedly as captain. He became their first black skipper, and did it with a style that was a credit to his country and his people.

To anyone who knew Frankie this came as no surprise. He exuded personal charm, was intelligent, understood his players and knew the game inside out. Although he led the West Indies to a convincing win in England, probably his finest service to the game was his captaincy in Australia which, despite the loss of the series, caught the imagination of the entire cricket world so that it led to a definite resurgence of interest in a bleak period.

His early death was a loss not only to the West Indies, but to cricket everywhere, as he surely would have become one of the game's finest administrators.

The massive Clyde, who came to England rather oddly as a wicketkeeper, will long be remembered for the power and the effectiveness of his batting. He had a very high backlift so that he appeared a natural candidate for the yorker; yet always seemed to bring his bat down behind. His strength enabled him to hit a straight six off the back foot, and for a big man he was a surprisingly fine hooker and very frustrating to bowl against, as I frequently found to my cost.

During a double century he made against England in Barbados, I sent down what in many respects was the most unusual maiden of my career. The first ball pitched on a length and would have hit middle. Clyde drove it on the up off his front foot along the ground, and only a superb stop in the covers prevented the boundary it deserved. The next delivery was identical, only fractionally shorter, and he played the same stroke, only this time off his back foot, with the same result. The same thing occurred for the remaining four balls, with Clyde hitting me off front foot then back foot straight and to the on. I maintain that on that perfect pitch I could not possibly have sent down a better over; yet only brilliant fielding, including two full-length stops, prevented his scoring 24 runs.

After the three Ws, from nowhere, came 'those two little pals of mine, Ramadhin and Valentine', who were to be the only pair of spinners from overseas to decide a four-Test series in England since the war. Sonny Ramadhin was a diminutive little man. He bowled his off-breaks with an unusually open action and varied his pace cleverly, but what made him so effective was that he could bowl a leg-break without much discernible change. This automatically created doubts in the minds of the batsmen, rather in the same way as the googly had first done. It took English players a couple of tours to work him out, or to be more accurate to wear him out; while the Australians typically adopted a more positive approach, took a calculated risk and launched a violent counterattack, which undermined the bowler's confidence.

The West Indians themselves were amazed that English players had difficulty in not instantly picking his leg-break, or what was really closer to a leg-cutter. I can recall sitting with Clyde Walcott during an Essex v. the West Indians match while he unfailingly nominated it from the pavilion.

Alf Valentine was a left-arm spinner who most definitely did not come from a coaching manual. He bowled wide of the crease, did not use his height, and his action was somewhat crab-like. There was little flight, but he did have the ability to turn the ball appreciably on a really good wicket. He was at his most effective in his early twenties, when he really was a very fine bowler, and why he went back rather than forward will always remain one of those mysteries. Perhaps he tried to think about it too much, instead of just bowling them over.

The West Indies next unearthed another trio of young players, who in their way were just as exciting as the three Ws—Gary Sobers, Rohan Kanhai and Collie Smith. All but the last were eventually to captain their country and Collie almost certainly would have done so had he not been killed in a car crash before he reached his peak. We shall never know how good a player Collie would have become, but there is no doubt in my mind that he would have been a world class all-rounder.

Quite simply, Sir Gary is the greatest rounder the game has ever seen. As a batsman he has scored more runs in Test cricket than

Holding has a long flowing run up of quite remarkable beauty and, as can be seen in this splendid photograph, a model action, combining both power and grace, which enables him to bowl very fast. Whether he will be able to maintain his pace and his hostility over the years, time alone will tell, but there can be no question that his performance in the Oval Test against England in 1976 was an immortal piece of fast bowling. On a featherbed of a wicket, which emasculated bowlers, frustrating Roberts and making Willis look a medium pacer, he took 8 for 92 runs in the first innings and 6 for 57 in the second, the outcome of his exceptional speed through the air and refusal to allow himself to be defeated by the conditions. The result was an overwhelming victory for his team on a pitch very similar to that which had blunted both Lillee and Thomson in the previous year

Vivian Richards, currently the finest batsman in the world, hits another boundary during his breath-taking 291 at the Oval in 1976, when he tore the English attack to shreds with a devastating display of positive batting

anybody else, although it will be appreciated he took part in nearly twice as many Tests as, for example, Sir Don Bradman, and has hit the highest individual Test score, 365 not out against Pakistan at Kingston, Jamaica. In many respects far more important than the grand total is the number of runs he scored on the occasions when he came to the aid of his side when it was apparently beaten. As a batsman he was world class, both in execution and performance. As a bowler he was good enough to be selected for international cricket in three entirely different styles—quick left-hander who moved the ball in the air and off the pitch, wrist-spinner and orthodox slow left-arm—something which nobody else has ever approached. He was, in addition, a fine all-purpose fieldsman and a brilliant short leg and slip, and before the team started to decline he was a highly successful captain.

Gary has booked for himself a permanent place among the game's immortals, and it is safe to say there will never be another like him. What is even more delightful is that it has been achieved by a genuine sportsman, truly a knight without meanness or malice.

Rohan Kanhai, once he had established himself as a Test cricketer, proceeded to dazzle with the virtuosity and the range of his stroke-making, which contained several shots with his own special stamp. Originally, Rohan had a rather volatile temperament, but he mellowed over the years and this enabled him to come back into the international scene when it seemed that he had just burnt himself out. Inevitably, he lost some of the gay abandon which characterized his batting in his early twenties, but he has blossomed forth into a master craftsman on a difficult pitch and a shrewd tactician.

Although the West Indies has a tradition for fast bowling which stretches back to the turn of the century and was very much in evidence in the 1930s with Constantine, Martindale and Francis, their pacemen of the 1940s and early 1950s were unexceptional. The first really quick bowler to emerge after the war was Gilchrist, who was very fast and frequently extremely nasty. A basic lack of self-control led to an early departure from the international scene, but the fact that in a very short career, which contained only thirteen

Tests, he took 57 wickets is an indication of his menace. He was to be followed by that fine and sharply contrasting pair, Wes Hall and Charlie Griffith. The former, tall, lithe and laughing, would come bounding from some green patch near the sightscreen with all the beauty of a thoroughbred in full flight before moving into that fine body action and full follow-through. The latter, built like a heavyweight slugger with a smoky, sometimes mean temperament to match, would amble up with an armoury which included a deadly yorker, a vicious bouncer and a well concealed slower ball. They indeed made a formidable pair, especially when it is remembered that Gary Sobers, who could be distinctly sharp when he wanted, was there to back them up. Wes was faster than Charlie and moved the ball more, but Charlie was generally considered to be the nastier and had greater control.

Since then the West Indies have found a number of good fast bowlers and won the 1976 series in England with a battery of four, which although effective proved rather monotonous for the spectators. These included Andy Roberts, with the brisk approach and, oh so slow, slouch back, who has proved for both the West Indies and his adopted county, Hampshire, the value of bowling straight. He is a natural match-winner at any level, because he is capable of bowling out good batsmen on good wickets and is fast enough to frighten and then polish off the tail.

Wayne Daniel, although raw and lacking in control, illustrates the value of sheer speed. Providing a bowler is fast enough, he is bound to upset batsmen and pick up some wickets, while many of his loose deliveries are for the same reason liable to go unpunished.

Holding, at the Oval in the final Test, produced one of the historic feats of fast bowling by capturing sixteen wickets on what was a featherbed. He has pace, heart, a lovely action and a run up that is poetry in motion, even if the average spectator would prefer it to be a sonnet rather than a long narrative poem.

EASTERN MAGIC

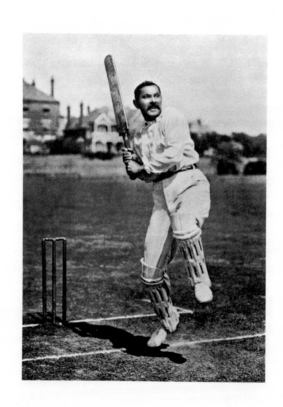

Photographs of cricketers at the turn of the century tend to be posed: it is difficult to imagine that the immortal Ranjitsinhji jumped out to drive in this fashion. Such a supreme artist must surely have glided down the wicket. To become outstanding at anything, great natural ability alone will never suffice, and in this connection C. B. Fry's comments about Ranji are particularly enlightening: 'Apropos of Ranjitsinhji's "genius" I should like to remark that whatever his inborn afflatus, he certainly took pains—I know no man who worked harder to make himself a batsman. He used to engage half a dozen bowlers in April, and even in March, and he practised often two hours in the morning and two hours in the afternoon. I do not believe in "geniuses" who have not worked hard; they do not exist.' The bowlers employed by the prince, even in his university days, were among the best in the land. It helps to be very rich

The Early Days of Indian Cricket

The beginning of Indian and Pakistan cricket belong to the days when the whole of the Indian continent was part of the British Empire. It was brought there by the colonial administrators, settlers and troops. Initially the inhabitants of this vast land learned the rudiments of the game by watching it being played by the British, but they gradually discovered that this strange pastime contained something special which appealed to their temperament.

They liked the guile and the grace, the lack of hurry, the sudden bursts of excitement between long periods of peace, the thrust and counter thrust, when sheer physical strength could be crushed by speed and eye, the beauty and the style.

In the early days Indian cricket owed much to the Indian princes, who not only gave it the blessing and the respectability of their personal patronage but also became keen and active participants. Their considerable financial backing enabled local players to savour its peculiar charm and then Ranjitsinhji burst on to the international scene at the turn of the century with a batting style which enchanted everybody by its artistry. He might be said to have brought a new dimension to the game.

Ranji became a legend in his lifetime and was largely responsible for creating the myth that all Indian batsmen have eyes like hawks, wrists of steel and lightning reflexes. This belief was to be carried on by his nephew, Duleepsinhji, who in his short career delighted the world with what came to be known as Indian magic.

Despite the patronage of princes like Patiala, who brought out English coaches and built grounds, the powerful influence of Lord Harris, who was governor from 1890–5, and the obvious practical advantages it provided to the numerous Anglo-Indians, who were the land's administrators, cricket did well to survive.

It had to withstand not only the normal growing pains, but the far more complex problems of different races, religions and languages, a highly involved caste system, and an entirely alien culture. These all threatened the natural development of the game in a way which did not apply in other parts of the British Empire to anything like the same extent.

The most significant years in Indian cricket were 1926–7, when the MCC made their first official tour and really sowed the seeds that were eventually to make cricket in India and Pakistan a major sport for the people of both countries.

At that time it must be realized that although there was an ever increasing number of native teams, the game was still largely dominated by the European residents, both from the playing and the administrative angles. It is significant that when the Calcutta CC picked the Indian XI to meet the MCC in the unofficial second Test no fewer than seven Europeans were included, despite the fact that an entirely native Indian XI had almost defeated the tourists earlier. C. K. Nayudu had also hit a remarkable 153 out of 187 in only 115 minutes against them to show that Indian cricket had something important to offer, while Wazir Ali had taken three centuries off the visitors and was another indication of the increasing power of the Indian players, even if their fielding was poor and much of their bowling undistinguised.

The next important stage was the formation of the Indian Board of Control, which was to be responsible for the welfare of the game throughout the continent. This owed much to the drive of the first secretary, de Mello, a natural 'go-getter' who refused to be dismayed by the many rivalries and factions that existed and continued to exist. The outcome was that internal cricket improved and in 1932 India sent a team to tour England. Although this contained more than its share of Ruritanian, or rather oriental farce, it did mark another stage forward.

The original team was as follows: the Maharaja of Patiala (captain), Prince Gyanashyamsinhji (deputy captain), the Maharajkumar of Vizianagram (deputy vice captain), C. K. Nayudu, Wazir Ali, Ghulam Mahomed, Navle, B. Kapadia, Godambe, Colah, Marshall, Palia, Naoomal, Amar Singh, Nissar, Lal Singh and Joginder Singh. This was clearly not the best team available, but it did provide a superb diplomatic balance between Hindus, Moslems, Sikhs and Parsees.

The captaincy stakes also represented a

compromise, because there was no way in which Patiala could afford to absent himself from Indian politics for six months, while nobody seriously believed that Vizzy would go on the tour unless he was the skipper, and it came as no surprise when he withdrew from the tour. In the long run this was rather fortunate, as it allowed Jahangir Khan to be included in the party, and in any case Vizzy was not even by Indian standards a good captain.

Finding the right captain has always tended to be one of India's, and later Pakistan's problems, and stemmed from what was basically a feudal system. The obvious leaders were the princes, who had inherited a tradition for command which, combined with their position, guaranteed them the respect of their team, at least until the days of independence. As a result it is difficult to think of an Indian or Pakistan captain to compare with Bradman, Benaud, Worrell or Illingworth. In the main they have lacked real flair and have tended to be either tactically sound but short of imagination, or good disciplinarians, lacking tact and often playing ability as well.

Eventually Patiala also declined the captaincy, which went to Porbandar, the ruler of a small state, with no cricketing qualifications except that he was the brother-in-law of Limbdi and had the practical advantage of being acceptable to all parties. Unfortunately, in England he became incensed by press criticism of his fairly obvious lack of ability on the field which was emphasized by a total of 2 runs in three innings, and he announced that he had been ordered to rest by his doctor and would take no further active part in the tour.

With Limbdi out of action with a bad back, the captaincy for the first ever Test was entrusted to C. K. Nayudu, who suffered from two disadvantages. He was no diplomat and he was also a commoner, so that other members of the party resented him. This eventually led to a portion of his side waking up Porbandar in the small hours of the morning, immediately prior to the match, to announce that they would not play under Nayudu. It was hardly the ideal start to a Test, though they did rather better than many had expected when they lost to what was anyway a stronger team, but were not disgraced.

Internal squabbles continued for the rest of the tour with players even refusing to try and only too anxious to blame somebody else, with the unlucky Nayudu the prime target of everyone. Amar Singh, a bowler of real quality, would not even speak to his captain and Nissar, a fine fast bowler, was convinced that many of the slip catches were being deliberately put down by his colleagues.

With this lack of team spirit it was not surprising that the Indians did not do as well as their ability warranted, but there were some fine individual performances, including some robust batting from the much maligned Nayudu, while Jahangir with his sort approach and beautiful body action was an outstanding seamer.

Both Duleep and the Nawab of Pataudi, the two finest batsmen in India, certainly under English conditions, declined to make the tour. They believed that their future lay in English cricket and considering that shambles of a tour and all the political ramifications that existed at that time in Indian cricket it is easy to understand their reasoning.

Despite all the upsets on that first tour to England, it did much to popularize the game in India and it had shown the cricket world that there were many fine Indian players.

The next MCC side to tour India in 1933–4 under D. R. Jardine was a powerful combination, though not the strongest available. They found that Indian cricket had improved despite its many internal problems. There were still not enough top class players and like their predecessors they found themselves meeting the same opponents all over the country. The idea of strengthening the local XI by importing talent naturally reduced the chances of defeat, but it did not encourage local players who needed experience against First Class opposition.

India managed to draw the first two Tests before going down in the third, despite their captain Nayudu, who was a fine fighter himself, having to put up with players who often would not try and an erratic Selection Committee. However, in Amarnath and Merchant India had clearly discovered two exceptionally talented young players.

The rivalries between the different centres and the religious factions which continued to

Above The All-India team which visited England in 1936. It was not a successful tour, as they managed to win only four First Class matches out of the twenty-eight played and lost two of the three Tests, the other being drawn. This was to some extent due to internal dissension, but in spite of these problems Mohamed Nissar Singh turned in some excellent performances with the ball and Merchant and Mushtaq Ali played some fine innings

plague Indian cricket were very much in evidence when a not over-strong Australian team toured there in 1935–6. The statement issued by Nayudu, who had been replaced as captain by the Yuvraj of Patiala for the first Test against the tourists, that he was pleased to play under him and asking for a united front went largely unanswered because India itself was so very divided. There was the India of Bombay, the India of Calcutta, and India of the British, the India of the princes, the India of Ghandi, the India of the Moslems, the India of the northern provinces and many more.

The resulting lack of harmony was to be seen all too clearly during the 1936 tour to England, under the Maharajkumar of Vizianagram. As a result, the team failed to live up to its considerable potential, winning only four of the twenty-eight First Class matches. In addition, it was beset by injuries and the weather was frequently unkind, while the sending home of their best all-rounder, Amarnath, cannot have assisted. Team spirit cannot have been helped by no fewer than four players joining up with the main party during the course of the tour.

The last team representing the whole of the continent to tour England was in 1946. They did better than their two previous teams, winning eleven and losing only four of their twenty-nine First Class matches, and under the captaincy of the experienced and respected Nawab of Pataudi were a very popular party, but it must be remembered that English cricket was at a low ebb. However, for the first time the Indians did present that 'united front' for which Nayudu had unsuccessfully appealed back in 1936. This is what Wisden had to say about them:

'In one important particular India's sixteen cricketers who had visited England in 1946 accomplished more towards raising the status and dignity of their country's sport than was achieved by either of the two previous touring sides. While the politicians at home argued the rights of independence, the cricketers abroad showed the world that they could put aside differences of race and creed and join together on the field as a single unit, working as one for the same cause. These young men came as

Right Duleepsinhji batting at the nets in Sussex at the start of the season. A nephew of Ranji, Duleep was a very graceful batsman, who normally played with the sleeves of his silk shirt buttoned up, as his uncle had done before him. He was slightly built and his power came from his sense of timing and his wrists. Illness forced him to retire from the game after only eight full seasons, but in this all too brief period he averaged over 50 in both First Class and international cricket

their country's ambassadors. By their cricket they won the hearts of the English public; by their modesty and bearing they earned the respect and admiration of everyone with whom they came into contact.'

It could be claimed that India had firmly established itself among the cricket-playing countries of the world.

Merchant showed himself to be one of the great batsmen, scoring over 2,000 runs with style, determination, immaculate technique, and a wide range of strokes, including a delicious, late late-cut. The Nawab of Pataudi was never fully fit and only gave occasional reminders of his pre-war charm, but Mankad showed himself to be his country's greatest all-rounder by completing the 'double', last achieved by a tourist (Learie Constantine) in 1928. His orthodox, slow left-arm bowling was relatively more effective on good pitches and his control was so good that he was seldom collared. His weapons included a devastating quicker ball which came on with his arm. His batting was efficient rather than attractive and he had the ability to score runs consistently in whatever position he batted, which varied from opener to number nine.

The team also included two other above-average all-rounders in Hazare and Amarnath. The former was a conscientious, painstaking batsman and a useful medium-paced seamer, who nagged away. The latter injured his eye in the first match so that his batting, which at its best could be so dazzling, suffered, but he bowled his medium-paced in-swingers off the wrong foot and the occasional leg-cutter very well. Like so many bowlers who hop on to their front foot in their delivery stride Amarnath came off the pitch a shade quicker than the batsman expected, but an attack which really revolved around Mankad, Amarnath and Hazare could at Test level only be described as friendly.

Cricket in Pakistan

Since becoming an independent nation Pakistan has made rapid strides forward and in a very short space of time has produced a remarkable number of world class cricketers. At the time of writing their strongest team is probably second only to the West Indies, but

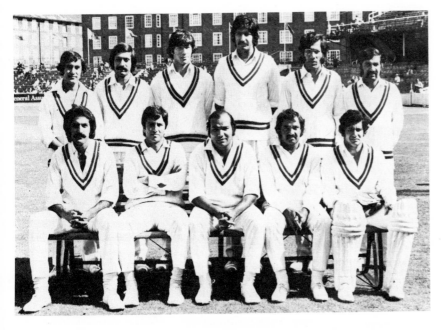

Above The Pakistan team for the Oval Test in 1974. They went through this short tour without defeat, but all three Tests were drawn: the first could have gone either way; the second, thanks to Underwood's exploitation of a damp patch where the water had got under the covers, went very much in England's favour, and the final Test was killed by a feather bed pitch at the Oval after Pakistan had batted extremely well

Top left Duleepsinhji pushes a ball to leg for the South of England during a Test Trial at Old Trafford

Left The Nawab of Pataudi captained the Indian team that toured England in 1946. He was still an accomplished batsman, but not as fluent as he had been in his thirties, when he had scored a century for England in his first Test against Australia. He also made 106 and 84 in his first University Match, in 1929, and 238 not out in his last, in 1931

the defection of so many of their finest players to the Packer circus is likely to set them back several years.

The one big criticism of Pakistan cricket is that it has probably been run rather too rigidly. Although this discipline has its good points, it has inevitably been responsible for several clashes between the authorities and the players, especially those who have become accustomed to the easier and financially more rewarding life of a top class cricketer in England.

Some of their managers appeared to be under the impression that they were leading a platoon rather than a group of cricketers from very different backgrounds. This would not have mattered if they had possessed a greater knowledge of the game or the psychology of cricketers, who are often temperamental and sometimes difficult. Some players will respond well to tight discipline, others, frequently the most talented, need to be cajoled. The ability to command an air squadron is not necessarily of use when organizing a deep sea rescue operation!

Pakistan made their first tour to England in 1954 and with what was basically a limited team did considerably better than might have been expected by winning nine and losing only three of the thirty First Class matches they

played, but the highlight of the trip was their defeat of England at the Oval in the final Test. This meant that they were the only side to win a Test on their first visit to this country, even if this was largely due to the courtesy of the England Selectors, who underrated the opposition and decided to experiment before the outcome of the rubber had been decided.

Unlike the Indian touring party of 1952, who unconditionally surrendered before fast bowling, Pakistan, under A. H. Kardar, the former Oxford Blue, were not afraid of pace and fought all the way. The first Test, which was restricted to about eight hours, not surprisingly ended in a draw. The second was won by England by the substantial margin of an innings and 129 runs. In the third the weather saved Pakistan from another heavy defeat, as with only 6 wickets in their second innings standing they still required another 244 to make England bat again.

For the final Test the England Selectors decided to give experience to Tyson and Loader, which left an ultra long tail, but the fatal step was the omission of Alec Bedser, who would surely have enjoyed himself on a pitch where Fazal Mahmood was able to take 12 wickets in a match which Pakistan were to win by a mere 24 runs.

This victory did much for the morale of Pakistan cricket, but was possibly a handicap to their future teams, who were expected to emulate this feat without the necessary resources.

The Kardar side itself did not have sufficient class players to back up Hanif Mohammad, the first great batsman from the most remarkable cricketing family the game has ever seen; Fazal Mahmood; Khan Mohammad; their wicketkeeper batsman, Imtiaz Ahmed, and the captain himself.

Hanif, who went on to score nearly 4,000 runs in Test cricket including 12 centuries and a mammoth, in time as well as runs, 337 against the West Indies, was a master craftsman. This diminutive opener possessed a beautifully organized defence, intense powers of concentration and a fine temperament. On the rare occasions that a ball beat his bat, his pads would automatically be forming a second line of defence. It has been suggested by several who have returned without an l.b.w. that in front of his own umpires these were just as effective. He normally took on the sheet anchor role for his country but occasionally, though not often, he showed that he also had plenty of attacking strokes to back up his rock-like defence, and like most little men he could hook very well.

If Hanif was the greatest, most prolific and certainly the soundest of Pakistan batsmen, Fazal Mahmood was the finest bowler and on the mat was for a period just about the most deadly executioner in the world. He could cut the ball either way at a pace just around fast-medium. In addition to his ability to make the ball bite on most surfaces, he was also blessed with immense stamina and an outsize heart, which enabled him to keep going for long periods. There have been occasions when he has kept going on one leg. Of the post war bowlers only Alec Bedser had a more deadly leg-cutter and it would have been interesting if one could have seen them both operating on the mat. His final tally of 139 wickets in international cricket for under 25 apiece taken on pitches throughout the world, many batting paradises, serves as a reminder of his outstanding ability.

Imtiaz Ahmed, although not in the same class as Alan Knott as a wicketkeeper, was an extremely efficient performer who missed very few chances and was also well above average as a batsman. It would be hard to exaggerate his all-round value to his national XI. For more than forty Tests he was an indispensable member of the team, while his hooking was frequently both a tonic and an inspiration. After the success of that first tour Pakistan cricket tended to stand still, and this included the boredom brought about by ten successive drawn Tests with India. The dread of defeat and lifeless wickets conspired to produce what was surely the most soulless international cricket of all time. They found some good new players including Saeed Ahmed, a fine stroke-maker, if somewhat suspect against extreme pace; Mushtaq Mohommad, who was to blossom forth into their most successful all-rounder; and Intikhab, a very accurate leg-spinner and forcing bat, who hit with remarkable power. The last three were able to provide the experience and the ability needed when in the late 1960s Pakistan began to put together

what by the early 1970s had become their strongest national team, with more balance, class and depth than any of their previous XIs.

This renaissance was to some extent started by the surprising defeat by New Zealand which shook the country and led to some drastic rethinking by the game's administrators. The number of national tournaments was doubled and the players responded to the increased competition.

The 1968–9 tour saw two brilliant stroke-makers, Majid Khan and Asif Iqbal, but finished in the confusion of a major riot in Karachi which robbed Knott, 96 not out, of what should have been his first Test century. It was also a reminder that the game was very vulnerable to the large demonstrations which have become a too familiar sight.

The Pakistan team which came to England in 1974 played sixteen First Class matches, won nine and drew seven, thus becoming the first visitors since Sir Don Bradman's party of 1948 to leave without a defeat.

They played very positive cricket throughout and the way they tried to beat every county made a very welcome change from the approach of too many Australian sides, who use these games mainly for batting practice. Although all three Tests were drawn, there was little to choose between the stars of the two teams, apart from Underwood, who was able to exploit a wet pitch to greater effect than anyone else.

Their batting had rather more class than England's and was also far more attractive, as Majid, Asif and Zaheer were all exciting strokemakers with Sadiq and Mushtaq, neither of whom are short of shots, providing the sound support.

There was also the promise of Wasim Raja, a left-hander with aggressive intentions. Sarfraz, despite a somewhat ugly action, was a fine fast bowler with a strong physique and he was well supported by Asif Masood, who was less reliable but swung the ball more. With the young and improving Imran Khan in the role of seamer the tourists were well served in this department, but they did lack a good finger-spinner, especially as the pitches of the 1970s did not make two wrist-spinners, Intikhab and Mushtaq, though very different in style,

Above The little master: Hanif Mohammad, the number one member of Pakistan's greatest cricketing family. Hanif was for many years the most reliable batsman in Pakistan, with a superb defence and great powers of concentration. He was only seventeen when he made his first appearance for his country. He hit the highest individual First Class score, 499 in 1958–9 for Karachi against Bahawalpur, and also made 337 in a Test against the West Indies. This was the longest innings in First Class cricket, lasting more than sixteen and a half hours

Right Mushtaq Mohammad (Hanif's brother) was the youngest player ever to be picked for a Test. He was not sixteen when he was chosen to play against the West Indies in 1958–9. Originally an aggressive batsman, particularly fond of the cut and the hook, he later became more defensive in outlook, and provided his country with much needed substance in their middle order. He is also a positive leg-break and googly bowler, who really spins the ball, and he has captained both Pakistan and Northants

Right Imran Khan is a fluent, free scoring batsman with a wide range of strokes. He is also a distinctly lively opening bowler and a brilliant all-purpose fielder, and could well develop into the finest all-rounder in the history of Pakistan cricket

the ideal combination for cricket in England.

With the continued advance of Imran Khan, who could well become a great all-rounder, and the arrival of Miandad, who has shown for Sussex that here is another batsman of enormous potential, the immediate future of Pakistan looked very bright even though the rows between the players and the Board were frequent and included one prior to the 1976–7 West Indian trip, until Kerry Packer succeeded in signing most of their brightest and most experienced players.

However, there is such a wealth of talent, much of it untapped, in Pakistan that there is good cause to suppose that they will find replacements in the not too far distant future. The snag could well be not the shortage of the basic material but rather the shortage of cash to develop it. Pakistan has numerous political and financial problems. There are no longer the princes and the patrons around who had the money and were willing to spend it on the game.

Unlike football, cricket is a costly sport. The equipment, the preparation of pitches, accommodation, and the basic administration all take time and money. Although the future Hanifs, Imrans and Fazals may be naturally gifted, they cannot hope to reach the top in world cricket without the necessary facilities. Even when they have reached the top, they still need to earn sufficient money and in Pakistan, with no professional cricket and an overall shortage of good jobs, this cannot be easy for a player, unless he is taken on by an English county. Even if this occurs, then other snags are likely. The Pakistan professional knows what his English and Australian counterparts receive for an overseas tour and this is likely to make him dissatisfied with what his Board is prepared to pay him for tours and Tests in his homeland. Pakistan has also acquired the reputation of being the 'land of the perpetual draw'.

Indian Cricket
The fundamental weakness of Indian cricket since independence has been the inability to produce fast bowlers, because the climate, the food and the normal build of the inhabitants do not make for big men with a physique which enables them to propel a cricket ball at

over eighty miles per hour in extreme heat. They are to be found in Pakistan and the north but they are in very short supply in India. This absence of pace bowling puts them at a serious disadvantage when they meet other countries on a pitch with pace and bounce, not only because they have not the bowlers to exploit these conditions, but also because their own batsmen are more prone to failure through lack of experience against real pace. They are also handicapped by the fact that many of their batsmen are small, so that a normal lifter from just short of a length is often tantamount to a bouncer, and far more unpleasant and difficult to negotiate.

As a result the Indian attacks have had to be built around spin and guile and they have produced more outstanding slow bowlers since the war than any other country. Mankad, whom we have discussed earlier, Prasanna, Gupte, Bedi, Chandrasekhar, Venkataraghavan, and Nadkarni have all in their different ways and very different styles been fine slow bowlers, at their most effective on their own pitches, but good enough to win matches on anything but very green wickets.

Watching for the first time the short, rolypoly little figure sidling up to the stumps with his rather low, inoffensive arm action, one could be forgiven for thinking that perhaps the bowler had just come from a factory and had been put on either because they were short, or because they wanted to give some runs away, or because he happened to be the foreman. One certainly would not imagine that here was an international cricketer, at his best on a good, dry pitch and one of the most feared off-spinners in the world. Prasanna is an absolute master of his chosen craft. He uses spin and flight, drifts the ball away from the unwary batsman, possesses endless patience and has great control. Unhurried, apparently unworried, he is content to wheel away over after over, not just waiting for the mistake, but striving to cause it.

Gary Sobers rated Gupte very highly and thought he was among the best, possibly the best leg-spinner he had ever encountered. He was the complete wrist-spinner, with a natural looping flight, the ability to turn the ball on almost any wicket and a well disguised googly which was exceptionally hard to pick. A natural attacking bowler, Gupte was at his most effective on dry pitches, preferably with pace and bounce. He found the Caribbean wickets far more sympathetic to his style than those in England, where he was disappointing.

Two things made Bedi different from most modern slow left-armers; his gay turbans, and his style, which is essentially old fashioned and ageless and would be effective in any era. Unlike so many left-hand spinners, who are potential match winners on helpful wickets and are steady, slightly negative bowlers on other occasions, Bedi will set problems for batsmen anywhere in the world and on any wicket, because in addition to his finger-spin, he flights the ball in the classical tradition of the Golden Era. Although Bishen is in some respects easier to hit, because he gives the ball air, than the bowlers who push the ball through flat, this is one of the reasons why he has been so successful in international cricket on perfect pitches. He challenges the opposition to attack him and hopes to trap them in the process. A joy to watch, he is a true weaver of spells.

Chandrasekhar is the fastest leg-break bowler since Doug Wright. He pushes his leg-breaks and googlies through at a pace closer to medium than slow and has the happy knack of producing from time to time the near unplayable delivery even on a placid pitch. His speed through the air, combined with his spin and high arm action, enables him to achieve a considerable amount of bounce, with the result that a number of batsmen are caught in the leg trap off his top-spinner and googly. He is a natural match winner, but distinctly unpredictable, because there are occasions when he simply cannot drop into his groove. He is then erratic and something of a moon bowler.

Venkataraghavan is very much an English style off-spinner, relying more upon line and break than flight for his effectiveness, while Nadkarni epitomized accuracy. His left-arm bowling was flat, gave nothing away and was very difficult to get after, a defensive, rather than an attacking bowler.

Having beaten an admittedly rather weak MCC in Madras in the previous winter, the first tour of England since independence in 1952 proved to be a big disappointment, when

The Nawab of Pataudi, 'Tiger', followed in his father's footsteps, becoming captain of India. Here, he is leading the Indian team on to the Manuka Oval at Canberra during their Australian tour of 1967–8

the Indians were routed in the Tests and only gained four victories in the First Class programme. Their batting was formidable until confronted by pace, their bowling, apart from Ghulam Ahmed, an excellent off-spinner, lacked the penetration needed to bowl out opposing sides, and their overall approach was too defensive. This pattern could be said to apply to Indian cricket for many yeàrs except in India, where the heat and the lack of pace in their pitches tended to neutralize the speed of visiting quickies. They have always been inclined to have problems with their captains, who have often been pleasant, shy, rather retiring and predictable individuals.

The change occurred in 1971 and continued for the three greatest years in the history of Indian Test cricket. In this golden period they beat the West Indies in the Caribbean one nil, with the other four Tests drawn, beat England in England one nil with the other two Tests drawn, and beat England in India two one.

What was the secret of their success? First, and foremost, they had in Bedi, Prasanna, Chandrasekhar and Venkataraghavan four world class spinners. This was supported by the best fielding, especially close catching, probably ever seen from an Indian XI. Over the years it could be said that fielding has not been India's strongest department. Their captain Wadekar must take much of the credit for this improvement and he also led his team sensibly throughout. Their batting, especially in the West Indies when Gavaskar and Sardesai were in wonderful form, was impressive, but it was no stronger than that of many previous Indian teams except that in times of stress it showed more character and determination. The success also brought that vital ingredient of confidence, so that the team began to think in terms of winning, rather than merely avoiding defeat.

Although it is true that both West Indian and English cricket was in a transitional stage and at a low ebb, India did very well to exploit the situation and by so doing increased still further both the general interest in and the enthusiasm for the game. To celebrate their first ever triumph in the West Indies and England, an enormous bat some sixty foot high and inscribed with the names of all the players was erected at Indore.

Top calibre spin bowling has always been one of the strongest features of Indian cricket. Prasanna is one of their finest off-break bowlers, indeed possibly their finest

Chandrasekhar, here about to deliver the ball, bowls his leg-breaks and googlies at medium pace, but is still able to turn the ball on plumb wickets. His high arm action, combined with the spin which he imparts, enables him to achieve a surprising amount of bounce. He can be both erratic and expensive, but he is a real match winner on his day

All the euphoria was brought down with a big bump in 1974, when India was not only beaten in England, but was completely outplayed in all three Tests. This rout cruelly exposed certain technical deficiencies against high quality seam bowling and in Wadekar's captaincy. It also underlined, sadly, that even great spin bowling is seldom the key factor in Test series in England, because the conditions, particularly the well grassed pitches and outfields which do so much to protect the shine, give the seamers so much help.

The Prudential World Cup also showed that India has not yet come to terms with the special requirements of limited overs cricket. At present it lacks two essentials, the necessary pace bowlers and defensive spinners.

There has been no shortage of fine Indian batsmen since the war and one of the most fascinating features has been the marked difference in style and technique of so many of them. The most brilliant and naturally gifted must surely have been the young Pataudi, 'Tiger', as he was known on the English county circuit. Nobody knows just how good he would have become if he had not partially lost the sight of one eye as a passenger in a car crash in Sussex, shortly after the University match and long before he had reached his peak as a batsman.

Despite this very serious handicap, which forced him to adopt an open stance, he showed a quite remarkable determination to continue playing and was still good enough to make many runs in international cricket and to captain his country, like his father before him. How many more runs 'Tiger' would have made with two good eyes is impossible to estimate, but the odds must be that he would have become a cricketing immortal, instead of just a very good batsman.

It is hard to imagine a batsman less like the accepted idea of an Indian player, than 'Polly' Umrigar. 'Polly' was a big, powerful man with a clumsy, almost awkward style, who had problems against short pitched bowling, but often demoralized opposing attacks, especially on slow pitches. He put together numerous really big scores and had a distinct partiality for double centuries. A keen student of the game, he made a better second in command than captain.

Although originally a dashing strokemaker and a spectacular hooker, Manjrekar cut out some of his more audacious strokes and for years was his country's most prolific run-getter and most complete batsman, equally at home against pace and spin.

As well as being a highly successful accumulator of runs with unlimited patience and plenty of determination. Hazare was also a useful medium-paced bowler, especially on the mat. A career average in Test cricket of over 47, the highest of any Indian batsman, underlines his prowess; a very efficient fighter rather than exciting entertainer, who invariably had to be dug out.

When Gavaskar scored 774 runs in four Tests against the West Indies, a new batting genius appeared to have arrived on the scene, but he has never again approached that type of form though he has played some fine innings. A neat and attractive opening batsman, he is inclined to lose his wicket too often, when apparently well set, which suggests that his concentration does not match his ability. Viswanath is a delightful strokemaker who could develop into a great player, although his lack of inches has proved something of a handicap when facing the lifting ball.

THE SPRINGBOKS

The South African team chosen to take part in the Triangular Tournament of 1912, between South Africa, Australia and England. The idea of bringing together the three strongest countries was excellent, but the outcome was not a great success. The biggest snag was the weather, as it was one of the wettest English summers. The Australians did not have their strongest team because of a dispute between their Board and the players, while the South African batting proved a big disappointment, despite a century by Faulkner in the first Test. Although Pegler captured 29 wickets, their batting was rather expensive

Cricket was first introduced into South Africa by British soldiers, settlers and administrators during the first half of the nineteenth century. It gradually grew and prospered without ever attaining the same momentum as in Australia. One reason was that it did not attract the Boers, who much later were to discover such a fierce passion for rugby football. The outcome was that cricket, which was to play a far from inconspicuous part in gradually reducing ethnic barriers in other parts of the world, did not have the same effect in South Africa. If the Dutch settlers had liked the game, history might have been very different.

The first side to visit South Africa was taken by C. A. 'round-the-corner' Smith—later to become a Hollywood institution—under the patronage of the founder of the Union Castle Line in 1888–9. Two years later a party captained by W. W. Read went there. In 1894 a South African team of limited capabilities visited England, but by now their cricket was steadily improving, helped by the internal competition of the Currie Cup. In 1895–6 and 1898–9 two tours were made by powerful sides under Lord Hawke, who promoted the game with all the zeal of a Victorian missionary. However, it was not until the Golden Age that South Africa eventually emerged as opponents of true international calibre, able to meet both England and Australia on equal terms.

Despite some impressive performances in 1902 against an Australian XI led by Joe Darling, and the successes of the 1904 South African side which lost only three matches and defeated a powerful England XI, nobody realized that a sudden upsurge was about to occur. Their 1904 side, under Frank Mitchell, who had originally gone to South Africa with Lord Hawke, contained some good batsmen. Kotze was as fast as anyone in England apart from Kortright of Essex, and Halliwell was a top class keeper, but most important of all was the all-rounder, Schwarz, who had been educated at St Paul's and had played on several occasions for Middlesex when Bosanquet had been experimenting with his googly. He was fascinated by this style of bowling, practised it quietly on his own, and suddenly introduced it on this tour against Oxford University, with dramatic results. Not only did his bowling

bring him a rich haul of victims, but he taught a number of other South Africans the art of leg-break and googly bowling, thus setting the scene and providing the ammunition for his country to shatter the complacency of English cricket.

The MCC sent a good side to South Africa in 1905–6 under Sir Pelham Warner. Everyone believed that they were more than capable of winning the series: they were to be proved so very wrong, as the tourists were routed by four Tests to one. South Africa had arrived!

Although the South Africans had several fine bats, including the graceful Sinclair, the solid Nourse, and White, and became a very close-knit unit with exceptional team spirit, because the same XI played in all five of the Tests, the real cause of England's downfall was the inability of their batsmen to cope with a quartet of wrist-spin bowlers on the mat. Schwarz, presumably because he lost his leg-break, as happened to so many leg-spinners in the years ahead, relied entirely on the googly and did the greatest damage. He was closely followed by Faulkner, whom the English players were unable to pick, and in reserve were White and Vogler. The most successful MCC batsman was F. L. Fane, who applied that old cricketing maxim 'when in doubt, push out' to good effect.

The outcome of this South African triumph was an invitation to visit England in 1907, including three Test matches. After the way they had annihilated Sir Pelham's team, the tour created enormous interest. Everyone wanted to see them in action, especially the four wrist-spinners. It was one of the few occasions in cricket that the big box office attraction did not depend upon either master batting or very fast bowling.

The South Africans were unlucky to encounter a very wet summer. This reduced the effectiveness of their batting, because they so often found themselves on pitches where the ball turned and stopped, and it also reduced to some extent the threat of their googly bowlers, although they did secure a large number of wickets.

All three Tests were rain-affected. England won the second, largely because Blythe took 15 wickets in the match, and the other two were drawn. However, there can be no disputing the impressive overall record of the visitors: of thirty-one matches, twenty-one were won outright and only four were lost.

Vogler, Schwarz, Faulkner and White so often bemused batsmen that English bowlers immediately began to copy the new style of attack and so eventually nearly every county could boast one genuine wrist-spinner. Now the wheel has gone full circle and, apart from the odd import, there are none to be seen.

Back on the mat the South Africans showed their supremacy by beating the MCC team, under H. D. G. Leveson Gower, by three Tests to two, with Vogler and Faulkner, now a world class all-rounder, the main executioners; but they were to be beaten in Australia, where their wrist-spinners were unable to gain as much turn, and were routed by the next English tourists, among whom Barnes reigned supreme.

In many respects South African cricket was at its zenith between 1905, when they burst so dramatically upon an unsuspecting international scene, and 1910. After that there was a slight decline. They produced some great sides and many outstanding players, but they were never to be quite so formidable again until well after World War II. Sadly, in the late 1960s and early 1970s, when they probably had the strongest team in the world, political considerations far removed from cricket prevented them from matching their strength against England and Australia.

It is difficult to assess the correct power of those early South African sides, because their effectiveness depended so much on their four googly bowlers, representing a novel form of attack. To some extent their success stemmed from the way the game was then played. The majority of batsmen of that period tended to be top-of-the-handle players, often using a long-handled bat. Their approach was, in the main, positive. They were accustomed to scoring runs by hitting firmly through the line of the ball, which presented problems if they were uncertain which way it would turn.

Tests of only three days' duration also ensured that runs had to be acquired swiftly. This suited wrist-spinners, who are essentially attacking bowlers, because in general their accuracy cannot compare with that of the orthodox finger-spinner.

A policy of crease occupation and waiting to put the loose delivery away when it arrived, which eventually did so much to kill the wrist-spinner, especially on the slow, well grassed English pitches of modern times, was not in fashion. However, unquestionably the South African googly bowlers brought a new dimension and excitement. It is very sad that they now appear to be a dying species.

South Africa was able to include four googly bowlers in the same side because Schwarz and White were very good batsmen and Faulkner, apart from Graeme Pollock, was almost certainly the finest left-hander they have ever had. He scored over 2,000 runs on his tour to Australia, where he averaged more than 70 in the Tests and was spoken of in the same bated breath as Trumper.

After the 1914–18 war, South African cricket fell into something approaching a decline, despite the presence of Herbie Taylor, especially strong off his back foot and considered by Sir Pelham Warner to have been one of the best players in the world, and Nupen, who along with Vogler was rated their most difficult bowler on the mat. They were, in fact, to wait until 1935 before winning their first Test in England at Lord's, where Balaskas captured 9 wickets for 103 with his leg-breaks and googly, and the solid Bruce Mitchell played a dour, undefeated century.

In 1938–9 a strong England side, under Wally Hammond, won a very high scoring series, and for the first time all the Tests took place on grass wickets. This tour is best remembered for the so-called timeless Test, which after ten days remained undecided because the England party, only 42 runs short of victory and with 5 wickets still standing, had to catch their boat home. It provided a classic example of a pitch which was too good, made batting too easy and emasculated the bowlers.

Like World War I, World War II had an adverse effect on the Springbok game. Compton and Edrich enjoyed an incredible run spree against Alan Melville's side, which was defeated easily by an England who were to be slaughtered the following year by Sir Donald Bradman and company. A far from formidable MCC touring party accounted for the Springboks in South Africa, and they lost the

H. J. Tayfield was known as 'Toey' because of his habit of always tapping the ground with his toe before setting off on his short, economical run. An off-spinner of the highest class, he took 170 wickets in thirty-seven Tests, and was at his most effective from over the wicket. This helped him to drift the odd ball away from the bat as a contrast to the break-back. Toey was not such a big spinner as Athol Rowan, but on the good batting pitches of Australia he was the best slow bowler South Africa had produced since their band of wrist-spinners in the golden era. Few have come closer to the ideal of never bowling a really bad ball. His line and length were exemplary, and he often used two forward short legs, who were placed straight and fairly deep to catch hard hit drives by batsmen who were tied down by his relentless accuracy

Heine, Adcock, McGlew and McLean celebrating the South African victory in the Test at Old Trafford in 1955, which they won by 3 wickets with only five minutes to spare after a magnificent match. Heine and Adcock were a much feared and respected opening pair of pace bowlers; McGlew was a tough little opening batsman, who always had to be dug out, while McLean was a natural attacking player, who was prepared to take chances, a match winner, but somewhat lacking in consistency

1951 series in England by three Tests to one, on a tour in which they could only manage five victories in thirty First Class matches.

The revival was to come in 1955, when Jack Cheetham brought one of the finest South African sides to Britain, and though they lost a wonderful series, they won both the third and fourth Tests and, perhaps even more important, the affection of the cricketing public. They had some good batsmen and a well balanced attack, but what transformed them by the end of the tour from a good team into a very good one was their brilliant fielding, which they had really worked at.

In 1956–7 they held the MCC, under Peter May, to a drawn series, but by 1960 they had lost some of their finest players and they were beaten again by England in 1964–5, the last time a representative MCC side was to have the good fortune to make this trip. Their last visit here was for a short tour in 1965, when they gave ample evidence of the promise to come. Politics intervened, and this promise was not allowed to reach fruition, but before the dark clouds finally enveloped their cricket, South Africa had the infinte satisfaction of annihiliating the Australians under Lawry.

The Tests between England and South Africa, which began during the Golden Age, ended with the d'Oliveira Affair, which was not without moments of unintentional farce.

Basil learned his cricket in South Africa and became the best non-European player in the country, but as he was a Cape Coloured he was not eligible to take part in the Currie Cup, or represent the national XI. His performances were sufficiently impressive for Middleton, the Lancashire League Club, to offer him a contract and he quickly proved his worth to them with bat and ball. In 1964 he joined Worcestershire, who not only acquired a fine all-rounder, but also a charming person, and a year later he became eligible for County Championship matches, where he immediately made his mark as a class performer.

Basil became a British citizen and was chosen to play for England. In terms of ability there is no doubt that he more than justified selection, though personally I have never been in favour of including mercenaries from overseas, who have learned their cricket abroad, in our national XI. This view has nothing to do with colour and applies equally to a number of white South Africans in county cricket at the present time, who could take up British nationality and would certainly walk into the England team. Like Basil, they are also debarred from participating in home Test cricket because of politics.

Having established himself in the England side, 'Dolly' was obviously in the running to be selected for the MCC team due to tour South Africa in the winter of 1968–9, although his inclusion would inevitably have been something of an embarrassment to all parties.

This snag appeared to have disappeared when Basil had a bad summer and lost his place, but fate decided otherwise. Prideaux dropped out of the final Test at the Oval against the Australians and Basil was recalled. Always a man for the big occasion, he responded with a splendid century, which had much to do with England winning the game. Nevertheless, when the Selectors chose the touring party the following day, Basil was not included. It was a somewhat surprising decision, but no more than many others made by Selectors over the years, and it was based on purely cricket, not political considerations. All might still not have been lost if D. J. Insole, the chairman, had not seen fit to say that overseas they regarded d'Olivera primarily as a batsman, rather than an all-rounder, and that having put him alongside seven chosen batsmen they had decided to leave both him and Colin Milburn out.

Although difficult to believe, this was acceptable, but it became absolute nonsense when Cartwright, a bowler, was forced to cry off and d'Oliveira was then invited to take his place. The South African Government simply could not comprehend such naivety and understandably believed that undercover intrigue was responsible. Mr Vorster described d'Oliveira as a 'Political Cricket Ball', which he undoubtedly was, albeit an unintentional one, and declared that he would not be welcome in South Africa. This left the MCC with no alternative but to call off the tour.

Whether d'Oliveira would have been allowed to tour South Africa, although clearly not wanted—a fact of which he himself must have been only too well aware—if he had been

a straightforward selection, will always remain a matter of opinion, but there can be no doubt that a delicate situation was thoroughly mis-handled.

This was not to be the end of the affair. A Special General Meeting of the MCC was called by twenty members, led by the Rev. David Sheppard. The aim of the meeting was to sever links with white South African cricket. Although the three motions were heavily defeated, it all added fuel to the growing campaign against South African apartheid policies. The game found itself reluctantly involved in a political issue. There were demonstrations during a short unofficial tour of England by a South African side organized by Wilfred Isaacs, a businessman; the formation of an evocative and emotional 'Stop the Seventy Tour Committee', and eventually the 1970 full South African tour was called off.

This was certainly not the wish of ninety per cent of the cricketers of England, but was forced upon the Cricket Council by the government of the day, under Harold Wilson, and meant that probably the best South African team in history was never seen in this country. It also served to emphasize the weakness of law and order when confronted by sufficient demonstrators.

From the social angle the most enjoyable of all cricket tours were those to South Africa. The hospitality was on a scale unequalled anywhere else in the world, the country varied and fascinating, the climate beautiful and the cricket excellent. They have produced some magnificent players and I have been lucky enough since the war to have played against all the most outstanding, before they were banished from the international scene.

The South African cricketers, as a species, were inclined to be different from their counterparts in other countries. They were immensely keen and talented, but their basic approach was very reminiscent of that of Public School sides.

I shall always remember my incredulity when I heard the South African captain say: 'On your toes, Tony Pithey.' It was exactly what I might have said to one of my school team, but not to Fred Trueman or Tom Graveney. This grown-up schoolboy streak

Eddie Barlow driving Veivers through the covers in the fifth Test against Australia at Sydney in 1964, watched by his captain Trevor Goddard, another highly efficient all-rounder. Eddie has been a Test class all-rounder, a tough, rather ugly batsman, who could be relied upon to score runs when they were most needed. He was a far better bowler than he looked (always an advantage) and an excellent slip field. He has shown for Derbyshire that he is also a shrewd positive captain. His misfortune is that South Africa was excluded from the challenge of international cricket when he was in his prime

meant that their captain resembled a prefect, with more authority over his players than an Australian or an English skipper, so that the discipline was stricter.

It all stemmed from a life style, which, though very materially rewarding, is at the same time rather narrow and isolated. As a result there were times when I felt I was on an entirely different wave length.

A classic example occurred in 1965 when I captained T. N. Pearce's XI against Van der Merwe's side in their last match of the tour. I had done this against numerous touring sides and previously had had no difficulty in explaining the best way to provide an entertaining match and, above all, to avoid anything even vaguely resembling a final Test, for touring teams do not like to end their trip with a loss. My format was simple. The pitch at Scarborough was good, and covered throughout, while the hours of play were short. Therefore, the obvious thing was for my side to bat first, declare before the close, and on the final day set the tourists a generous target, with the object of providing an exciting finish as close as possible to the last over. If the visitors thought my declaration was unfair, then they could simply bat out time. If they were unable to do that, then they had only themselves to blame.

I never had any difficulty in putting this across to a whole series of touring skippers, including some from Asia, who were understandably suspicious of an Englishman bearing gifts. It had worked because it did not matter if my team lost providing there were three full days of entertaining cricket. However, I failed with Van der Merwe. He made the mistake of batting first, did not appreciate that it was customary to employ seamers in the first session, especially if you had been given four, and ended by losing in two days, convinced that he had been conned. Nothing was further from my mind, especially as we had then to play a one-day game. Yet Van der Merwe was a good South African captain, though not the best since the war. That title must surely to to Jack Cheetham, who did so much to transform a highly competent side into an outstanding one.

If I were asked to name a model for any aspiring young batsman, I would unhesitatingly choose Barry Richards. In terms of sheer technique and style, he is closer to absolute perfection than any other player I have ever encountered. Equally at home off either foot, he always seems to have an inordinately long time in which to employ a vast range of strokes, all eloquently executed. His only weakness is that he has been known to become bored with batting because he has been denied the stimulus of international cricket, apart from four Tests in which, incidentally, he scored over 500 runs though he had not reached his peak. He finds himself in the same type of position as Jack Nicklaus would be in if his golf were restricted to the English circuit, and to some extent his game and his enthusiasm have suffered.

How does Barry compare with Graeme Pollock, whose Test career was also drastically shortened? This pair are unquestionably the finest batsmen South Africa have produced since the war, and probably of all time. Tall, powerfully built and wielding an immensely heavy bat with the grace and ease of a rapier. Graeme was the more devastating, because he hit the ball harder. He would smash it to the boundary, whereas Barry caressed it.

A century made by left-handed Graeme against a West Indian side at Scarborough was impressive enough for their bowlers to say: 'Man, he's as good as Sobers'—both a wonderful tribute and an indication of his ability. His finest asset was his front foot driving off good length bowling, which was so majestic and effective that it recalled memories of the Golden Age. He was more of a destroyer and less of an artist than Barry; while he was not so impressive on his back foot. However, both possessed the class and panache which divides the great batsmen from the very good ones, who in the case of South Africa included stocky Dudley Nourse, rather short on style but full of fight and determination, and the dashing Roy McLean, who attacked with relish and cut with a viciousness that can seldom have been surpassed.

The most outstanding Sprinkbok allrounder since Aubrey Faulkner, and for a time, after Gary Sobers was injured, the best in the world, is Mike Procter. He is a genuine, slightly unusual fast bowler, a fine field and a high calibre batsman. Mike's very open action will not be found in any coaching manual, but the important point is that it suits him, because it not only enables him to bowl very fast, but is also responsible for an in-swinger which is so big that on occasions he is able to go round the wicket and secure l.b.w. decisions. Although Trevor Goddard was just not in the same class as Procter, and far less spectacular, he became a vital and integral part of the South African team, a dependable left-hander, a stock bowler always difficult to score against who could shut an end up for long periods, and a brilliant field.

Fast bowlers are at their most effective when they are able to work in pairs, and Heine and Adcock formed a distinctly hostile opening attack. Both were tall and had high actions, so that although they were not as quick through the air as Frank Tyson or Dennis Lillee, they had the ability to make the ball lift unpleasantly from only just short of a length on a good wicket. Heine quite clearly did not like batsmen, live ones, and although Adcock was less aggressive, he developed a very late out-swinger, which with his pace and height was able to account for anyone.

Peter Pollock, the elder brother of Graeme, was another fine fast bowler with a nasty bouncer and a volatile temperament which contrasted sharply with Graeme's rather languid charm.

Despite their tradition for wrist-spinners and their obvious value in South Africa, as shown by the successes of 'Roly' Jenkins and Johnny Wardle out there, they have not had an outstanding one since the war, their two finest spinners, Athol Rowan and 'Toey' Tayfield, both being off-spinners. Athol was an off-break bowler in the English mould. He was a big spinner with a classical action and excellent control, who was often hampered by a damaged knee. 'Toey' was, relatively speaking, at his best on good wickets overseas and in these conditions was fit to rank alongside Jim Laker and Lance Gibbs. He liked bowling over the wicket, when his left foot would come down in line with about the middle stump, and he was able to make the odd ball leave the bat appreciably. His length and line were invariably immaculate; he was willing to nag

Peter Pollock is one of a number of fine hostile fast bowlers produced by South Africa since World War II, of whom the most aggressive was probably Peter Heine and the best Adcock. Peter bowled with fire and pace during the South African tour to England in 1965, but he suffered at that time from the lack of a partner with equal venom at the other end. He had a nasty bouncer and plenty of stamina, which enabled him to keep going for long spells. Peter was a very determined character and a tough competitor

Graeme Pollock, Peter's younger brother, pulling the ball to the boundary against Hampshire. A tall, extremely powerful batsman, his driving off his front foot on the up was something never to be forgotten. If his Test career had not been cut short by politics, he must assuredly have produced figures which would have substantiated his justifiable claim to be numbered among that small band of truly great batsmen with the ability to destroy a Test attack with a two-hour hundred

away for hours, and he always bowled to his field, which often included two rather deep forward short legs, placed there for the full on-drive which had been lofted rather than pushed. When a pitch was taking a lot of spin, especially after rain, and he was forced to go round the wicket, Tayfield, like Lance Gibbs until he had settled down with Warwickshire, did not exploit these conditions to anywhere near the same extent as Jim Laker.

No mention of South African cricket would be complete without paying tribute to their fielding, which was first lifted to heights of excellence by Jack Cheetham. Players like Jackie McGlew, who did so much to carry on the tradition, were prepared to throw themselves about in a fashion formerly done only by a few eccentrics. Fielding, especially backing up, became a tight drill, so that there were never easy runs to be had against them, and the short single became a luxury few could afford, especially when Colin Bland arrived on the scene. Colin turned himself into one of the greatest covers of all time. He usually patrolled the area between cover and mid-off so spectacularly that it is no exaggeration to say spectators came to see him field. Subsequently, it could be argued that Clive Lloyd has been equally outstanding in this position, but nobody, in my opinion, has been able to surpass the accuracy and speed of Colin's returns. He aimed to hit the stumps and did so with a regularity which delighted everyone, except the unhappy batsman.

What the future of South African cricket will be at international level is impossible to say at the moment. Until their national team is multi-racial it appears that they will be condemned to isolation. However, the county form shown here by such youngsters as Rice and McEwan, who would both go straight into the England side if they became British citizens, indicates that the standard of their domestic cricket is still high, even though it lacks of spur of Tests.

THE KIWIS

The Wellington Ground, where in 1978 New Zealand at long last secured that elusive victory over England. Boycott, who had put the opposition in to bat, had the unenviable distinction of being the first England captain to suffer defeat at the hands of the Kiwis

Although cricket was well established in New Zealand before 1900 with the first provincial match in 1860, and several sides had toured there, it has the least impressive record of all the Test-playing countries and did not succeed in beating England in a Test until 1978. There are various reasons for this, and for the comparatively small number of outstanding Kiwi players who have been produced over the years.

New Zealand is a small country with a population of some three million, but this does not entirely explain why their overall standard has not risen both faster and higher. After all, Barbados is much smaller yet has turned out far more world class players. What has held back the development of cricket is not merely the size of the country and the population, but the isolation. Apart from Australia, there are no other cricketing nations close by to stimulate interest and to provide opponents. It must also be admitted that the Australian authorities did not assist New Zealand cricket as much as they might have until well after the last war when air travel had opened up the world, and distances could be measured in hours rather than days and weeks. For instance, Sir Donald Bradman never batted there, and his presence in his prime would have given the game a tremendous boost.

To their credit the MCC did visit New Zealand every four years, but these tours usually took place after the battle for the Ashes and were therefore both short and, with the tourists already thinking of home, inevitably something of an anticlimax. This was a pity as New Zealand has much to offer any visitor, while the game itself would have benefited if more matches could have been played and more areas covered, even if the increased expenditure had not been covered by match receipts.

The amount of First Class cricket in New Zealand is strictly limited. Outside the Tests and games against touring teams, both of which have increased a lot in recent years, and the occasional trial, a player has to depend upon Plunket Shield contests, which provide him with only fifteen days of cricket in a season, insufficient training for a future international. Apart from that, he has to rely on club cricket. Although the standard is reasonable if not exceptional in the main cities, it is not very high in some of the country districts where the game is still played on the mat.

The financial resources of New Zealand cricket have always been small. The gate receipts, apart from Tests, are seldom enough to meet the running costs. As a result their players are amateurs, because there is not the money available to pay wages to a professional.

Nor is it a wealthy country, so the sporting sponsorships which have done so much for the game and its participants in England and Australia are on a much smaller scale. This is also reflected in the comparatively small remuneration given to their players when touring abroad.

New Zealand pitches are closer to those encountered in England than anywhere else in the world, usually on the slow side and inclined towards greenness and a low bounce. But their Test wickets are seldom as good because they do not and cannot receive as much attention.

Three of their Test grounds—Christchurch, Dunedin and Auckland—are used for rugby football in the winter, while soccer is played on the one at Wellington, which means the curator does not have the time in that climate to prepare an ideal international wicket. Although the same basic problem confronts the Australian groundsmen, they have the blessing of much more and far hotter sunshine. As a result they are able to transform what were muddy pieces of football ground into pitches with pace and bounce that will easily stand up to the demands of a five-day Test.

The slow, green Test wickets of New Zealand are a natural breeding ground for steady seamers and grafting batsmen. It is no surprise that they have produced a high quota of each. These conditions, of course, do not encourage the dashing stroke-maker who hits through the line of the ball, or the spinner, and both are in short supply.

Despite a continual battle to remain solvent, the sporting bodies in New Zealand are very efficient and methodical. Cricket is organized with almost as much thoroughness as is shown in their second religion, rugby, with the clubs formed into leagues and junior leagues.

Possibly the pursuit of points has become too intense and may be partially responsible for a rather serious and utilitarian approach, which encourages the reliable performer with bat and ball more than the romantic. As a result it might be said that New Zealand cricket is keen and honest, but short on panache and rather too stolid.

This contrasts sharply with the first New Zealand team to visit England in 1927 under Tom Lowry. It was not a great side, but it possessed a gaiety and sense of adventure far in excess of the Congdon team of 1973 which, though it was much stronger, was intrinsically rather dull and lacking in colour. Nevertheless, this 1973 side was arguably their strongest to tour England and came very close to obtaining that elusive victory in the first Test, when having been set to score a mammoth 479 to win, they eventually failed by a mere 38 runs, thanks very largely to 176 from Congdon, 116 from Pollard and 46 from Wadsworth. It was a gallant effort, made the more memorable by that fact that they had been shot out for a mere 97 in their first knock.

They followed this by having much the better of the second Test at Lord's, where they amassed 551 for 9, having first dismissed England for 253. England were saved by a long defensive innings of 178 from Fletcher, but it was still very close, as when Arnold the number ten joined Fletcher there were two hours remaining and the lead stood at a mere 70. Had the Surrey bowler not been put down behind the stumps off the third ball he received, the barrier against England would surely have been broken. Once again, it was Congdon with 178 who led the run-making after the first 2 wickets had gone for only 10. He received splendid support from his middle order, especially Hastings, Burgess and the battling Pollard.

To have twice gone so near was a bitter psychological blow, so it really was not surprising that the Kiwis should have blown up in the final match to be beaten by an innings. Thus, the series ended with them losing by two matches to nil with one match drawn, a scoreline which did not do them justice or adequately reflect the small difference between the teams.

In terms of results, the most successful to visit England was Walter Hadlee's side of 1949, who lost only one match and drew all four Tests. But it must be remembered that these Tests were all of only three days' duration, and the weather and the pitches were all plumb. England, too, were still recovering from the effects of the war, which apart from the deaths of two of their finest bowlers, Hedley Verity and Ken Farnes, had put them back a long way.

Nevertheless, Hadlee's team, which he led and nursed so well, did contain two master batsmen in Donnelly and Sutcliffe; above average batting support; two fine bowlers in Cowie, fastish, and Burtt, slow left-arm; the first view of Reid who was to become their greatest all-rounder, and excellent fielding.

Although there will be endless arguments about the respective merits of Martin Donnelly and Bert Sutcliffe, both were world class left-handers. Martin was the more brilliant, not unreminiscent of Neil Harvey at his best. He had the ability to destroy the opposition, would use the occasional unconventional stroke to hit a good length ball to the boundary, and thrived on the big occasion and extra pressure. He relied to a considerable extent on a combination of a wonderful eye and timing, which explains why, when he made a few appearances for Warwickshire and was not in full practice, it was hard to understand how he had come to be rated so highly.

Bert Sutcliffe was also an outstanding stroke-maker, who initially was prone to flirt dangerously outside the off stump, but his basic technique was more correct and more flowing. He would have served as a wonderful model for any aspiring player. Later, largely due to a nasty injury from a bouncer, he came to be suspect against real pace. Bert, like all New Zealand batsmen of the period, suffered from insufficient world class cricket, and when his team mates became over-dependent upon his runs, he lost some of his original freedom.

Although Cowie was thirty-seven when he went to England under Walter Hadlee and his pace was no more than fast-medium, he still proved extremely effective. In his pre-war prime 'Bull' was probably the best fast bowler New Zealand had ever had with a heart, strength and body action to match.

The New Zealand team which toured India, Pakistan and England in 1965 was led by John Reid and managed by Walter Hadlee, whose two sons were subsequently to play for their country. This was a useful side with the usual quota of competent seamers and some good batsmen, but a shade short of class at the highest level

One that got away: Ken Wadsworth, who was to die at the tragically early age of twenty-nine, drops Arnold second ball at Lord's in the second Test in 1973. If this chance had been taken, New Zealand would probably not have had to wait until 1978 for their first win over England

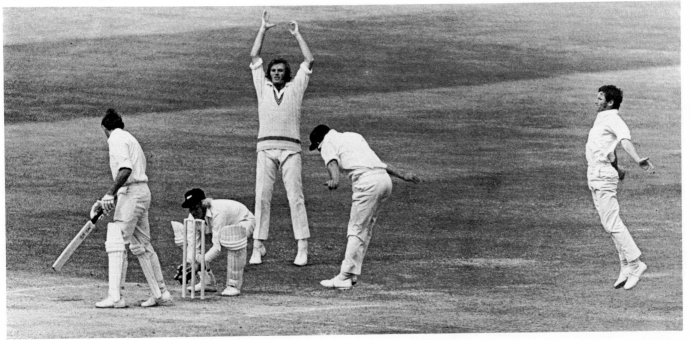

Tom Burtt was a classical slow left-armer with exceptional control and a natural flight. It is difficult to compare him with Hedley Howarth, who filled this role later, as conditions for the latter were in general less sympathetic to an orthodox spinner. It might be said that Tom's figures were better than expected and Hedley's not quite so good. Both were that New Zealand rarity, quality spinners, and to them could be added the fine leg-break bowler of the 1930s, Bill Merritt.

Undoubtedly New Zealand's best all-rounder was John Reid. A natural athlete, strongly built and a genuine competitor, he first came to the fore as a hard-hitting batsman and outstanding fielder, and later turned himself into a nagging medium-paced seamer-cum-off-cutter with a flat trajectory and rather ugly delivery, who gave little away, and picked up 85 wickets in Test cricket, which, taken in conjunction with nearly 3,500 runs from his bat, puts him among the great international all-rounders.

He will be remembered more for his batting than his bowling, and he suffered for most of his international career from playing for a team who were normally struggling. This is reflected by the fact that he went to the wicket 108 times in his fifty-eight appearances for his country. John would have done better if it had been possible for him to adopt his aggressive attacking approach more frequently. As a captain he was a sound, rather than a brilliant opponent, who never stopped fighting, but was handicapped by the material at his disposal and had to try to hide obvious deficiencies in both his team's batting line up and attack by his own tireless efforts.

Bevan Congdon was a very effective accumulator, who kept within his limitations, never gave his wicket away lightly, and always had to be prized out. One gained the impression he had made himself into a better batsman than his basic ability warranted through sheer unstinting application to the job in hand, not losing his wicket, and therefore inevitably scoring runs. His captaincy was similar to his batting. It lacked personal charisma and was sensible, serious and tactically rather predictable.

New Zealand have produced a number of competent batsmen who have scored plenty of

Bruce Taylor was a tall, rather ungainly, but very effective fast medium bowler. He had a wonderfully successful tour in the Caribbean in 1971–2, when he captured 27 wickets in 4 Tests. He was also a dangerous hard-hitting batsman

Above Glenn Turner, the most prolific run-getter ever produced by New Zealand, forces the ball through the covers. He is the latest man to make 1,000 runs before the end of May, and has proved a run-machine for Worcestershire

Below Bevan Congdon and Ian Chappell, two extremely determined protagonists, who never gave anything away, shaking hands prior to the first Test at Melbourne in December 1973

runs at international level, but have fallen a little short of true greatness. They include Dowling, a most impressive opener; Hastings, handsome and dashing; Burgess, colourful; and Pollard, somewhat cramped, but very tenacious.

Their most complete player after, or probably ahead of Bert Sutcliffe, is unquestionably Glenn Turner, who made his first tour to England in 1969 as a young novice and immediately showed an admirable defensive technique, with an exceptional application which enabled him to carry his bat for 43 at Lord's in the first Test. Although he had an insatiable appetite for batting, at that stage his repertoire of strokes was very limited. Subsequently he joined Worcestershire for whom he has scored heavily and consistently. When he played for New Zealand on their England tour in 1973, he became the first batsman to reach 1,000 runs before the end of May for thirty-five years. It was a remarkable performance, but his purple run spree did not eventually prove an asset to his side, for Glenn lost his edge and failed to enjoy the success in the ensuing Tests which had been expected and which might well have been the decisive factor. The vast quantity of runs he has accumulated over the years, as well as the highest Test average of any New Zealander, show Glenn to be a player of very high quality and one of the most accomplished openers in the world. In one-day cricket for his adopted country he has shown he has the ability to score quickly and improvise, but for such a fine craftsman the one criticism that could be made is that he does not dominate often enough in international matches, even though he makes the runs. But then the same could be said to apply to another exceptional acquirer of runs, Geoff Boycott. Both possess enormous powers of concentration and defences that make life very unpleasant for bowlers.

The weakness of New Zealand cricket since the last war might be termed a basic lack of experience, a shortage of high calibre stroke-makers, spin-bowlers and wicketkeepers to round off what have normally been good fielding sides. Their chief strength has been in the number of dependable seamers, normally brisk rather than genuinely fast.

For the most part they have tended to be tall, often gangling men with high arm actions, who have consequently been able to extract considerable bounce. Most of them have depended more upon movement off the pitch than through the air. One of the best was Tony McGibbon, who was also a stubborn batsman in the lower order and, although he took his cricket very seriously, never forgot that it was intended to be fun to play.

Bruce Taylor had practically no First Class experience when he was chosen to take part in one of the most ambitious of all overseas tours: India with four Tests, Pakistan with three Tests and finally England with three. His international debut could scarcely have been more impressive. At Calcutta against India, he not only struck a spectacular maiden century, but followed it up with 5 for 86. This suggested Bruce might develop into a great all-rounder, rather than the extremely good seamer and dangerous left-handed striker he became. One gains the impression he never quite reached his true potential, although his bowling throughout New Zealand's first tour of the Caribbean in 1971–2 was of the very best class.

In four Tests—a selectorial quirk caused him to be omitted from the first—Bruce took 27 wickets at only 17 apiece. The fact that all five Tests were drawn provided another example of the cautious streak which inhibits Kiwi cricket. Even so, to hold the West Indies was in itself a considerable achievement.

Dick Motz and the two Hadlee brothers, D. R. and R. J., were all well above average right-arm pace bowlers, and there was Collinge, a quick left-armer who never mastered the art of moving the ball back into a right-hand batsman from outside his off stump when operating from over the wicket. However, it could be said they were no better, and no worse, than a whole string of English country seamers who have made occasional appearances in the national team.

In recent years the NZCA have embarked on numerous tours abroad in an effort to raise the overall standard of their Test cricket. It has been partially successful. Their reasoning was sound: if they provided their best players with more experience at top level they would improve, and in the long run this would be reflected by a general raising of standards throughout their domestic cricket. But they have encountered one serious snag, the employers. In the past these had usually been only too willing to release men to play in the Plunket Shield and the Tests, and to make the rare overseas tour. Now that the demands on the time of the leading Kiwi cricketers are so greatly increased, employers have become understandably more reluctant. The outcome has been that many players have been forced to decline trips abroad and have retired too early because they were unwilling to jeopardize their future for the love of a game whose financial rewards are severely restricted. There are no large perks to be had from cricket in New Zealand as there are in Australia nor from a professional county system as in England. Also there are far fewer employers who can afford to be philanthropic.

Although New Zealand touring teams have always lacked sufficient world class players, they have been universally popular, and would walk away with a 'best tourist' title. They do not have the inborn aggressiveness and, sometimes, arrogance of the Australian, while they are less assured than the English cricketer, who has often played rather too much and has frequently acquired an exaggerated estimation of his ability and importance. To the New Zealander, a tour represents a chance to play the game he loves, and although his approach has become increasingly professional his basic outlook has remained amateur. This was typified by one of their bowlers in 1949. He measured out his run and then put down his cap as a marker, just as he might have done in some remote up-country game.

They may not have been able to teach their hosts very much about cricket, although they did win a series in Pakistan, but they could teach them plenty about modesty and manners not forgetting courage, epitomized in a never-to-be-forgotten day against South Africa in Johannesburg. Bob Blair was left behind in the hotel on hearing that his fiancée had been killed in a massive train disaster. Lawrie Miller and Bert Sutcliffe, badly injured by Neil Adcock, had retired hurt, and John Reid withstood a hammering that would have felled most men. At 57 for 5 the match looked over, but first Miller came in again and then Sutcliffe, his head swathed in bandages, hit a remarkable 80 not out.

At the fall of the ninth wicket everybody started to leave the field. Then Blair, putting aside personal tragedy, emerged to assist Bert to add a further 33 for the last wicket in what must have been emotionally one of the most remarkable stands in the history of the game.

THE PACKER REVOLUTION

Z97420077 Kerry Packer and Tony Greig on their way to the High Court for the hearing of their case against the ICC and the TCCB

The Packer Revolution of 1977, like all other revolts, did not just blow up overnight. Discontent among the professional players, mainly about financial rewards, had been simmering for a considerable time. To some extent this was due to an increasingly materialistic world, where grab had become the operative word and virtues such as honour and loyalty had been thrust into the background.

The game's rulers failed to recognize the danger signs and were caught unprepared when a human catalyst, in the shape of Kerry Packer, provided the rebels with the arms and the backing which all successful revolutions need.

The sun appeared to be smiling down on cricket in the summer of 1977. The recession of the 1960s was in the past and the future looked bright. The Centenary Test in Melbourne had exceeded even the dreams of the organizers, and was probably the most momentous occasion in the entire history of the game, when the vast majority of living cricketers who had taken part in an Anglo-Australian series in Australia were reunited under ideal conditions. The match itself provided excitement, entertainment and a wonderful finish. The fact that the only rain to fall came on the rest day and that the eventual Australian victory was by exactly the same margin as in the first encounter, one hundred years earlier, seemed to indicate that the Almighty also loves the game.

It was on this happy scene that a large cloud in the shape of the Packer Affair suddenly appeared out of what everyone believed to be a clear blue sky, and developed into the biggest international row cricket had ever experienced.

The origins were purely Australian, a dispute between Kerry Packer, a wealthy Australian TV Magnate, and the Australian Board of Control. He wanted the exclusive rights to televise Test cricket in Australia, but the Board sold these to the Australian Broadcasting Corporation, although, judging by the amount of money Packer paid to the TCCB for the Anglo-Australian series in England, he was more than prepared to outbid the ABC.

Packer was unhappy that his offer should have been rejected. He realized that international cricket was not only good televison, but that considering the amount of hours it used up it was also relatively cheap. He therefore decided to run his own series, and secretly signed up many of the finest cricketers in the world.

There were several reasons why he was able to do this with so little difficulty. First and foremost, the rewards for playing professional cricket were comparatively small and for some time the Test players had been casting envious eyes on the large attendances at international matches, the television receipts and the ever increasing sponsorship, of which only a very minute proportion was finding its way back into their own pockets.

In Australia, Ian Chappell had for many years been actively campaigning for a bigger slice of the cake, and Australian players, at least the star performers, were doing increasingly well out of the game, although most of them had other jobs. There was also a corps of cricketing mercenaries from overseas, who made their livelihood from county cricket during the summer and played for or in their own country during the winter. Not unnaturally, they were keen for more money.

A cricketer's remuneration certainly compared most unfavourably with what was available in most other professional sports, especially the individual ones like tennis and golf. Although it is also true that soccer players earn considerably more, the crowds are larger, while it should not be forgotten that the Football League is also some £14,000,000 in the red.

The fact of the matter is that cricket, as has been mentioned elsewhere, is economically a bad game. The controlling bodies, who are responsible for the welfare of the sport at all levels, had used the considerable sums that had come to them via Test matches, television and sponsorship for the game as a whole, rather than to pay the high wages which the leading participants could with much justification claim they deserved. The authorities based their argument on the fact that the normal three-day county match simply could not occur if it was not subsidized from other sources.

The players signed for Packer because his contract gave them more money than they

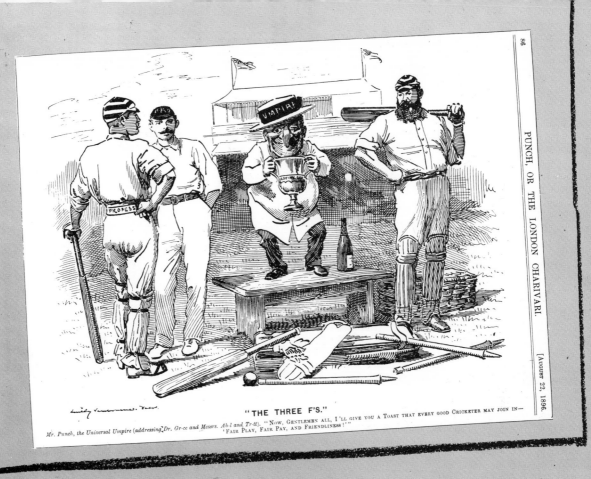

PUNCH, OR THE LONDON CHARIVARI.

[AUGUST 22, 1896.

"THE THREE F'S."

Mr. Punch, the Universal Umpire (addressing Dr. Gr-ce and Messrs. Ab-l and Tr-tt). "NOW, GENTLEMEN ALL, I'LL GIVE YOU A TOAST THAT EVERY GOOD CRICKETER MAY JOIN IN— 'FAIR PLAY, FAIR PAY, AND FRIENDLINESS!'"

could otherwise have hoped to make at the time directly from cricket.

The second reason for Packer's success was that he acquired the services of Tony Greig, the current England captain who, eloquent and charming, was the ideal person to convince any players with reservations about the deal. They knew for a start that he was already doing extremely well out of the game, so that if he was prepared to take the risk, it should surely be worth their while.

Tony started by obtaining the services of Underwood and Knott, the two other members of the England XI who were of genuine international class and had enjoyed large, lucrative, tax-free Benefits. He also had no problems with Snow, who was in the twilight of his career and must have thought of Packer as Father Christmas.

After the Centenary Test, Tony flew to the Caribbean, where the West Indies were playing Pakistan. He had little difficulty in convincing players in both teams of the obvious financial advantages in joining the Packer brigade.

The South African contingent, who were barred from Test cricket, were an even easier

target, while the Chappell brothers were ideally equipped to quell any doubts among Australian cricketers, some of whom, judging by their performances in England, really should be paying Packer to be allowed to take part.

Third, the ICC, who represent the Test playing countries of the world, were caught sleeping, because like most amateur controlling bodies they were conservative in outlook, honest, narrow and absolutely convinced that they were invariably right. It had never occured to them that anyone would attempt to run a pirate series, which was not under their jurisdiction, undermined their authority, and was in their eyes a threat to the future of the game, because it would inevitably have an adverse effect on the India *v.* Australia series, and must also lessen interest in England's tours to Pakistan and New Zealand.

Finally, the whole operation was carried out with a secrecy which in itself was remarkable, as cricket gossip tends to travel fast. This was the result of a most attractive downpayment to the players with a heavy penalty clause for betrayal.

The intention was to announce the pirate

series in mid-June, by which time two of the principal participants, Tony Greig and Greg Chappell, would have been the respective captains in the fight for the Ashes, and the ICC would then have been presented with what was virtually a coup d'état.

However, the story broke in the *Daily Mail* in early May, though it had leaked out two weeks earlier in South Africa. An astonished cricket world learned that Kerry Packer had clandestinely signed up, with the active assistance of the captains of England, Australia, Pakistan and the West Indies, a large number of the finest players in the world for an unofficial Test series in Australia during the following winter.

The TCCB and the Selectors, not surprisingly, felt that Tony Greig's role as an undercover agent was scarcely fitting for the England captain, and promptly appointed Mike Brearly in his place. They then, quite logically, decided that defectors to the Packer camp would be available for selection against Australia that summer, as a high percentage of the opposition had done likewise. It could also be argued that the actions of the Australian players were far more serious, in that they were deliberately taking part in an exercise which obviously posed a serious threat to the welfare of their own cricket in their own country.

Tony Greig claimed that his actions were for the good of county players, arguing that if the stars received more money, this would eventually filter down to the lower ranks. His argument overlooked two points, the extent that existing international matches subsidized the game at all levels, and the danger of following the disastrous course of English League Football, where the players had been allowed to take more out of the game than the game has to give. He would have been more convincing if he had admitted that he had taken the opportunity of making a great deal of money in a short period, and that with his South African background, Australia was the ideal place to plan for his ultimate future. Nobody could blame him for that decision, though it is feasible that he was naive enough to believe he was leading a genuine crusade, as distinct from a well organized revolt which suited Packer's economic plans. After all, his use of the word 'grovel' about the West Indies

Caricature of W. G. Grace by Max Beerbohm. Grace is holding a cheque signed by the Editor of the *Daily Telegraph*, who ran a highly successful fund on his behalf in 1895

had suggested a certain simplicity in matters which were unconnected with money. It showed again when Greig said that he had not consulted Lord's before signing because they could not have kept the matter quiet. This was perfectly true, but he expected them to compromise or to surrender unconditionally so that he could enjoy the best of all worlds.

Kerry Packer also talked glibly about compromise with all the confidence of a poker player holding a running flush and a limitless supply of cash to back it up. In the light of future events in the high court, this confidence proved to be well justified.

The ICC, never noted for haste, or singleness of purpose, eventually met at Lord's and issued a long statement underlining the threat which they considered the unofficial series represented to the international cricket world. They felt that it could well undermine the status of Tests on which the game was so dependent, but they did agree to meet Kerry Packer to see if an arrangment satisfactory to all parties could be achieved.

The meeting between Packer and representatives of the ICC took place at Lord's in late June. The ICC were prepared to give the Packer series their practical support, providing he was prepared to abide by the following five conditions:

1 The programme and venues were to be acceptable to the home authority and the length of programme was to be six weeks, unless otherwise agreed. The matches would be under the control of the home authority and played in accordance with the Laws of Cricket.

2 No player was participate in these games without the permission of his home authority; this permission would not be withheld unreasonably.

3 No teams taking part in these matches could be represented as national teams (i.e. not Australia; possibly an Australian XI).

4 Players contracted to Mr Packer were to be available for Test matches, First Class fixtures and other home authority sponsored matches where there was no clash.

5 The home authority must be able to honour all contractual commitments to existing sponsors and advertisers.

Whether these reasonable requests could have been acceptable will never be known, because Packer demanded that his company be given the absolute guarantee of the exclusive television rights to cover Australian cricket when the present contract expired in 1978–9. This was not within the powers of the ICC to grant, and the meeting broke up, which was tantamount to war between the Packer organization and the governing bodies of cricket: a view which was substantiated by Packer's bellicose pronouncements immediately afterwards.

Before the ICC met again to decide what action to take against the rebels, Packer announced that he would be taking legal action against anyone who banned his players, claiming restrait of trade. He also claimed that the authorities were using double standards, in that they were allowing his players to perform in the present series without a penalty, conveniently overlooking one point, that until such time as the Packer Circus actually took place there was no logical reason for banning them.

The ICC met in late July and acted with complete and very unusual unamimity. They formally disapproved of any matches which took place without their consent. They stated that any player who took part in games of this nature after October would automatically be ineligible for Test cricket, and these games would not rank as First Class, or appear in the official records. They also strongly recommended individual contries to extend this ban to all cricket under their jurisdiction.

The conference took this strong line because they believed that the Packer circus and any other future venture of the same type would seriously damage the entire structure of the game.

This decision had one immediate effect. Jeff Thomson announced his withdrawal from the Packer series, and he was followed shortly afterwards by Alvin Kallicharran.

The situation inevitably saddened anybody who really cared for cricket. If the ICC were allowed to implement their new laws, the game would be devalued at international level, because England, Australia, Pakistan and especially the West Indies would not be able to field their strongest team. Conversely, it could be argued that it was unsatisfactory that cricket should be run by businessmen like Packer, whose interests, as he repeatedly emphasized, were above all commercial. He certainly did not possess the same love and knowledge of the game as any of the representatives of the ICC, though he did have considerably more money and business acumen.

From the point of view of England Test cricketers, the Packer threat was responsible, almost immediately, for a considerable increase in their earnings for representing their country both at home and abroad. If this had occurred earlier Underwood and Knott might possibly have had second thoughts about signing for Packer.

The cricket authorities suddenly realized that they might lose even more players if the rewards did not improve, and that others might follow those who had already signed, which was particularly worrying because the team was showing a considerable improvement.

The first positive move to change this trend originated from a Mr Evans, who ran an office cleaning business. His proposal was that England Test cricketers should receive £1,000 per Test, while an additional £1,000 per annum should be paid to a squad of fifty chosen by the Selectors. This proposal was sensible in conception, but unsatisfactory in

practice, when it became clear that the half million pounds which his organization was prepared to invest in the project was dependent upon it receiving an additional million pounds' worth of business per annum.

With two defections from his squad and possible further English recruits carefully weighing up the pros and cons, Packer reappeared in London and announced that he would start legal proceedings against the ICC and the TCCB on the grounds that the new laws passed by the ICC constituted a restraint of trade. He was obviously on a good wicket, but the cricket authorities failed to appreciate this, a costly mistake.

If they wanted to ban the Packer players from county cricket, all they needed to do (assuming that the individual counties were prepared to abide by the recommendation of their controlling body) was to pay them their summer wages—this would have cost about £75,000 and would have been provided out of TCCB funds—and then sent them off to play in their 2nd XI. It might have been a nasty solution, but would have been far less expensive than a court case.

During the Final Test at the Oval, the Cornhill Insurance Company announced that they would sponsor England cricket to the tune of £200,000 per annum for the next three years on the proviso that payments to Test players would be substantially increased, both at home and abroad.

Although the TCCB had been talking about Test Match sponsorship for several years, and had been seriously looking for the previous eighteen months, it is safe to say that the Cornhill Insurance Company would never have come in at the end of the season if Mr Evans had not drawn their attention to the problems caused by Packer and the need for an immediate injection of cash if the national team was not to be in serious danger of losing more key players to the lure of big money in Australia.

The legal proceedings which Packer instigated against the ICC and the TCCB were brought by his company, World Series Cricket Pty Ltd, and three individual members of his World XI, Tony Grieg, John Snow and Mike Procter. They claimed that the proposed ban by the ICC and the TCCB constituted unjustified restraint of trade and

"Most of the cricketers dropped out, Kerry—but I got a couple of footballers at half a million each!"

"I regret I can no longer continue with this case. Kerry Packer has just signed me up as an umpire."

CAPTAIN'S KNOCK!

an unlawful inducement to players to break contracts with Mr Packer.

On 25 November 1977, after a High Court battle which had dragged on for thirty-one days, Mr Justice Slade predictably ruled that the ban introduced by the TCCB was illegal because it represented an unreasonable restraint on trade and an inducement for players to break their contracts with Mr Packer.

The judge underlined the cricketer's rights to make a living, and he rejected the argument that it was morally wrong for players to sign for Packer. It was 'straining the concept of loyalty', he said, to expect cricketers to enter into self denying ordinances during the winter.

He could see no reason why the players—'with the possible exception of Mr Greig'—could be criticized on moral grounds for secretly signing contracts with Mr Packer.

Mr Justice Slade said that a challenge to the conventional structure of First Class cricket from a private promoter had been 'bound to come sooner rather than later', but the risk of it happening might have been less if official cricket had offered the most talented players a secure and more remunerative career structure.

Although Mr Packer had bowled out the cricket rulers expensively in the High Court and had won his case, the game itself was certainly the poorer, but whether it will in the long run also be the loser, time alone will tell.

While Mr Justice Slade was pronouncing judgement, the Packer Circus had already started in Australia to the accompaniment of the biggest publicity barrage ever. Despite this the crowds, except for the new innovation, night cricket, were fairly small, and few would now be able to recall the results of that first Australian summer. It was also significant that the Packer Programme for 1978-9 was deliberately designed not to clash with the Anglo-Australian Tests—not, one feels, to placate the Australian Board of Control, but to avoid the competition.

However, the success of the Packer Circus will ultimately depend not on gate receipts but on the number of television viewers and whether advertisers will be prepared to buy space on the programme.

The considerable ingenuity which Packer

has displayed in staging his pirate series, despite numerous problems and the vast amount of money he has expended, suggest that he has something to offer cricket. The pity is that he has been working against the game's rulers rather than with them.

The four Test-playing countries which originally lost players to the WCS were Australia, England, Pakistan and the West Indies. Predictably, the reactions of the four boards were different. The first two decided to exclude those who had signed for Packer from the Test teams for the forseeable future. They really had no alternative, as apart from anything else the other players would not have accepted them. It was also true that while both countries might miss their Packer men, they were not essential.

Pakistan, with fewer quality cricketers to select and short of the money needed to compete with the WCS, tried to do without their Packer men. They paid the price of a disastrous tour to England and have predictably recalled them for the Tests against India.

The West Indies wanted to compromise. Not only did they lose virtually the whole of the strongest side in the world to the WCS, but the majority of their players were already cricket mercenaries. It was therefore logical that the West Indies should have included their Packer men when Australia toured the Caribbean in 1978. What was slightly surprising was that the Australian players met them without the vigorous protest that the England players would have made. But a major row developed over the composition of the side for the third Test. Lloyd resigned the captaincy and those with Packer contracts refused to play. It was a classic example of the new player power and stemmed from the dropping of Murray, the group's unofficial shop steward, and a lack of discipline from the WCS administrators, who managed to upset the only board which was sympathetic.

At a meeting of the Cricketers Association, representing all the county players, before the commencement of the 1978 season, many urged that WCS players should be excluded from the county and the international circuits, while others favoured a compromise.

After the Slade judgement, the county clubs had to offer contracts to all their Packer players, but there was a curious lack of unanimity. Some, like Gloucestershire, wanted them back. Others, like Warwickshire, who did not renew the contract of Amiss at the end of the summer although he was the only player to score 2,000 runs, had them on sufferance.

Midway through the summer the President and Secretary of the MCC secretly met two Packer representatives in New York to discuss a compromise. It was hardly surprising that the WCS proposal—as much as ten months of WCS cricket in one calendar year with the full approval and recognition of the ICC—was rejected by the ICC. Later, however, the two WCS men claimed that their proposals had only been intended as a starting point for negotiations and that their real aim was an officially recognized six-week World Cup competition in Australia after the end of the traditional Test series, though the WCS would presumably continue to operate at other periods in Australia.

The long term danger of the Packer Revolution is that it could harm the game. By seriously weakening the governing bodies of the sport, it has opened the way for financial exploitation. Once the players, or sponsorships, become more important than the game itself it is heading for oblivion, for power without responsibility leads to anarchy. Although the Laws of Cricket are not perfect, they have been gradually drawn up over the years for the benefit of the game. If amendments were made to suit the particular requirements of television this would not be healthy.

Erratum

The right-hand illustration on page 94 is of Barry, not Vivian, Richards. The caption should read:
'Barry Richards is a master of playing a technically correct scoring stroke in a slightly unusual manner. In this picture, against Kent in a Benson and Hedges match, he is giving himself a little extra room to force a ball from on off his stumps through a gap in the offside.'

RECORDS
compiled by Bill Frindall

These Records are correct up to the end of September 1978.

First Class Cricket

TEAM RECORDS

HIGHEST TOTALS

1,107	**Victoria** v. New South Wales Melbourne	1926-27
1,059	Victoria v. Tasmania Melbourne	1922-23
951-7d.	Sind v. Baluchistan Karachi	1973-74
918	New South Wales v. South Australia Sydney	1900-01
912-8d.	Holkar v. Mysore Indore	1945-46
910-6d.	Railways v. Dera Ismail Khan Lahore	1964-65
903-7d.	England v. Australia The Oval	1938
887	Yorkshire v. Warwickshire Birmingham	1896

LOWEST TOTALS

12†	**Oxford U.** v. MCC and Ground Oxford	1877
12	**Northamptonshire** v. Gloucestershire Gloucester	1907
13	Wellington v. Nelson Nelson	1862-63
13	Auckland v. Canterbury Auckland	1877-78
13	Nottinghamshire v. Yorkshire Nottingham	1901
15	MCC v. Surrey Lord's	1839
15†	Victoria v. MCC Melbourne	1903-04
15†	Northamptonshire v. Yorkshire Northampton	1908
15	Hampshire v. Warwickshire Birmingham	1922

†*One batsman was absent*

HIGHEST AGGREGATES

Runs	Wkts		
2,376	38	**Maharashtra** v. Bombay Poona	1948-49
2,078	40	Bombay v. Holkar Bombay	1944-45
1,981	35	England v. South Africa Durban	1938-39
1,929	39	New South Wales v. South Australia Sydney	1925-26
1,911	34	New South Wales v. Victoria Sydney	1908-09
1,905	40	Otago v. Wellington Dunedin	1923-24

LARGEST MARGINS OF VICTORY

Largest Innings Victories

Inns and 851 runs	**Railways (910-6d)** v. Dera Ismail Khan Lahore	1964-65
Inns and 666 runs	Victoria (1,059) v. Tasmania Melbourne	1922-23
Inns and 656 runs	Victoria (1,107) v. New South Wales Melbourne	1926-27
Inns and 605 runs	New South Wales (918) v. South Australia Sydney	1900-01
Inns and 579 runs	England (903-7d.) v. Australia The Oval	1938
Inns and 575 runs	Sind (951-7d.) v. Baluchistan Karachi	1973-74
Inns and 527 runs	New South Wales (713) v. South Australia Adelaide	1908-09
Inns and 517 runs	Australians (675) v. Nottinghamshire Nottingham	1921

Largest Victories by Runs Margins

685 runs	**New South Wales (235 and 761-8d.)** v. Queensland Sydney	1929-30
609 runs	Muslim Commercial Bank (575 and 208-0d) v. W.A.P.D.A. Hyderabad	1977-78
675 runs	England (521 and 342-8d.) v. Australia Brisbane	1928-29
638 runs	New South Wales (304 and 770) v. South Australia Adelaide	1920-21
571 runs	Victoria (304 and 649) v. South Australia Adelaide	1926-27
562 runs	Australia (701 and 327) v. England The Oval	1934

Victory Without Losing a Wicket

Lancashire (166-0d. and 66-0) beat Leicestershire by 10 wkts. Manchester	1956
Karachti 'A' (277-0d.) beat Sind 'A' by an inns and 77 runs Karachi	1957-58
Railways (236-0d. and 16-0) beat Jammu and Kashmir by 10 wkts Srinagar	1960-61
Karnataka (451-0d.) beat Kerala by an inns and 186 runs Chickmagular	1977-78

BATTING RECORDS
HIGHEST CAREER AGGREGATES (30,000 RUNS)

(*Not Out)	Career	I.	N.O.	H.S.	Runs	Av.	100
J. B. Hobbs	1905-34	1,315	106	316*	**61,237**	.50.65	197
F. E. Woolley	1906-38	1,532	85	305*	58,969	40.75	145
E. H. Hendren	1907-38	1,300	166	301*	57,611	50.80	170
C. P. Mead	1905-36	1,340	185	280*	55,061	47.67	153
W. G. Grace	1865-1908	1,493	105	344	54,896	39.55	126
W. R. Hammond	1920-51	1,004	104	336*	50,493	56.10	167
H. Sutcliffe	1919-45	1,087	123	313	50,135	52.00	149
T. W. Graveney	1948-71	1,223	159	258	47,793	44.91	122
T. W. Hayward	1893-1914	1,138	96	315*	43,551	41.79	104
M. C. Cowdrey	1950-76	1,130	134	307	42,719	42.89	107
A. Sandham	1911-37	1,000	79	325	41,283	44.82	107
L. Hutton	1934-60	814	91	364	40,140	55.51	129
M. J. K. Smith	1951-75	1,091	139	204	39,832	41.84	69
W. Rhodes	1898-1930	1,528	237	267*	39,802	30.83	58
J. H. Edrich	1956-78	979	104	310*	39,790	45.47	103
R. E. S. Wyatt	1923-57	1,141	157	232	39,404	40.04	85
D. C. S. Compton	1936-64	839	88	300	38,942	51.85	123
E. Tyldesley	1909-36	961	106	256*	38,874	45.46	102
J. T. Tyldesley	1895-1923	994	62	295*	37,897	40.66	86
J. W. Hearne	1909-36	1,025	116	285*	37,252	40.98	96
L. E. G. Ames	1926-51	950	95	295	37,245	43.56	102
D. Kenyon	1946-67	1,159	59	259	37,002	33.63	74
W. J. Edrich	1934-58	964	92	267*	36,965	42.39	86
J. M. Parks	1949-76	1,227	172	205*	36,673	34.76	51
D. Denton	1894-1920	1,163	70	221	36,479	33.37	69
G. H. Hirst	1889-1929	1,215	151	341	36,323	34.13	60
W. G. Quaife	1894-1928	1,203	186	255*	36,021	35.41	72
R. E. Marshall	1946-72	1,053	59	228*	35,725	35.94	68
G. Gunn	1902-32	1,061	82	220	35,208	35.96	62
D. B. Close	1949-78	1,217	169	198	34,833	33.23	52
John Langridge	1928-55	984	66	250*	34,380	37.45	76
C. Washbrook	1933-64	906	107	251*	34,101	42.67	76
G. Boycott	1962-78	696	103	261*	33,690	56.81	109
M. Leyland	1920-48	932	101	263	33,659	40.50	80
H. T. W. Hardinge	1902-33	1,021	103	263*	33,519	36.51	75
R. Abel	1881-1904	994	73	357*	32,669	35.47	74
C. A. Milton	1948-74	1,078	125	170	32,150	33.73	56
J. D. B. Robertson	1937-59	897	46	331*	31,914	37.50	67
J. Hardstaff, jr.	1930-55	812	94	266	31,847	44.35	83
James Langridge	1924-53	1,058	157	167	31,716	35.20	42
K. F. Barrington	1953-68	831	136	256	31,714	45.63	76
C. B. Fry	1892-1921	658	43	258*	30,886	50.22	94
D. Brookes	1934-59	925	70	257	30,874	36.10	71
P. Holmes	1913-35	810	84	315*	30,574	42.11	67
R. T. Simpson	1944-63	852	55	259	30,546	38.32	64
L. G. Berry	1924-51	1,056	57	232	30,225	30.25	45
K. G. Suttle	1949-71	1,064	92	204*	30,225	31.09	49

HIGHEST SEASON AGGREGATES (3,000 RUNS)

(*Not Out)	Season	I	N.O.	H.S.	Runs	Av.	100s
D. C. S. Compton	1947	50	8	246	**3,816**	90.85	18
W. J. Edrich	1947	52	8	267*	3,539	80.43	12
T. W. Hayward	1906	61	8	219	3,518	66.37	13
L. Hutton	1949	56	6	269*	3,429	68.58	12
F. E. Woolley	1928	59	4	198	3,352	60.94	12
H. Sutcliffe	1932	52	7	313	3,336	74.13	14
W. R. Hammond	1933	54	5	264	3,323	67.81	13
E. H. Hendren	1928	54	7	209*	3,311	70.44	13
R. Abel	1901	68	8	247	3,309	55.15	7
W. R. Hammond	1937	55	5	217	3,252	65.04	13
M. J. K. Smith	1959	67	11	200*	3,245	57.94	8
E. H. Hendren	1933	65	9	301*	3,186	56.89	11
C. P. Mead	1921	52	6	280*	3,179	69.10	10
T. W. Hayward	1904	63	5	203	3,170	54.65	11
K. S. Ranjitsinhji	1899	58	8	197	3,159	63.18	8
C. B. Fry	1901	43	3	244	3,147	78.67	13
K. S. Ranjitsinhji	1900	40	5	275	3,065	87.57	11
L. E. G. Ames	1933	57	5	295	3,058	58.80	9
J. T. Tyldesley	1901	60	5	221	3,041	55.29	9
C. P. Mead	1928	50	10	180	3,027	75.67	13
J. B. Hobbs	1925	48	5	266*	3,024	70.32	16
E. Tyldesley	1928	48	10	242	3,024	79.57	10
W. E. Alley	1961	64	11	221*	3,019	56.96	11
W. R. Hammond	1938	42	2	271	3,011	75.27	15
E. H. Hendren	1923	51	12	200*	3,010	77.17	13
H. Sutcliffe	1931	42	11	230	3,006	96.96	13
J. H. Parks	1937	63	4	168	3,003	50.89	11
H. Sutcliffe	1928	44	5	228	3,002	76.97	13

RECORD SEASON AGGREGATES OUTSIDE ENGLAND

(*Not Out)	Season	I.	N.O.	H.S.	Runs	Av.	100s
In Australia							
D. G. Bradman	1928-29	24	6	340*	**1,690**	93.88	7
In South Africa							
J. R. Reid	1961-62	30	2	203	**1,915**	68.39	7
In West Indies							
E. H. Hendren	1929-30	18	5	254*	**1,765**	135.76	6
In New Zealand							
G. M. Turner	1975-76	20	4	177*	**1,244**	77.75	5
In India							
C. G. Borde	1964-65	28	3	168	**1,604**	64.16	6
In Pakistan							
Zaheer Abbas	1973-74	24	5	174	**1,597**	84.05	5

RECORD SEASON BATTING AVERAGES IN ENGLAND

(Qualification: 12 innings)

(*Not Out)	Season	I.	N.O.	H.S.	Runs	Av.	100s
D. G. Bradman	1938	26	5	278	2,429	**115.66**	13
W. A. Johnston	1953	17	16	28*	102	102.00	0
G. Boycott	1971	30	5	233	2,503	100.12	13
D. G. Bradman	1930	36	6	334	2,960	98.66	10
H. Sutcliffe	1931	42	11	230	3,006	96.96	13
R. M. Poore	1899	21	4	304	1,551	91.23	7
D. R. Jardine	1927	14	3	147	1,002	91.09	5
D. C. S. Compton	1947	50	8	246	3,816	90.85	18

HIGHEST INDIVIDUAL SCORES

(*Not Out)

Score	Player	Match	Venue	Season
499	**Hanif Mohammad**	Karachi v. Bahawalpur	Karachi	1958-59
452*	D. G. Bradman	New South Wales v. Queensland	Sydney	1929-30
443*	B. B. Nimbalkar	Maharashtra v. Kathiawar	Poona	1948-49
437	W. H. Ponsford	Victoria v. Queensland	Melbourne	1927-28
429	W. H. Ponsford	Victoria v. Tasmania	Melbourne	1922-23
428	Aftab Baloch	Sind v. Baluchistan	Karachi	1973-74
424	A. C. MacLaren	Lancashire v. Somerset	Taunton	1895
385	B. Sutcliffe	Otago v. Canterbury	Christchurch	1952-53
383	C. W. Gregory	New South Wales v. Queensland	Brisbane	1906-07
369	D. G. Bradman	South Australia v. Tasmania	Adelaide	1935-36
365*	C. Hill	South Australia v. New South Wales	Adelaide	1900-01
365*	G. St A. Sobers	West Indies v. Pakistan	Kingston	1957-58
364	L. Hutton	England v. Australia	The Oval	1938
359*	V. M. Merchant	Bombay v. Maharashtra	Bombay	1943-44
359	R. B. Simpson	New South Wales v. Queensland	Brisbane	1963-64
357*	R. Abel	Surrey v. Somerset	The Oval	1899
357	D. G. Bradman	South Australia v. Victoria	Melbourne	1935-36
356	B. A. Richards	South Australia v. Western Australia	Perth	1970-71
355	B. Sutcliffe	Otago v. Auckland	Dunedin	1949-50
352	W. H. Ponsford	Victoria v. New South Wales	Melbourne	1926-27
350	Rashid Israr	Habib Bank v. National Bank	Lahore	1976-77
345	C. G. Macartney	Australians v. Nottinghamshire	Nottingham	1921
344*	G. A. Headley	Jamaica v. Lord Tennyson's XI	Kingston	1931-32
344	W. G. Grace	MCC v. Kent	Canterbury	1876
343*	P. A. Perrin	Essex v. Derbyshire	Chesterfield	1904
341	G. H. Hirst	Yorkshire v. Leicestershire	Leicester	1905
340*	D. G. Bradman	New South Wales v. Victoria	Sydney	1928-29
338*	R. C. Blunt	Otago v. Canterbury	Christchurch	1931-32
338	W. W. Read	Surrey v. Oxford U.	The Oval	1888
337*	Pervez Akhtar	Railways v. Dera Ismail Khan	Lahore	1964-65
337	Hanif Mohammad	Pakistan v. West Indies	Bridgetown	1957-58
336*	W. R. Hammond	England v. New Zealand	Auckland	1932-33
336	W. H. Ponsford	Victoria v. South Australia	Melbourne	1927-28
334	D. G. Bradman	Australia v. England	Leeds	1930
333	K. S. Duleepsinhji	Sussex v. Northamptonshire	Hove	1930
332	W. H. Ashdown	Kent v. Essex	Brentwood	1934
331*	J. D. B. Robertson	Middlesex v. Worcestershire	Worcester	1949
325*	H. L. Hendry	Victoria v. New Zealanders	Melbourne	1925-26
325	C. L. Badcock	South Australia v. Victoria	Adelaide	1935-36
325	A. Sandham	England v. West Indies	Kingston	1929-30
324	J. B. Stollmeyer	Trinidad v. British Guiana	Port-of-Spain	1946-47
324	Waheed Mirza	Karachi Whites v. Quetta	Karachi	1976-77
323	A. L. Wadekar	Bombay v. Mysore	Bombay	1966-67
322	E. Paynter	Lancashire v. Sussex	Hove	1937
321	W. L. Murdoch	New South Wales v. Victoria	Sydney	1881-82
319	Gul Mahomed	Baroda v. Holkar	Baroda	1946-47
318*	W. G. Grace	Gloucestershire v. Yorkshire	Cheltenham	1876
317	W. R. Hammond	Gloucestershire v. Nottinghamshire	Gloucester	1936
316*	V. S. Hazare	Maharashtra v. Baroda	Poona	1939-40
316*	J. B. Hobbs	Surrey v. Middlesex	Lord's	1926
316	R. H. Moore	Hampshire v. Warwickshire	Bournemouth	1937
315*	T. W. Hayward	Surrey v. Lancashire	The Oval	1898
315*	P. Holmes	Yorkshire v. Middlesex	Lord's	1925
315*	A. F. Kippax	New South Wales v. Queensland	Sydney	1927-28
314*	C. L. Walcott	Barbados v. Trinidad	Port-of-Spain	1945-46
313	H. Sutcliffe	Yorkshire v. Essex	Leyton	1932
312*	W. W. Keeton	Nottinghamshire v. Middlesex	The Oval	1939
312*	J. M. Brearley	MCC Under-25 v. N. Zone	Peshawar	1966-67
311	J. T. Brown	Yorkshire v. Sussex	Sheffield	1897
311	R. B. Simpson	Australia v. England	Manchester	1964
311	Javed Miandad	Karachi Whites v. National Bank	Karachi	1974-75
310*	J. H. Edrich	England v. New Zealand	Leeds	1965
310	H. Gimblett	Somerset v. Sussex	Eastbourne	1948
309	V. S. Hazare	The Rest v. Hindus	Bombay	1943-44
308*	F. M. M. Worrell	Barbados v. Trinidad	Bridgetown	1943-44
307	M. C. Cowdrey	MCC v. South Australia	Adelaide	1962-63
307	R. M. Cowper	Australia v. England	Melbourne	1965-66
306*	A. Ducat	Surrey v. Oxford U.	The Oval	1919
306*	E. A. B. Rowan	Transvaal v. Natal	Johannesburg	1939-40
305*	F. E. Woolley	MCC v. Tasmania	Hobart	1911-12
305*	F. R. Foster	Warwickshire v. Worcestershire	Dudley	1914

305*	W. H. Ashdown	Kent v. Derbyshire Dover	1935
304*	P. H. Tarilton	Barbados v. Trinidad Bridgetown	1919-20
304*	A. W. Nourse	Natal v. Transvaal Johannesburg	1919-20
304*	E. de C. Weekes	West Indies v. Cambridge U. Cambridge	1950
304	R. M. Poore	Hampshire v. Somerset Taunton	1899
304	D. G. Bradman	Australia v. England Leeds	1934
303*	W. W. Armstrong	Australians v. Somerset Bath	1905
303*	Mushtaq Mohammad	Karachi Blues v. Karachi U. Karachi	1967-68
302*	P. Holmes	Yorkshire v. Hampshire Portsmouth	1920
302*	W. R. Hammond	Gloucestershire v. Glamorgan Bristol	1934
302	W. R. Hammond	Gloucestershire v. Glamorgan Newport	1939
302	L. G. Rowe	West Indies v. England Bridgetown	1973-74
301*	E. H. Hendren	Middlesex v. Worcestershire Dudley	1933
301	W. G. Grace	Gloucestershire v. Sussex Bristol	1896
300*	V. T. Trumper	Australians v. Sussex Hove	1899
300*	F. Watson	Lancashire v. Surrey Manchester	1928
300*	Imtiaz Ahmed	P.M.'s XI v. Commonwealth XI Bombay	1950-51
300	J. T. Brown	Yorkshire v. Derbyshire Chesterfield	1898
300	D. C. S. Compton	MCC v. N.E. Transvaal Benoni	1948-49
300	R. Subba Row	Northamptonshire v. Surrey The Oval	1958

Mansell Collection

MOST HUNDREDS IN A CAREER (100 OR MORE)

	Career	100s	First	100th	Last	Inns for 100
J. B. Hobbs	1905-34	**197**	1905	1923	1934	821
E. H. Hendren	1907-38	170	1911	1928	1937	740
W. R. Hammond	1920-51	167	1923	1935	1947	679
C. P. Mead	1905-36	153	1906	1927	1936	892
H. Sutcliffe	1919-45	149	1919	1932	1939	700
F. E. Woolley	1906-38	145	1906	1929	1938	1,031
L. Hutton	1934-60	129	1934	1951	1955	619
W. G. Grace	1865-1908	126	1866	1895	1904	1,113
D. C. S. Compton	1936-64	123	1936	1952	1964	552
T. W. Graveney	1948-71	122	1948	1964	1970	940
D. G. Bradman	1927-49	117	1927	1947	1948	295
G. Boycott	1962-78	109	1963	1977	1978	645
M. C. Cowdrey	1950-76	107	1951	1973	1975	1,035
A. Sandham	1911-37	107	1913	1935	1937	871
T. W. Hayward	1893-1914	104	1893	1913	1914	1,076
J. H. Edrich	1956-78	103	1959	1977	1978	945
L. E. G. Ames	1926-51	102	1926	1950	1951	915
E. Tyldesley	1909-36	102	1912	1934	1935	919

MOST HUNDREDS IN A SEASON

18 **D. C. S. Compton** in 1947
16 J. B. Hobbs in 1925

SIX HUNDREDS IN SUCCESSION

C. B. Fry in 1901
D. G. Bradman in 1938-39
M. J. Procter in 1970-71

FASTEST INNINGS

50:	8 min. C. Inman	Leicestershire v. Nottinghamshire Nottingham	1965
100:	35 min. P. G. H. Fender	Surrey v. Northamptonshire Northampton	1920
200:	120 min. G. L. Jessop	Gloucestershire v. Sussex Hove	1903
	120 min. C. H. Lloyd	West Indians v. Glamorgan Swansea	1976
300:	181 min. D. C. S. Compton	MCC v. North-Eastern Transvaal Benoni	1948-49

MOST BOUNDARIES IN AN INNINGS

68 **P. A. Perrin** (343*) Essex v. Derbyshire Chesterfield 1904

MOST SIXES IN AN INNINGS

15 **J. R. Reid** (296) Wellington v. Northern Districts Wellington 1962-63

MOST RUNS OFF ONE OVER

36 **G. St A. Sobers** Nottinghamshire v. Glamorgan Swansea 1968
(Hit six sixes off M. A. Nash)

RECORD PARTNERSHIPS FOR EACH WICKET

(*Unbroken)

1st	561	Waheed Mirza, Mansoor Akhtar	Karachi Whites v. Quetta Karachi	1976-77
2nd	465*	J. A. Jameson, R. B. Kanhai	Warwickshire v. Gloucestershire Birmingham	1974
3rd	456	Khalid Irtiza, Aslam Ali	United Bank v. Multan Karachi	1975-76
4th	**577**	**V. S. Hazare, Gul Mahomed**	Baroda v. Holkar Baroda	1946-47
5th	405	S. G. Barnes, D. G. Bradman	Australia v. England Sydney	1946-47
6th	487*	G. A. Headley, C. C. Passailaigue	Jamaica v. Lord Tennyson's XI Kingston	1931-32
7th	347	D. St E. Atkinson, C. C. Depeiza	West Indies v. Australia Bridgetown	1954-55
8th	433	A. Sims, V. T. Trumper	Australian XI v. Canterbury Christchurch	1913-14
9th	283	A. Warren, J. Chapman	Derbyshire v. Warwickshire Blackwell	1910
10th	307	A. F. Kippax, J. E. H. Hooker	New South Wales v. Victoria Melbourne	1928-29

BOWLING RECORDS

HIGHEST CAREER AGGREGATES (2,000) WICKETS)

	Career	Wkts	Runs	Av.
W. Rhodes	1898-1930	4,187	69.993	16.71
A. P. Freeman	1914-36	3,776	69,577	18.42
C. W. L. Parker	1903-35	3,278	63,821	19.46
J. T. Hearne	1888-1923	3,061	54,342	17.75
T. W. Goddard	1922-52	2,979	59,116	19.84
W. G. Grace	1865-1908	2,876	51,545	17.92
A. S. Kennedy	1907-36	2,874	61,044	21.24
D. Shackleton	1948-69	2,857	53,303	18.65
G. A. R. Lock	1946-71	2,844	54,710	19.23
F. J. Titmus	1949-78	2,812	62,731	22.30
M. W. Tate	1912-37	2,783	50,544	18.16
G. H. Hirst	1889-1929	2,739	51,300	18.72
C. Blythe	1899-1914	2,506	42,136	16.81
W. E. Astill	1906-39	2,431	57,784	23.76
J. C. White	1909-37	2,356	43,759	18.57
W. E. Hollies	1932-57	2,323	48,656	20.94
F. S. Trueman	1949-69	2,304	42,154	18.29
J. B. Statham	1950-68	2,260	36,995	16.36
R. T. D. Perks	1930-55	2,233	53,770	24.07
J. Briggs	1879-1900	2,221	35,390	15.93
D. J. Shepherd	1950-72	2,218	47,298	21.32
G. E. Dennett	1903-26	2,147	42,568	19.82
T. Richardson	1892-1905	2,105	38,794	18.42
T. E. Bailey	1945-67	2,082	48,170	23.13
A. Shaw	1864-97	2,072	24,827	11.97
F. E. Woolley	1906-38	2,068	41,066	19.85
G. Geary	1912-38	2,063	41,339	20.03
D. V. P. Wright	1932-57	2,056	49,305	23.98
J. Newman	1906-30	2,032	51,211	25.20
R. Illingworth	1951-78	2,031	40,485	19.93
S. Haigh	1895-1913	2,012	32,091	15.94

F. R. SPOFFORTH,

"The Demon" or Imp-etuous Bowler, representing Cricket
on t'other side of the H-earth.

HIGHEST SEASON AGGREGATES (200 WICKETS)

	Season	Wkts	Runs	Av.
A. P. Freeman	1928	304	5,489	18.05
A. P. Freeman	1933	298	4,549	15.26
T. Richardson	1895	290	4,170	14.37
C. T. B. Turner	1888	283	3,307	11.68
A. P. Freeman	1931	276	4,307	15.60
A. P. Freeman	1930	275	4,632	16.84
T. Richardson	1897	273	3,945	14.45
A. P. Freeman	1929	267	4,879	18.27
W. Rhodes	1900	261	3,606	13.81
J. T. Hearne	1896	257	3,670	14.28
A. P. Freeman	1932	253	4,149	16.39
W. Rhodes	1901	251	3,797	15.12

MOST WICKETS IN A MATCH

19-90	J. C. Laker	England v. Australia Manchester	1956
17-48	C. Blythe	Kent v. Northamptonshire Northampton	1907
17-50	C. T. B. Turner	Australians v. England XI Hastings	1888
17-54	W. P. Howell	Australians v. Western Province Cape Town	1902-03
17-56	C. W. L. Parker	Gloucestershire v. Essex Gloucester	1925
17-67	A. P. Freeman	Kent v. Sussex Hove	1922
17-89	W. G. Grace	Gloucestershire v. Nottinghamshire Cheltenham	1877
17-89	F. C. L. Matthews	Nottinghamshire v. Northamptonshire Nottingham	1923
17-91	H. Dean	Lancashire v. Yorkshire Liverpool	1913
17-91	H. Verity	Yorkshire v. Essex Leyton	1933
17-92	A. P. Freeman	Kent v. Warwickshire Folkestone	1932
17-103	W. Mycroft	Derbyshire v. Hampshire Southampton	1876
17-106	G. R. Cox	Sussex v. Warwickshire Horsham	1926
17-106	T. W. Goddard	Gloucestershire v. Kent Bristol	1939
17-119	W. Mead	Essex v. Hampshire Southampton	1895
17-137	W. Brearley	Lancashire v. Somerset Manchester	1905
17-159	S. F. Barnes	England v. South Africa Johannesburg	1913-14
17-201	G. Giffen	South Australia v. Victoria Adelaide	1885-86
17-212	J. C. Clay	Glamorgan v. Worcestershire Swansea	1937

MOST WICKETS IN A DAY

17-48	C. Blythe	Kent v. Northamptonshire Northampton	1907
17-91	H. Verity	Yorkshire v. Essex Leyton	1933
17-106	T. W. Goddard	Gloucestershire v. Kent Bristol	1939
16-38	T. Emmett	Yorkshire v. Cambridgeshire Hunslet	1869
16-52	J. Southerton	South v. North Lord's	1875
16-69	T. G. Wass	Nottinghamshire v. Lancashire Liverpool	1906
16-38	A. E. E. Vogler	Eastern Province v. Griqualand West Johannesburg	1906-07
16-103	T. G. Wass	Nottinghamshire v. Essex Nottingham	1908
16-83	J. C. White	Somerset v. Worcestershire Bath	1919

BOWLERS WHO HAVE TAKEN ALL TEN WICKETS IN AN INNINGS

E. Hinkly	Kent v. England Lord's	1848
J. Wisden	North v. South Lord's	1850
V. E. Walker	England v. Surrey The Oval	1859
E. M. Grace	MCC v. Gentlemen of Kent Canterbury	1862
V. E. Walker	Middlesex v. Lancashire Manchester	1865
G. Wootton	All England v. Yorkshire Sheffield	1865
S. E. Butler	Oxford U. v. Cambridge U. Lord's	1871
Jas. Lillywhite	South v. North Canterbury	1872
W. G. Grace	MCC v. Kent Canterbury	1873
A. Shaw	MCC v. North Lord's	1874
E. Barrett	Players v. Australians The Oval	1878
G. Giffen	Australian XI v. The Rest Sydney	1883-84
W. G. Grace	MCC v. Oxford U. Oxford	1886
G. Burton	Middlesex v. Surrey The Oval	1888
A. E. Moss	Canterbury v. Wellington Christchurch	1889-90
S. M. J. Woods	Cambridge U. v. Thornton's XI Cambridge	1890
T. Richardson	Surrey v. Essex The Oval	1894
H. Pickett	Essex v. Leicestershire Leyton	1895
E. J. Tyler	Somerset v. Surrey Taunton	1895
W. P. Howell	Australians v. Surrey The Oval	1899
C. H. G. Bland	Sussex v. Kent Tonbridge	1899
J. Briggs	Lancashire v. Worcestershire Manchester	1900
A. E. Trott	Middlesex v. Somerset Taunton	1900
A. Fielder	Players v. Gentlemen Lord's	1906

G. E. Dennett	Gloucestershire v. Essex	1906
	Bristol	
A. E. E. Vogler	Eastern Province v. Griqualand West	1906-07
	Johannesburg	
C. Blythe	Kent v. Northamptonshire	1907
	Northampton	
A. Drake	Yorkshire v. Somerset	1914
	Weston-s-Mare	
F. A. Tarrant	Maharaja of Cooch Behar's XI v. Lord Willingdon's XI	1918-19
	Poona	
W. Bestwick	Derbyshire v. Glamorgan	1921
	Cardiff	
A. A. Mailey	Australians v. Gloucestershire	1921
	Cheltenham	
C. W. L. Parker	Gloucestershire v. Somerset	1921
	Bristol	
T. Rushby	Surrey v. Somerset	1921
	Taunton	
J. C. White	Somerset v. Worcestershire	1921
	Worcester	
G. C. Collins	Kent v. Nottinghamshire	1922
	Dover	
H. Howell	Warwickshire v. Yorkshire	1923
	Birmingham	
A. S. Kennedy	Players v. Gentlemen	1927
	The Oval	
G. O. B. Allen	Middlesex v. Lancashire	1929
	Lord's	
A. P. Freeman	Kent v. Lancashire	1929
	Maidstone	
G. Geary	Leicestershire v. Glamorgan	1929
	Pontypridd	
C. V. Grimmett	Australians v. Yorkshire	1930
	Sheffield	
A. P. Freeman	Kent v. Essex	1930
	Southend	
H. Verity	Yorkshire v. Warwickshire	1931
	Leeds	
A. P. Freeman	Kent v. Lancashire	1931
	Manchester	
V. W. C. Jupp	Northamptonshire v. Kent	1932
	Tunbridge Wells	
H. Verity	Yorkshire v. Nottinghamshire	1932
	Leeds	
T. W. Wall	South Australia v. New South Wales	1932-33
	Sydney	
T. B. Mitchell	Derbyshire v. Leicestershire	1935
	Leicester	
J. Mercer	Glamorgan v. Worcestershire	1936
	Worcester	
T. W. Goddard	Gloucestershire v. Worcestershire	1937
	Cheltenham	
T. F. Smailes	Yorkshire v. Derbyshire	1939
	Sheffield	
E. A. Watts	Surrey v. Warwickshire	1939
	Birmingham	
W. E. Hollies	Warwickshire v. Nottinghamshire	1946
	Birmingham	
J. M. Sims	East v. West	1948
	Kingston	
T. E. Bailey	Essex v. Lancashire	1949
	Clacton	
J. K. R. Graveney	Gloucestershire v. Derbyshire	1949
	Chesterfield	
R. Berry	Lancashire v. Worcestershire	1953
	Blackpool	
S. P. Gupte	Bombay v. Combined XI	1954-55
	Bombay	
J. C. Laker	Surrey v. Australians	1956
	The Oval	
J. C. Laker	England v. Australia	1956
	Manchester	

G. A. R. Lock	Surrey v. Kent	1956
	Blackheath	
K. Smales	Nottinghamshire v. Gloucestershire	1956
	Stroud	
P. Chatterjee	Bengal v. Assam	1956-57
	Jorhat	
J. D. Bannister	Warwickshire v. Combined Services	1959
	Birmingham	
A. J. G. Pearson	Cambridge U. v. Leicestershire	1961
	Loughborough	
N. I. Thomson	Sussex v. Warwickshire	1964
	Worthing	
P. J. Allan	Queensland v. Victoria	1965-66
	Melbourne	
I. J. Brayshaw	Western Australia v. Victoria	1967-68
	Perth	
Shahid Mahmood	Karachi Whites v. Khairpur	1969-70
	Karachi	

MOST HAT-TRICKS

7   D. V. P. Wright
6   T. W. Goddard, C. W. L. Parker

TWO HAT-TRICKS IN A MATCH

A. Shaw	Nottinghamshire v. Gloucestershire	1884
	Nottingham	
A. E. Trott†	Middlesex v. Somerset	1907
	Lord's	
T. J. Matthews	Australia v. South Africa	1912
	Manchester	
C. W. L. Parker	Gloucestershire v. Middlesex	1924
	Bristol	
R. O. Jenkins	Worcestershire v. Surrey	1949
	Worcester	
J. S. Rao†	Services v. Northern Punjab	1963-64
	Amristar	
	(†twice in the same innings)	

FIVE WICKETS WITH SIX CONSECUTIVE BALLS

W. H. Copson	Derbyshire v. Warwickshire	1937
	Derby	
W. A. Henderson	North-Eastern Transvaal v. Orange Free State	1937-38
	Bloemfontein	
P. I. Pocock	Surrey v. Sussex	1972
	Eastbourne	

ALL ROUND RECORDS

CAREER AGGREGATES OF 20,000 RUNS AND 2,000 WICKETS

	Career	Runs	Av.	Wkts	Av.	'Doubles'
W. E. Astill	1906-39	22,726	22.54	2,431	23.76	9
T. E. Bailey	1945-67	28,642	33.42	2,082	23.13	8
W. G. Grace	1865-1908	54,896	39.55	2,876	17.99	8
G. H. Hirst	1891-1929	36,323	34.13	2,739	18.72	14
R. Illingworth	1951-78	23,977	28.40	2,031	19.93	6
W. Rhodes	1898-1930	39,802	30.83	4,187	16.71	16
M. W. Tate	1912-37	21,698	25.02	2,783	18.16	8
F. J. Titmus	1949-78	21,534	23.17	2,812	22.30	8
F. E. Woolley	1906-38	58,969	40.75	2,068	19.85	8

MOST SEASON 'DOUBLES' (1,000 RUNS AND 100 WICKETS)

16	W. Rhodes
14	G. H. Hirst

NOTABLE SEASON 'DOUBLES'

2,000 Runs and 200 Wickets: G. H. Hirst—2,385 runs and 208 wickets in 1906
3,000 Runs and 100 Wickets: J. H. Parks—3,003 runs and 101 wickets in 1937
1,000 Runs and 200 Wickets:

	Runs	Wkts	Season
A. E. Trott	1,175	239	1899
A. E. Trott	1,337	211	1900
A. S. Kennedy	1,129	205	1922
M. W. Tate	1,168	219	1923
M. W. Tate	1,419	205	1924
M. W. Tate	1,290	228	1925

NOTABLE MATCH 'DOUBLES'

Century and Ten Wickets in an Innings

V. E. Walker	England v. Surrey The Oval	1859
E. M. Grace	MCC v. Gentlemen of Kent Canterbury	1862
W. G. Grace	MCC v. Oxford University Oxford	1886
F. A. Tarrant	Maharaja of Cooch Behar's XI v. Lord Willingdon's XI Poona	1918-19

Double-Century and a Hat-Trick

W. E. Roller	Surrey v. Sussex The Oval	1885

WICKETKEEPING CAREER RECORDS

Most Dismissals

J. T. Murray	1952–75	1,527

Most Catches

J. T. Murray	1952–75	1,270

Most Stumpings

L. E. G. Ames	1926–51	415

Most Season Dismissals

127 (79ct, 48st.)	L. E. G. Ames	1929
121 (69ct, 52st.)	L. E. G. Ames	1928
110 (62ct, 48st.)	H. Yarnold	1949
107 (77ct, 30st.)	G. Duckworth	1928
107 (96ct, 11st.)	J. G. Binks	1960
104 (82ct, 22st.)	J. T. Murray	1957
102 (70ct, 32st.)	F. H. Huish	1913
102 (95ct, 7st.)	J. T. Murray	1960
101 (85ct, 16st.)	R. Booth	1960
100 (62ct, 38st.)	F. H. Huish	1911
100 (36ct, 64st.)	L. E. G. Ames	1932
100 (91ct, 9st.)	R. Booth	1964

Most Dismissals in a Match

12 (8ct, 4st.)	E. Pooley	Surrey v. Sussex The Oval	1868
12 (9ct, 3st.)	D. Tallon	Queensland v. New South Wales Sydney	1938-39
12 (9ct, 3st.)	H. B. Taber	New South Wales v. South Australia Adelaide	1968-69

Most Dismissals in an Innings

8 (8ct)	A. T. W. Grout	Queensland v. Western Australia Brisbane	1959-60

Wicketkeepers' Hat-tricks

W. H. Brain	(3st.)	Gloucestershire v. Somerset Cheltenham	1893
G. O. Dawkes	(3ct)	Derbyshire v. Worcestershire Kidderminster	1958

FIELDING—CAREER RECORDS

Most Catches:

F. E. Woolley	1906-38	**1,015**

Most Season Catches

78	W. R. Hammond	1928
77	M. J. Stewart	1957
73	P. M. Walker	1961
71	P. J. Sharpe	1962
70	J. Tunnicliffe	1901

Most Catches in a Match

10	W. R. Hammond	Gloucestershire v. Surrey Cheltenham	1928

Most Catches in an Innings

7	M. J. Stewart	Surrey v. Northamptonshire Northampton	1957
7	A. S. Brown	Gloucestershire v. Nottinghamshire Nottingham	1966

CRICKET.

A GRAND MATCH

WILL BE PLAYED IN

LORD'S GROUND,

MARYLEBONE.

On MONDAY, JUNE 21st, 1841,

And following Day.

The Slow Bowlers of England against the Fast.

PLAYERS.

Slow Bowlers.	Fast Bowlers.
BAYLEY,	A. MYNN, Esq
COBBETT	C. G. WHITTAKER, Esq.
LILLYWHITE,	REDGATE,
The Hon. Capt. LIDDELL	N. BLAND. Esq.
E. BARNETT, Esq.	R. W. KEATE. Esq.
R. KYNASTON. Esq.	C W. A NAPIER, Esq.
C. G TAYLOR, Esq.	W. PICKERING, Esq.
F. THACKERAY, Esq.	Captain PRICE,
J. M. WYTHE, Esq.	W. WARD, Esq.
GUY,	BOX,
WENMAN.	PILCH,

MATCHES TO COME.

Monday, June 28, at Lord's, Nine Gentlemen old Etonians, with Lillywhite & Hillyar, against Eleven Gentlemen of England.

Thursday, July 1st, at Lord's, the Marylebone Club, against the Undergraduates of Cambridge

Monday, July 5th, at Lord's, the Marylebone Club & Ground, against the Nottingham Club and Ground.

Cricket Bats, Balls, Stumps, Score Papers and the Laws of Cricket as revised by the Marylebone Club in 1838, to be had of Mr. J. H. DARK, at the Pavilion, and at the Manufactory on the Ground.

AN ORDINARY AT THREE O'CLOCK.

Admittance 6d.   Good Stabling on the Ground.   No Dogs Admitted

MORGAN, Printer, 39, New Church Street, Portman Market.

J. Blackham   T. Horan   G. H. Bailey   J. Conway (Manager)   A. Bannerman   C. Bannerman   W. L. Murdoch
F. R. Spofforth   F. E. Allen   D. W. Gregory   W. Midwinter   T. W. Garrett   H. F. Boyle

THE AUSTRALIAN CRICKET TEAM

Mansell Collection

National Championships

RANJI TROPHY

SHEFFIELD SHIELD WINNERS (Australia)

COUNTY CHAMPIONS (England)

WINNERS (India)

1892-93	Victoria	1956-57	New South Wales
1893-94	South Australia	1957-58	New South Wales
1894-95	Victoria	1958-59	New South Wales
1895-96	New South Wales	1959-60	New South Wales
1896-97	New South Wales	1960-61	New South Wales
1897-98	Victoria	1961-62	New South Wales
1898-99	Victoria	1962-63	Victoria
1899-1900	New South Wales	1963-64	South Australia
1900-01	Victoria	1964-65	New South Wales
1901-02	New South Wales	1965-66	New South Wales
1902-03	New South Wales	1966-67	Victoria
1903-04	New South Wales	1967-68	Western Australia
1904-05	New South Wales	1968-69	South Australia
1905-06	New South Wales	1969-70	Victoria
1906-07	New South Wales	1970-71	South Australia
1907-08	Victoria	1971-72	Western Australia
1908-09	New South Wales	1972-73	Western Australia
1909-10	South Australia	1973-74	Victoria
1910-11	New South Wales	1974-75	Western Australia
1911-12	New South Wales	1975-76	South Australia
1912-13	South Australia	1976-77	Western Australia
1913-14	New South Wales	1977-78	Western Australia
1914-15	Victoria		
1919-20	New South Wales		
1920-21	New South Wales		
1921-22	Victoria		
1922-23	New South Wales		
1923-24	Victoria		
1924-25	Victoria		
1925-26	New South Wales		
1926-27	South Australia		
1927-28	Victoria		
1928-29	New South Wales		
1929-30	Victoria		
1930-31	Victoria		
1931-32	New South Wales		
1932-33	New South Wales		
1933-34	Victoria		
1934-35	Victoria		
1935-36	South Australia		
1936-37	Victoria		
1937-38	New South Wales		
1938-39	South Australia		
1939-40	New South Wales		
1946-47	Victoria		
1947-48	Western Australia		
1948-49	New South Wales		
1949-50	New South Wales		
1950-51	Victoria		
1951-52	New South Wales		
1952-53	South Australia		
1953-54	New South Wales		
1954-55	New South Wales		
1955-56	New South Wales		

New South Wales have won the Shield 36 times, Victoria 22, South Australia 11, Western Australia 7, and Queensland nil.

COUNTY CHAMPIONS (England)

1864	Surrey	1927	Lancashire
1865	Nottinghamshire	1928	Lancashire
1866	Middlesex	1929	Nottinghamshire
1867	Yorkshire	1930	Lancashire
1868	Nottinghamshire	1931	Yorkshire
1869	Nottinghamshire	1932	Yorkshire
	Yorkshire	1933	Yorkshire
1870	Yorkshire	1934	Lancashire
1871	Nottinghamshire	1935	Yorkshire
1872	Nottinghamshire	1936	Derbyshire
1873	Gloucestershire	1937	Yorkshire
	Nottinghamshire	1938	Yorkshire
1874	Gloucestershire	1939	Yorkshire
1875	Nottinghamshire	1946	Yorkshire
1876	Gloucestershire	1947	Middlesex
1877	Gloucestershire	1948	Glamorgan
1878	Undecided	1949	Middlesex
1879	Nottinghamshire		Yorkshire
	Lancashire	1950	Lancashire
1880	Nottinghamshire		Surrey
1881	Lancashire	1951	Warwickshire
1882	Nottinghamshire	1952	Surrey
	Lancashire	1953	Surrey
1883	Nottinghamshire	1954	Surrey
1884	Nottinghamshire	1955	Surrey
1885	Nottinghamshire	1956	Surrey
1886	Nottinghamshire	1957	Surrey
1887	Surrey	1958	Surrey
1888	Surrey	1959	Yorkshire
1889	Nottinghamshire	1960	Yorkshire
	Lancashire	1961	Hampshire
	Surrey	1962	Yorkshire
1890	Surrey	1963	Yorkshire
1891	Surrey	1964	Worcestershire
1892	Surrey	1965	Worcestershire
1893	Yorkshire	1966	Yorkshire
1894	Surrey	1967	Yorkshire
1895	Surrey	1968	Yorkshire
1896	Yorkshire	1969	Glamorgan
1897	Lancashire	1970	Kent
1898	Yorkshire	1971	Surrey
1899	Surrey	1972	Warwickshire
1900	Yorkshire	1973	Hampshire
1901	Yorkshire	1974	Worcestershire
1902	Yorkshire	1975	Leicestershire
1903	Middlesex	1976	Middlesex
1904	Lancashire	1977	Middlesex
1905	Yorkshire		Kent
1906	Kent	1978	Kent
1907	Nottinghamshire		
1908	Yorkshire		
1909	Kent		
1910	Kent		
1911	Warwickshire		
1912	Yorkshire		
1913	Kent		
1914	Surrey		
1919	Yorkshire		
1920	Middlesex		
1921	Middlesex		
1922	Yorkshire		
1923	Yorkshire		
1924	Yorkshire		
1925	Yorkshire		
1926	Lancashire		

RANJI TROPHY WINNERS (India)

1934-35	Bombay
1935-36	Bombay
1936-37	Nawanagar
1937-38	Hyderabad
1938-39	Bengal
1939-40	Maharashtra
1940-41	Maharashtra
1941-42	Bombay
1942-43	Baroda
1943-44	Western India States
1944-45	Bombay
1945-46	Holkar
1946-47	Baroda
1947-48	Holkar
1948-49	Bombay
1949-50	Baroda
1950-51	Holkar
1951-52	Bombay
1952-53	Holkar
1953-54	Bombay
1954-55	Madras
1955-56	Bombay
1956-57	Bombay
1957-58	Baroda
1958-73	Bombay (winners for 15 consecutive seasons)
1973-74	Karnatala (formerly Mysore)
1974-75	Bombay
1975-76	Bombay
1976-77	Bombay
1977-78	Karnatala

PLUNKET SHIELD WINNERS (New Zealand)

The trophy was presented in 1906-07 by Lord Plunket, then Governor-General of New Zealand, and awarded by the New Zealand Cricket Council to Canterbury. Until 1921, when the championship was organized on a league basis, the Shield was contested under the challenge match system.

		Challenges defeated
1906 to December 1907	Canterbury	0
December 1907 to February 1911	Auckland	7
February 1911 to February 1912	Canterbury	2
February 1912 to January 1913	Auckland	1
January 1913 to December 1918	Canterbury	9
December 1918 to January 1919	Wellington	0
January 1919 to January 1920	Canterbury	2
January 1920 to January 1921	Auckland	3
January 1921—challenge system ended	Wellington	0

1921-22	Auckland
1922-23	Canterbury
1923-24	Wellington
1924-25	Otago
1925-26	Wellington
1926-27	Auckland
1927-28	Wellington
1928-29	Auckland
1929-30	Wellington
1930-31	Canterbury
1931-32	Wellington
1932-33	Otago
1933-34	Auckland
1934-35	Canterbury
1935-36	Wellington
1936-37	Auckland
1937-38	Auckland
1938-39	Auckland
1939-40	Auckland
1945-46	Canterbury
1946-47	Auckland
1947-48	Otago
1948-49	Canterbury
1949-50	Wellington
1950-51	Otago
1951-52	Canterbury
1952-53	Otago
1953-54	Central Districts
1954-55	Wellington
1955-56	Canterbury
1956-57	Wellington
1957-58	Otago
1958-59	Auckland
1959-60	Canterbury
1960-61	Wellington
1961-62	Wellington
1962-63	Northern Districts
1963-64	Auckland
1964-65	Canterbury
1965-66	Wellington
1966-67	Central Districts
1967-68	Central Districts
1968-69	Auckland
1969-70	Otago
1970-71	Central Districts
1971-72	Otago
1972-73	Wellington
1973-74	Wellington
1974-75	Otago

Under the revised competition system, Wellington won the Plunket Shield 14 times; Auckland 12, Canterbury 9; Otago 9; Central Districts (admitted 1950-51) 4; and Northern Districts (admitted 1956-57) once.

In 1975-76, the Plunket Shield was replaced as the major competition by the Shell Series.

SHELL TROPHY WINNERS

1975-76	Canterbury
1976-77	Otago
1977-78	Auckland

CURRIE CUP WINNERS (South Africa)

1889-90	Transvaal
1890-91	Griqualand West
1892-93	Western Province
1893-94	Western Province
1894-95	Transvaal
1896-97	Western Province
1897-98	Western Province
1902-03	Transvaal
1903-04	Transvaal
1904-05	Transvaal
1906-07	Transvaal
1908-09	Western Province
1910-11	Natal
1912-13	Natal
1920-21	Western Province
1921-22	Transvaal
	Natal
	Western Province
1923-24	Transvaal
1925-26	Transvaal
1926-27	Transvaal
1929-30	Transvaal
1931-32	Western Province
1933-34	Natal
1934-35	Transvaal
1936-37	Natal
1937-38	Natal
	Transvaal
1946-47	Natal
1947-48	Natal
1950-51	Transvaal
1951-52	Natal
1952-53	Western Province
1954-55	Natal
1955-56	Western Province
1958-59	Transvaal
1959-60	Natal
1960-61	Natal
1962-63	Natal
1963-64	Natal
1965-66	Natal
	Transvaal
1966-67	Natal
1967-68	Natal
1968-69	Transvaal
1969-70	Transvaal
	Western Province
1970-71	Transvaal
1971-72	Transvaal
1972-73	Transvaal
1973-74	Natal
1974-75	Western Province
1975-76	Natal
1976-77	Natal
1977-78	Western Province

Outright winners: Transvaal 17 times; Natal 17; Western Province 11, and Griqualand West (then Kimberley) once.
Joint winners: Transvaal 4 times; Natal 3, and Western Province twice. No other province has won the Cup.

SHELL SHIELD WINNERS (West Indies)

1965-66	Barbados
1966-67	Barbados
1967-68	No competition
1968-69	Jamaica
1969-70	Trinidad
1970-71	Trinidad
1971-72	Barbados
1972-73	Guyana
1973-74	Barbados
1974-75	Guyana
1975-76	Barbados
	Trinidad
1976-77	Barbados
1977-78	Barbados

Test Match Cricket

Key to Abbreviations
E.—England   A.—Australia   S.A.—South Africa   W.I.—West Indies
N.Z.—New Zealand   I.—India   P.—Pakistan   * Not Out

SUMMARY OF TEST MATCH RESULTS 1876-77 TO 1977-78 (824 MATCHES)

Team	Tests	Won	Lost	Drawn	Tied	Toss won
England	536	199	137	200	–	264
Australia	380	172	103	104	1	187
South Africa	172	38	77	57	–	80
West Indies	183	60	56	66	1	100
New Zealand	130	10	60	60	–	62
India	157	28	65	64	–	80
Pakistan	90	15	24	51	–	51

		Tests	E.	A.	S.A.	W.I.	N.Z.	I.	P.	Tied	Drawn
						Won by					
England	v. Australia	230	74	88	–	–	–	–	–	–	68
	v. South Africa	102	46	–	18	–	–	–	–	–	38
	v. West Indies	71	21	–	–	22	–	–	–	–	28
	v. New Zealand	50	24	–	–	–	1	–	–	–	25
	v. India	53	25	–	–	–	–	7	–	–	21
	v. Pakistan	30	9	–	–	–	–	–	1	–	20
Australia	v. South Africa	53	–	29	11	–	–	–	–	–	13
	v. West Indies	46	–	25	–	10	–	–	–	1	10
	v. New Zealand	9	–	5	–	–	1	–	–	–	3
	v. India	30	–	19	–	–	–	5	–	–	6
	v. Pakistan	12	–	6	–	–	–	–	2	–	4
South Africa	v. New Zealand	17	–	–	9	–	2	–	–	–	6
West Indies	v. New Zealand	14	–	–	–	5	2	–	–	–	7
	v. India	37	–	–	–	17	–	4	–	–	16
	v. Pakistan	15	–	–	–	6	–	–	4	–	5
New Zealand	v. India	22	–	–	–	–	3	10	–	–	9
	v. Pakistan	18	–	–	–	–	1	–	7	–	10
India	v. Pakistan	15	–	–	–	–	–	2	1	–	12
TOTALS		824	199	172	38	60	10	28	15	1	301

HIGHEST TOTAL

903-7d.   **England** v. Australia   1938
The Oval

LOWEST TOTAL

26   **New Zealand** v. England   1954-55
Auckland

LARGEST MARGIN OF VICTORY

Innings and 579 runs   **England** beat Australia   1938
The Oval

TIED MATCH

Australia v. West Indies   1960-61
Brisbane

MOST TEST MATCH APPEARANCES

114   M. C. Cowdrey (England)   1954-55 to 1974-75

BATSMEN WHO HAVE SCORED 3,000 TEST RUNS

For England

	Tests	I.	N.O.	H.S.	Runs	Av.	100
M. C. Cowdrey	114	188	15	182	7,624	44.06	22
W. R. Hammond	85	140	16	336*	7,249	58.45	22
L. Hutton	79	138	15	364	6,971	56.67	19
K. F. Barrington	82	131	15	256	6,806	58.67	20
D. C. S. Compton	78	131	15	278	5,807	50.06	17
G. Boycott	74	128	17	246*	5,675	51.12	16
J. B. Hobbs	61	102	7	211	5,410	56.94	15
J. H. Edrich	77	127	9	310*	5,138	43.54	12
T. W. Graveney	79	123	13	258	4,882	44.38	11
H. Sutcliffe	54	84	9	194	4,555	60.73	16
P. B. H. May	66	106	9	285*	4,537	46.77	13
E. R. Dexter	62	102	8	205	4,502	47.89	9
A. P. E. Knott	89	138	14	135	4,175	33.66	5
D. L. Amos	50	88	10	262*	3,612	46.30	11
A. W. Greig	58	93	4	148	3,599	40.43	8
E. H. Hendren	51	83	9	205*	3,525	47.63	7
F. E. Woolley	64	98	7	154	3,283	36.07	5

For Australia

	Tests	I.	N.O.	H.S.	Runs	Av.	100
D. G. Bradman	52	80	10	334	6.996	99.94	29
R. N. Harvey	79	137	10	205	6,149	48.41	21
W. M. Lawry	67	123	12	210	5,234	47.15	13
I. M. Chappell	72	130	9	196	5,187	42.86	14
K. D. Walters	68	116	12	250	4,960	47.69	14
R. B. Simpson	62	111	7	311	4,869	46.81	10
I. R. Redpath	66	120	11	171	4,737	43.45	8
G. S. Chappell	51	90	13	247*	4,097	53.20	14
A. R. Morris	46	79	3	206	3,533	46.48	12
C. Hill	49	89	2	191	3,412	39.21	7
V. T. Trumper	48	89	8	214*	3,163	39.04	8
C. C. McDonald	47	83	4	170	3,107	39.32	5
A. L. Hassett	43	69	3	198*	3,073	46.56	10

For South Africa

	Tests	I.	N.O.	H.S.	Runs	Av.	100
B. Mitchell	42	80	9	189*	3,471	48.88	8

For West Indies

	Tests	I.	N.O.	H.S.	Runs	Av.	100
G. St A. Sobers	93	160	21	365*	8,032	57.78	26
R. B. Kanhai	79	137	6	256	6,227	47.53	15
C. H. Lloyd	65	113	8	242	4,594	43.75	11
E. de C. Weekes	48	81	5	207	4,455	58.61	15
R. C. Fredericks	59	109	7	169	4,334	42.49	8
F. M. M. Worrell	51	87	9	261	3,860	49.48	9
C. L. Walcott	44	74	7	220	3,798	56.68	15
A. I. Kallicharran	45	76	7	158	3,331	48.27	10
C. C. Hunte	44	78	6	260	3,245	45.06	8
B. F. Butcher	44	78	6	209*	3,104	43.11	7

For New Zealand

	Tests	I.	N.O.	H.S.	Runs	Av.	100
B. E. Congdon	61	114	7	176	3,448	33.22	7
J. R. Reid	58	108	5	142	3,428	33.28	6

For India

	Tests	I.	N.O.	H.S.	Runs	Av.	100
P. R. Umrigar	59	94	8	223	3,631	42.22	12
S. M. Gavaskar	37	71	5	220	3,226	48.87	13
V. L. Manjrekar	55	92	10	189*	3,208	39.12	7
G. R. Viswanath	43	82	7	139	3,154	42.05	5
C. G. Borde	55	97	11	177*	3,061	35.59	5

For Pakistan

Hanif Mohammad	55	97	8	337	3,915	43.98	12	
Mushtaq Mohammad	49	88	7	201	3,283	40.53	10	

MOST RUNS IN A SERIES

Runs	Batsman	Series		Tests	I.	N.O.	H.S.	Av.	100
974	D. G. Bradman	A. v. E.	1930	5	7	0	334	139.14	4
905	W. R. Hammond	E. v. A.	1928-29	5	9	1	251	113.12	4
834	R. N. Harvey	A. v. S.A.	1952-53	5	9	0	205	96.66	4
829	I. V. A. Richards	W.I. v. E.	1976	4	7	0	291	118.42	3
827	C. L. Walcott	W.I. v. A.	1954-55	5	10	0	155	82.70	5
824	G. St A. Sobers	W.I. v. P.	1957-58	5	8	2	365*	137.33	3
810	D. G. Bradman	A. v. E.	1936-37	5	9	0	270	90.00	3
806	D. G. Bradman	A. v. S.A.	1931-32	5	5	1	299*	201.50	4

MOST RUNS IN A TEST MATCH

380	G. S. Chappell (247*, 133)	Australia v. N.Z. Wellington	1973-74

HIGHEST INDIVIDUAL SCORES

365*	G. St A. Sobers	West Indies v. Pakistan Kingston	1957-58
364	L. Hutton	England v. Australia The Oval	1938
337	Hanif Mohammad	Pakistan v. West Indies Bridgetown	1957-58
336*	W. R. Hammond	England v. New Zealand Auckland	1932-33
334	D. G. Bradman	Australia v. England Leeds	1930
325	A. Sandham	England v. West Indies Kingston	1929-30
311	R. B. Simpson	Australia v. England Manchester	1964
310*	J. H. Edrich	England v. New Zealand Leeds	1965
307	R. M. Cowper	Australia v. England Melbourne	1965-66
304	D. G. Bradman	Australia v. England Leeds	1934
302	L. G. Rowe	West Indies v. England Bridgetown	1973-74

BOWLERS WHO HAVE TAKEN 100 TEST WICKETS

For England

	Tests	Balls	Runs	Wkts	Av.	5 w. I.
F. S. Trueman	67	15,178	6,625	307	21.57	17
D. L. Underwood	74	18,979	6,600	265	24.90	16
J. B. Statham	70	16,056	6,261	252	24.84	9
A. V. Bedser	51	15,918	5,876	236	24.89	15
J. A. Snow	49	12,021	5,387	202	26.66	8
J. C. Laker	46	12,027	4,101	193	21.24	9
S. F. Barnes	27	7,873	3,106	189	16.43	24
G. A. R. Lock	49	13,147	4,451	174	25.58	9
M. W. Tate	39	12,523	4,055	155	26.16	7
F. J. Titmus	53	15,118	4,931	153	32.22	7
R. G. D. Willis	41	7,887	3,653	151	24.19	10
H. Verity	40	11,143	3,510	144	24.37	5
A. W. Greig	58	9,802	4,541	141	32.20	6
T. E. Bailey	61	9,712	3,856	132	29.21	5
W. Rhodes	58	8,231	3,425	127	26.96	6
R. G. D. Davies	35	6,759	3,191	126	25.32	8
C. M. Old	40	7,540	3,510	125	28.08	4
D. A. Allen	39	11,297	3,779	122	30.97	4

R. Illingworth	61	11,934	3,807	122	31.20	3
J. Briggs	33	5,332	2,094	118	17.74	9
G. G. Arnold	34	7,650	3,254	115	28.29	6
G. A. Lohmann	18	3,821	1,205	112	10.75	9
D. V. P. Wright	34	8,135	4,224	108	39.11	6
R. Peel	20	5,216	1,715	102	16.81	6
J. H. Wardle	28	6,597	2,080	102	20.39	5
C. Blythe	19	4,438	1,863	100	18.63	9

For Australia

R. Benaud	63	19,108	6,704	248	27.03	16
G. D. McKenzie	60	17,681	7,328	246	29.78	16
R. R. Lindwall	61	13,650	5,251	228	23.03	12
C. V. Grimmett	37	14,513	5,231	216	24.21	21
A. K. Davidson	44	11,587	3,819	186	20.53	14
D. K. Lillee	32	8,783	4,017	171	23.49	12
K. R. Miller	55	10,461	3,906	170	22.97	7
W. A. Johnston	40	11,048	3,826	160	23.91	7
W. J. O.Reilly	27	10,024	3,254	144	22.59	11
H. Trumble	32	8,099	3,072	141	21.78	9
J. R. Thomson†	32	7,158	3,699	145	25.51	6
M. H. N. Walker	34	10,094	3,792	138	27.47	6
A. A. Mallett	35	9,136	3,494	125	27.95	6
M. A. Noble	42	7,109	3,025	121	25.00	9
I. W. Johnson	45	8,780	3,182	109	29.19	3
G. Giffen	31	6,325	2,791	103	27.09	7
A. N. Connolly	29	7,818	2,981	102	29.22	4
C. T. B. Turner	17	5,195	1,670	101	16.53	11

For South Africa

H. J. Tayfield	37	13,568	4,405	170	25.91	14
T. L. Goddard	41	11,736	3,226	123	26.22	5
P. M. Pollock	28	6,522	2,806	116	24.18	9
N. A. T. Adcock	26	6,391	2,195	104	21.10	5

For New Zealand

R. O. Collinge	34	7,473	3,309	114	29.02	3
B. R. Taylor	30	6,334	2,953	111	26.60	4
R. C. Motz	32	7,034	3,148	100	31.48	5

For West Indies

L. R. Gibbs	79	27,115	8,989	309	29.09	18
G. St A. Sobers	93	21,599	7,999	235	34.03	6
W. W. Hall	48	10,421	5,066	192	26.38	9
S. Ramadhin	43	13,939	4,579	158	28.98	10
A. L. Valentine	36	12,953	4,215	139	30.32	8
A. M. E. Roberts	27	6,858	3,298	134	26.81	9
V. A. Holder	34	7,877	3,079	101	30.48	3

For India

B. S. Bedi	58	19,135	6,615	246	26.89	14
B. S. Chandrasekhar	50	14,253	6,270	222	28.24	15
E. A. S. Prasanna	47	13,867	5,491	187	29.36	10
V. M. H. Mankad	44	14,865	5,236	162	32.32	8
S. P. Gupte	36	11,284	4,403	149	29.55	12
S. Venkataraghavan	37	10,301	3,796	113	33.59	3

For Pakistan

Fazal Mahmood	34	9,834	3,434	139	24.70	13
Intikhab Alam	47	10,475	4,492	125	35.93	3

IN AFFECTIONATE REMEMBRANCE

OF

ENGLISH CRICKET

WHICH DIED AT THE OVAL

ON

29th August 1882,

Deeply lamented by a large circle of sorrowing friends and acquaintances.

R. I. P.

N.B.—The body will be cremated, and the ashes taken to Australia.

MCC

RECORD PARTNERSHIPS FOR EACH WICKET

1st	413	V. Mankad (231), P. Roy (173)	I. v. N.Z. Madras	1955-56	
2nd	**451**	**W. H. Ponsford (266), D. G. Bradman (244)**	A. v. E. The Oval	1934	
3rd	370	W. J. Edrich (189), D. C. S. Compton (208)	E. v. S.A. Lord's	1947	
4th	411	P. B. H. May (285*), M. C. Cowdrey (154)	E. v. W.I. Birmingham	1957	
5th	405	S. G. Barnes (234), D. G. Bradman (234)	A. v. E. Sydney	1946-47	
6th	346	J. H. W. Fingleton (136), D. G. Bradman (270)	A. v. E. Melbourne	1936-37	
7th	347	D. St E. Atkinson (219), C. C. Depeiza (122)	W.I. v. A. Bridgetown	1954-55	
8th	246	L. E. G. Ames (137), G. O. B. Allen (122)	E. v. N.Z. Lord's	1931	
9th	190	Asif Iqbal (146), Intikhab Alam (51)	P. v. E. The Oval	1967	
10th	151	B. F. Hastings (110), R. O. Collinge (68*)	N.Z. v. P. Auckland	1972-73	

MOST WICKETS IN A TEST SERIES

	Tests	Wkts	Av.		
S. F. Barnes	4	**49**	10.93	England v. S. Africa	1913-14
J. C. Laker	5	46	9.60	England v. Australia	1956
C. V. Grimmett	5	44	14.59	Australia v. S. Africa	1935-36
A. V. Bedser	5	39	17.48	England v. Australia	1953
M. W. Tate	5	38	23.18	England v. Australia	1924-25
W. J. Whitty	5	37	17.08	Australia v. S. Africa	1910-11
H. J. Tayfield	5	37	17.18	S. Africa v. England	1956-57
A. E. E. Vogler	5	36	21.75	S. Africa v. England	1909-10
A. A. Mailey	5	36	26.27	Australia v. England	1920-21
G. A. Lohmann	3	35	5.80	England v. S. Africa	1895-96
B. S. Chandrasekhar	5	35	18.91	India v. England	1972-73

MOST WICKETS IN A TEST MATCH

19-90	**J. C. Laker**	England v. Australia Manchester	1956

MOST WICKETS IN A TEST INNINGS

10-53	**J. C. Laker**	England v. Australia Manchester	1956
9-28	G. A. Lohmann	England v. South Africa Johannesburg	1895-96
9-37	J. C. Laker	England v. Australia Manchester	1956
9-69	J. M. Patel	India v. Australia Kanpur	1959-60
9-95	J. M. Noreiga	West Indies v. India Port-of-Spain	1970-71
9-102	S. P. Gupte	India v. West Indies Kanpur	1958-59
9-103	S. F. Barnes	England v. South Africa Johannesburg	1913-14
9-113	H. J. Tayfield	South Africa v. England Johannesburg	1956-57
9-121	A. A. Mailey	Australia v. England Melbourne	1920-21

HAT-TRICKS

F. R. Spofforth	Australia v. England Melbourne	1878-79
W. Bates	England v. Australia Melbourne	1882-83
J. Briggs	England v. Australia Sydney	1891-92
G. A. Lohmann	England v. South Africa Port Elizabeth	1895-96
J. T. Hearne	England v. Australia Leeds	1899
H. Trumble	Australia v. England Melbourne	1901-02
H. Trumble	Australia v. England Melbourne	1903-04
T. J. Matthews (2)	Australia v. South Africa Manchester	1912
M. J. C. Allom	England v. New Zealand Christchurch	1929-30
T. W. J. Goddard	England v. South Africa Johannesburg	1938-39
P. J. Loader	England v. West Indies Leeds	1957
L. F. Kline	Australia v. South Africa Cape Town	1957-58
W. W. Hall	West Indies v. Pakistan Lahore	1958-59
G. M. Griffin	South Africa v. England Lord's	1960
L. R. Gibbs	West Indies v. Australia Adelaide	1960-61
P. J. Petherick	New Zealand v. Pakistan Lahore	1976-77

T. J. Matthews did the hat-trick in both innings.
M. J. C. Allom and P. J. Petherick were playing in their first Test matches.

WICKETKEEPING RECORDS

Wicketkeepers who have made 100 Dismissals

	Tests	Ct	St.	Total
A. P. E. Knott (England)	89	233	19	**252**
T. G. Evans (England)	91	173	46	219
R. W. Marsh (Australia)	52	190	8	198
A. T. W. Grout (Australia)	51	163	24	187
D. L. Murray (West Indies)	51	150	8	158
J. H. B. Waite (South Africa)	50	124	17	141
W. A. S. Oldfield (Australia)	54	78	52	130
J. M. Parks (England)	46	103	11	114
Wasim Bari (Pakistan)	42	94	15	109

Most Dismissals in a Test Series

26 (23ct, 3st.)	**J. H. B. Waite**	South Africa *v.* New Zealand	1961-62
26 (26ct)	**R. W. Marsh**	Australia *v.* West Indies (6 Tests)	1975-76

Most Dismissals in a Test Match

9 (8ct, 1st.)	**G. R. A. Langley**	Australia *v.* England Lord's	1956

Most Dismissals in a Test Innings

6 (6ct)	**A. T. W. Grout**	Australia *v.* South Africa Johannesburg	1957-58
6 (6ct)	**D. T. Lindsay**	South Africa *v.* Australia Johannesburg	1966-67
6 (6ct)	**J. T. Murray**	England *v.* India Lord's	1967
6 (5ct, 1st.)	**S. M. H. Kirmani**	India *v.* New Zealand Christchurch	1975-76

FIELDING RECORDS

Fielders who have made 100 Catches

	Tests	Catches
M. C. Cowdrey (England)	114	**120**
W. R. Hammond (England)	85	110
R. B. Simpson (Australia)	62	110
G. St A. Sobers (West Indies)	93	109
I. M. Chappell (Australia)	72	103

Most Catches in a Test Series

15	**J. M. Gregory**	Australia *v.* England	1920-21

Most Catches in a Test Match

7	**G. S. Chappell**	Australia *v.* England Perth	1974-75
7	**Yajurvindra Singh**	India *v.* England Bangalore	1976-77

Most Catches in a Test Innings

5	**V. Y. Richardson**	Australia *v.* South Africa Durban	1935-36
5	**Yajurvindra Singh**	India *v.* England Bangalore	1976-77

Mansell Collection

OUT!

So don't fatigue yourself. I beg Sir?

INDEX

Picture Credits

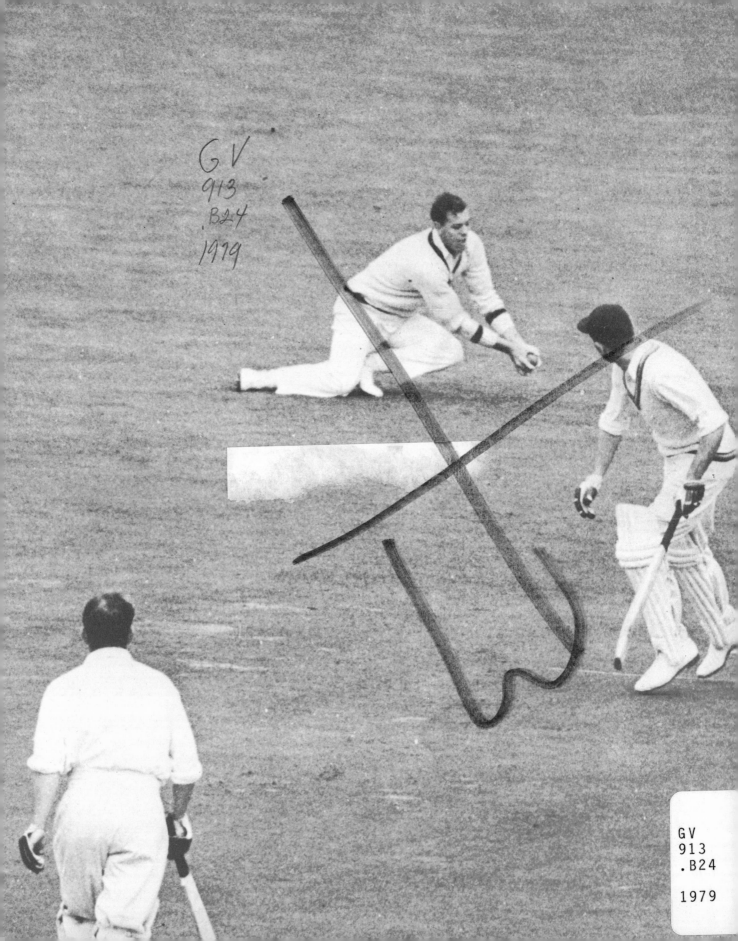